ARY

D0030188

ABOUT THE AUTHOR

Brahma Chellaney is one of India's leading strategic thinkers and analysts and a well-known television commentator on international affairs. He has written for the *International Herald Tribune, Wall Street Journal,* and *New York Times,* among other publications. He is a professor of strategic studies at the Centre for Policy Research, an independent think tank in New Delhi, and a member of the Policy Advisory Group headed by the foreign minister of India.

ASIAN JUGGERNAUT
The Rise of China, India and Japan

Brahma Chellaney

HARPER

BUSINESS

NEW YORK ● LONDON ● TORONTO ● SYDNEY

HARPER

BUSINESS

A hardcover edition of this book was published in 2006 by HarperCollins Publishers India, a joint venture with The India Today Group.

ASIAN JUGGERNAUT. Copyright © 2006 by Konrad Adenauer Stiftung. All rights reserved. Printed in the United States of America. No part of this book may be used or reproduced in any manner whatsoever without written permission except in the case of brief quotations embodied in critical articles and reviews. For information address HarperCollins Publishers, 10 East 53rd Street, New York, NY 10022.

HarperCollins books may be purchased for educational, business, or sales promotional use. For information please write: Special Markets Department, HarperCollins Publishers, 10 East 53rd Street, New York, NY 10022.

First U.S. edition published 2010.

Library of Congress Cataloging-in-Publication Data has been applied for.

ISBN 978-0-06-136308-5

10 11 12 13 14   RRD   10 9 8 7 6 5 4 3 2 1

Preface

U.S. President Barack Obama must face up to the qualitative reordering of power under way in the Asia-Pacific, with tectonic shifts challenging strategic stability. The impact of such shifts on U.S. foreign policy will be accentuated by America's own challenges, including economic troubles and the two separate wars overseas. Such challenges dictate greater U.S.-China cooperation to ensure both continued large Chinese capital inflows and Beijing's political support on contentious issues ranging from North Korea and Burma to Pakistan and Iran. Such calculations, in turn, are likely to have a bearing on America's dual role in Asia — 'as a resident power, and as the "straddle power" across the Asia-Pacific', to quote Defence Secretary Robert Gates.

Asia has come a long way since the creation of two Koreas, two Chinas, two Vietnams and India's partition. It has risen dramatically as the world's main creditor and economic locomotive. The ongoing global power shifts indeed are primarily linked to Asia's phenomenal economic rise, the speed and scale of which has no parallel in world history. How fast Asia has come up can be gauged from the 1968 book, *Asian Drama: An Inquiry Into the Poverty of Nations*, by Swedish economist and Nobel laureate Gunnar Myrdal, who bemoaned the manner impoverishment, population pressures and resource constraints were weighing down Asia. With the story of endemic poverty turning into a tale of spreading prosperity, today's Asian drama is very different.

Even so, Asia faces complex security, energy, and developmental challenges in this era of globalization and greater interstate competition. It has to cope with entrenched territorial and maritime disputes, sharpening competition over scarce resources, improved military capabilities, increasingly fervent nationalism and the spread of religious extremism. Diverse trans-border trends — from nuclear proliferation and terrorism, to illicit refugee flows and human trafficking — add to the challenges. At a time when several Asian countries are arming themselves at a fast pace, some disputes in Asia seem intractable and indeed conflict-prone. But Asia also is becoming more interdependent through trade, investment, technology and tourism. The economic renaissance has been accompanied by a growing international recognition of Asia's soft power, as symbolized by its arts, fashion and cuisine.

With the world's fastest-growing markets, fastest-rising military expenditures and most-volatile hot spots, a resurgent Asia today holds the key to the future global order. Central to this continent's own future is the strategic triangle made up of the largest Asian economic and military powers — China, India and Japan. Not since Japan rose to world-power status during the reign of the Meiji Emperor in the second half of the 19th century has another non-Western power emerged with such potential to alter the world order as China today. As the 2009 assessment by the U.S. intelligence community predicted, China stands to more profoundly affect global geopolitics than any other country. China's ascent, however, is dividing Asia, not bringing Asian states closer. A strong China, a strong Japan and a strong India need to move beyond historical legacies and find ways to reconcile their interests in order to peacefully coexist and achieve greater prosperity.

Actually, never before in history have China, India and Japan been strong at the same time. Despite the international attention on the two demographic titans, China and India, Japan still has a nearly $5-trillion economy, impressive high-technology skills and Asia's largest navy. Battered by its worst recession in post-war history, Japan, however, is losing its status as the world's second-largest economy to China. China already has overtaken Japan in having the world's biggest trade surplus and foreign-currency reserves, although its per-capita income still is less than a tenth that in Japan. Yet, for the foreseeable future, Japan will stay a strong nation. Against that background, ensuring that the Japan-China and China-India competition does not slide into strategic conflict remains a key challenge.

The United States, for its part, will remain a key player in Asia through its security arrangements and other strategic ties with an array of regional states. Its policies and actions will continue to have an important influence on the strategic calculus of the major Asian actors. The central U.S. interest in the Asia-Pacific still centres on a stable balance of power. During the first half of the Cold War, the United States chose to maintain a balance by forging security alliances with Japan and South Korea and also by keeping forward bases in Asia. By the time the Cold War entered the second phase, America's 'ping-pong diplomacy' led to the 1972 'opening' with Beijing, which was designed to reinforce the balance by employing a newly assertive, nuclear-armed China to countervail Soviet power in the Asia-Pacific region. 'The effect was to change the Cold War's global chessboard — to the disadvantage of the Soviet Union', according to Zbigniew Brzezinski. 'Indirectly, the normalization facilitated Chairman Deng Xiaoping's decision to undertake a comprehensive economic reform. China's growth would have been much harder without the expansion in U.S.-Chinese trade and financial relations that followed normalization'.

Now, according to the Pentagon's *Quadrennial Defence Review Report*, America's interests centre on 'maintaining a stable balance' in 'the East Asian littoral', given the likelihood that 'a military competitor with a formidable base will emerge in the region' — an allusion to China. Washington would not want Japan or India to kowtow to a China seeking to supplant the United States as the leading force in Asia. But America also would not want to see the rise of a combative India or Japan. For example, an overt Japan-China conflict in the East China Sea over the competing maritime and gas-exploration claims would compel Washington to side with Tokyo or risk wrecking the U.S.-Japanese security relationship, centred on U.S. forward deployment on Japanese soil. Similarly, India-China tensions or border skirmishes over the Himalayan territorial disputes would run counter to the U.S. interest to build closer ties with both sides and not to side with New Delhi. America's interests in Asia actually lie in hedging its own future options while balancing the various powers.

To be sure, the emergence of China as a global player with rising heft is not only transforming the geopolitical landscape in the Asia-Pacific, but also spurring greater American reliance on Beijing for financial and political support. But as the U.S.-China relationship acquires a wider and deeper base in the coming years, the strains in some of America's existing military or strategic partnerships could become pronounced. In fact, for the first time, building a stronger cooperative relationship with China is taking precedence in U.S. policy over the sale of advanced weaponry to Asian allies, lest the transfer of offensive arms raise Beijing's hackles. As a result, doubts could grow in Japan and Taiwan, for example, over the reliability of Washington's commitment to their security.

In the near term, rising Chinese assertiveness has had the unintended effect of persuading Japan to jettison its doubts about U.S. security commitments and to reinvigorate its military relationship with Washington. In the long run, however, Tokyo may seek to ease its security dependency on the United States. In recent years, the United States has worked hard to co-opt India in a "soft alliance" shorn of treaty obligations. But New Delhi is unlikely to get much comfort on China or Pakistan from American policy. In that light, the Indian ardour in recent years for closer defence ties with America could gradually give way to more sobering reality, even as U.S.-India ties continue to grow. By contrast, Australia's cosy relationship with distant China, especially under the Mandarin-speaking prime minister, Kevin Rudd, may mesh with the possible trajectory of U.S.-China ties. What Canberra pursues today — to balance its relations with Tokyo and Beijing — Washington could begin doing before long.

China's own future, however, remains more uncertain than ever, despite its dramatic rise. It faces a worrisome paradox: Because of an opaque, repressive political system, the more it globalizes, the more vulnerable it becomes internally. At the core of its challenges is how to make a political soft landing. Although China has come a long way since the 1989 Tiananmen Square massacre, with its citizens now enjoying property rights, the freedom to travel overseas and other rights that were unthinkable a generation ago, political power still rests with the same party and system responsible for the death of tens of millions of Chinese during the so-called Great Leap Forward, Cultural Revolution and other state-induced disasters. The greatest genocide in modern world history was not the Holocaust but the Great Leap Forward, a misguided charge toward industrialization that left 36 million people dead, according to *Tombstone*, a recent book by longtime Chinese communist Yang Jisheng.

Although China has moved from being a totalitarian state to being an authoritarian state, some things haven't changed since the Mao Zedong years. Some other things have changed for the worse, such as the whipping up of ultra-nationalism and turning that into the legitimating credo of continued communist rule. Attempts to bend reality to the illusions the state propagates through information control and online censors actually risk turning China into a modern-day Potemkin state. China's internal problems — best symbolized by the 2008 Tibetan uprising, the 2009 Uighur revolt and spreading peasant discontent — won't go away unless Beijing stops imposing cultural and political homogeneity and makes the transition to a more-open society.

Internationally, China's trajectory will depend on how its neighbours and other players like the United States manage its growing power. Such management — independently and in partnership — will determine if China stays on the positive side of the ledger, without its power sliding into arrogance. Against this background, the U.S.-China relationship — despite a deepening symbiosis — is likely to remain uneasy, but overt competition or confrontation suits neither side. For the United States, China's rising power actually helps validate American forward military deployments in the Asian theatre. It also helps America to keep existing allies and to search for new ones.

There are many books on the tangled China-India and China-Japan relationships. But *Asian Juggernaut* is the first wide-ranging study that examines Asia in totality, employing the broader framework to focus on the critical China-India-Japan strategic triangle. In that sense, it is a pioneering study, dissecting Asia's major challenges. Asia may be coalescing economically, but politically it remains deeply divided, with its major powers at loggerheads. The strategic dissonance between China and Japan and the underlying rivalry between China and India can hardly contribute to the building of a stable, secure Asia. Efforts to develop homogeny in Asia constantly run into the unresolved issue of hegemony. While the community in Europe was built among democracies, the political systems in Asia are so varied and some even so opaque that building interstate trust is not easy. In Europe, the bloody wars of the past century have made armed conflict unthinkable today. But in Asia, the wars of the past, such as China's wars with India and Vietnam, failed to resolve disputes. And while Europe has built institutions to underpin peace, Asia has yet to begin that process in earnest. In fact, in the absence of real institutions in Asia, the United States has sought to keep the peace.

Asian Juggernaut examines ways Asia can build cooperative approaches to tackle its security, energy, territorial, environmental, developmental and history challenges. Given Asia's fundamental diversity and weak institutional arrangements, the book offers policy-oriented ideas on developing wider cooperation by building upon existing bilateral and regional understandings and mechanisms. This analysis of Asia's cooperative future and pivotal role is intended for policy analysts, social scientists, military professionals, security experts, journalists, university students and others interested in knowing where Asia is headed.

Brahma Chellaney

Contents

The Asian Renaissance

WITH THE CENTRE OF GRAVITY IN WORLD AFFAIRS moving to a dynamic and thriving Asia, this continent's significance in international relations is beginning to rival that of Europe in the eighteenth and nineteenth centuries. More than half of the global population lives in Asia, a rapidly changing region that has come up dramatically in less than a quarter century. At the same time, the problems that confront Asia are evident from just one piece of information — the continent accounts for three-quarters of all terrorism casualties worldwide, placing it at the centre of the global war on terror.

Economically and politically, Asia appears poised to determine the new world order. With the world's fastest-growing markets, fastest-rising military expenditures and most serious hotspots (including the epicentre of international terrorism), Asia holds the key to the future global order.

The Asian renaissance is underscored by the high gross domestic product (GDP) growth rates of Asian states. Such rapid growth is likely to continue in large parts of Asia in the coming years. In fact, Asia is expected to remain the world's economic locomotive for the next couple of decades or more, with its larger economies increasingly scouring the world for energy and raw materials to feed their growth. The Asia-driven energy and resource competition has sharpened the political dynamics of the global energy markets. A twenty-first-century version of an energy-related Great Game is already on, although in more subtle ways than the colonial-era hunt for raw materials and other resources.

The Cold War produced two Koreas, two Chinas and two Vietnams. Today, with growing competition among the major Asian players and the rise of regional powers, Asia faces new challenges in an era of globalization, including how to move beyond historical legacies and tap the continent's dynamism and growth for greater security and prosperity. The colossal shift in global geopolitics presents an opportunity for Asia as well as tests its ability to assume a central role in international relations.

Broadly, Asia confronts two contradictory trends. On one side are the territorial and maritime disputes, competition over scarce resources, improved military capabilities and increasingly fervent nationalism that threaten to imperil security and growing prosperity. On the other side is the rising Asian interdependence through trade and investment, communications, technology and tourism. Asia also has to cope with resilient jingoism, protectionism and diverse kinds of negative transborder influences, including terrorism, subversion and illegal migration.

Starting with Japan's economic success, followed by the emergence of other continental tigers and now the rise of China and India, a resurgent Asia has been bouncing back from its historical decline. That decline began in the period after the nineteenth century, when Asia dropped behind Europe during the Industrial Revolution. The Asian Development Bank has estimated that Asia, after making up three-fifths of the world's GDP at the beginning of the industrial age in 1820, saw its stake decline to one-fifth in 1940, before dramatic economy recovery has helped bring it up to two-fifths today. By 2025, according to the same estimation, Asia might return to its 1820 position in terms of world product.

Simultaneously, with its rapid economic growth, Asia's arts, fashion and cuisine are now regaining international recognition. Even Japan's giant economy has finally rumbled back from the worst recession since the end of World War II. Asia as a whole is on the rise. As home to several information-technology giants, Asia, with its rising soft- and hard-power resources, is likely to help shape the future of globalization.

Indeed, the ascent of Asia, as symbolized by China, India and Japan, has in some quarters conjured up a perceived threat to Western pastures. This found an echo in a State of the Union address of then U.S. President George W. Bush, who said: 'In a dynamic world economy, we are seeing new competitors, like China and India, and this creates uncertainty, which makes it easier to feed people's fears. So we're seeing some old temptations return. Protectionists want to escape competition, pretending that we can keep our high standard of living while walling off our economy. Others say that the government needs to take a larger role in directing the economy, centralizing more power in Washington and increasing taxes'.[1] The reality is that the balance of economic power in the world has been changing recurrently in history, and will continue to do so.

The new international clout of Asia can be seen not only from China's long streak of fast economic growth but also from the fact that Japan, South Korea, Taiwan and Southeast Asia alone hold $2.5 trillion in Western debt. China in particular inspires both admiration and unease. As a U.S. national-security strategy report put it, 'China encapsulates Asia's dramatic economic successes, but China's transition remains incomplete. In one generation, China has gone from poverty and isolation to growing integration into the international economic system. China once opposed global institutions; today it is a permanent member of the UNSC (United Nations Security Council) and the WTO (World Trade Organization)'.[2] The report added: 'China's leaders must realize, however, that they cannot stay on this peaceful path while holding on to old ways of thinking and acting that exacerbate concerns throughout the region and the world. These old ways include: Continuing China's military expansion in a non-transparent way'.

The opportunities and challenges faced by Asia need to be seen in the context of the larger global trends and developments. Internationally, conflict remains rife, and only the forms and dimensions of conflict have changed,[3] as evidenced by the rise of both intrastate strife and unconventional aggression in the form of terrorism.[4] Interstate war, however, is unlikely to disappear as a feature of international relations. In fact, 'the only thing more common than predictions about the end of war has been war itself'.[5]

Equally significant is the manner momentous international events continue to be shaped by changes in political geography. The collapse of the Soviet Union, the crumbling of Yugoslavia and the separation of East Timor from Indonesia have had far-reaching ramifications. Despite the sanctity attached to existing interstate frontiers and the prevailing international norms against redrawing borders in blood, the desire of some states to extend their frontiers to territories they covet is a major cause of regional tensions. Examples in Asia of such irredentism include China's claims over Taiwan and India's Arunachal Pradesh and Pakistan's belligerence on Kashmir. Export of terror as an instrument of state policy is also tied to regional ambitions.

Centre of Transnational Terrorism

The scourge of transnational terrorism in the twenty-first century is both a response to, and derives assistance from, rapid technological change. Terrorism, drawing sustenance from murderous ideologies, seeks to get round the military-deterrent capabilities of target-states by employing unconventional means. The growing gap between the technologically advanced and backward nations also inspires terrorists to take recourse to unconventional methods in an asymmetrical situation.

The rise of extremism in totalitarian Muslim states is linked not only to the lack of avenues for free expression and debate but also to the sense of disillusionment over the widening technology gap between Islamic states and the rest of the world. The oil boom of the 1970s created an 'illusion that power had come to the Islamic world'.[6] Subsequent events have shown that despite their huge oil revenues, the oil-exporting Muslim states from West Asia to Southeast Asia face an increasing 'knowledge gap' with the West.[7] The internal dynamics in Islamic states — many trapped in a cauldron of political tyranny, religious bigotry and social tensions — have helped spur militancy. What the world is witnessing, according to Wafa Sultan, a Syrian-American psychiatrist, is not a clash of religions or civilizations, but a battle between modernity and barbarism — a battle that the forces of violent, reactionary Islam are destined to lose.[8] It is more a clash about civilization than a clash between civilizations.

Technological forces today are playing a greater role in shaping geopolitics than at any other time in history. In the same way textiles, railways and coal built up the power and wealth of some countries after the advent of the Industrial Revolution, information technology is at the centre of power and force today.[9] Real military prowess and dominance over the battlefield are now derived from the ability of a great power like the United States to collate, process, amalgamate and harness militarily useful information from space-based surveillance, high-speed computers and other instruments of the information age.

The unprecedented pace of technological progress can be seen from the fact that the globe has amassed more scientific knowledge after World War II than was generated in the previous 5000 years. The swiftest advances in technology, however, have been occurring since the late 1980s with the advent of the information age, with scientific information now increasing twofold about every five years.[10] Asia has impressive information-technology resources, and there is every possibility that by 2050, the global economy will be led, in addition to the United States, by Asia's three behemoths — China, India and Japan.

In the face of continual technological revolution, the tolerance for rapid change is one important characteristic distinguishing the successful cultures from the no-so-successful ones. Insular, conservative, inward-looking societies are less competent to rapidly exploit or absorb new innovations. A liberal culture and professional work ethics are certainly an advantage.

The more the world changes, however, the more it remains the same in some critical aspects. The information revolution and globalization have not changed the nature of international relations or the make-up of the international system, even as they have helped trigger fundamental changes in polity, economy and security. The rapid pace of technological change is itself a consequence of nations competing fiercely and seeking relative advantage in an international system based not on collective security but on national security. While state sovereignty remains paramount,[11] the principle of non-interference in the internal affairs of another state has come under open pressure as a result of internal wars, externally driven ideological battles and transborder challenges. State sponsorship or protection of terrorism makes this principle even more difficult to uphold.

As Asia illustrates, the rise of international terrorism is a reminder that the information age is both an integrating and a dividing force. Greater public awareness flowing out of the advances in information and communications technologies has encouraged individuals in many societies to search for their roots and more clearly define their identity. At a time of greater international fluidity and uncertainty,[12] the rise of religious orthodoxy, ethnic or localist affiliation, jingoism and even xenophobia in some societies in an era of supposed internationalism and a single 'global village' raises troubling questions about international peace and stability. So does the location of four-fifths of the world's oil resources in politically troubled areas,[13] especially when international competition for oil and other natural resources is sharpening as a consequence of the rapid economic growth in Asia.

Terrorism is a challenge that stares squarely at Asia, which is home to several failed or failing states. Asia, which already accounted for 75 per cent of all terrorism casualties worldwide by 2000,[14] has been facing mounting terrorist and extremist violence in recent years. Growing terrorism carries the risk of economic disruption, besides threatening the freedoms and tolerant spirit of pluralistic societies. The challenges Asia faces are apparent from the fact that the epicentre of international terrorism is located in the Pakistan–Afghanistan belt. The U.S. State Department has diplomatically called South Asia 'a central theatre of the global war on terrorism',[15] while Steven Hadley, the then U.S. national security adviser, characterized a nuclear, Talibanized, Sunni Pakistan as 'both an ally in the war on terror and, in some sense, a site where the war is being carried about'.[16]

The U.S. occupation of Iraq made the world forget that the September 11, 2001, terrorist strikes in the United States happened not because of Iraq but because of the terrorist nurseries in the Pakistan–Afghanistan belt, some of which remain in business, especially in the northern and western parts of Pakistan. Pakistan remains a principal recruiting ground and logistical centre for global terrorists. As the Pakistani military ruler, General Pervez Musharraf, acknowledged on July 21, 2005, in an address to the nation after the London subway bombings, 'Wherever these extremist or terrorist incidents occur in the world, a direct or indirect connection is established with this country'.[17] Ominously, Pakistan has emerged as a common thread in the investigations of most acts of international terrorism.

The global spread of the *jihad* culture is rooted in the Afghan war of the 1980s and the U.S. and Saudi funnelling of arms to the anti-Soviet guerrillas through Pakistan's Inter-Services Intelligence (ISI) agency. To fight Soviet-style atheism, then U.S. President Ronald Reagan did not hesitate to use Islam in Afghanistan, just as he readily utilized the Catholic Church in his intense anti-Marxist campaign in Central America. Islam was employed to unite the Muslim world and spur the spirit of *jihad* against the Soviet intervention in Afghanistan. Terrorism and the modern-day Frankensteins are the haunting byproducts of the war against atheism and communism that the West was supposed to have won.

The Afghan war veterans came to haunt the security of India, the West and several Muslim states. Many members of the Afghan war alumni returned to their homelands to wage terror campaigns against governments they viewed as tainted by Western influence. Egyptian President Anwar Sadat's 1981 assassination was one of the first to be linked to such inspired terror. Large portions of the multibillion-dollar military aid to the anti-Soviet Afghan rebels by the U.S. Central Intelligence Agency (CIA) was siphoned off by the conduit[18] — the ISI — to ignite a bloody insurgency in Indian Kashmir from 1990 after the agency had failed to trigger an uprising in India's Punjab state despite arming Sikh dissidents.

Against that background, draining the existing terrorism-breeding swamps in Asia will not be easy, given the way the culture of *jihad* is now deeply woven into the social fabric of certain communities. For instance, some of Pakistan's 15,000 *madrasas* are not just seats of medieval theology but also schools imparting training in arms. What has made this incendiary radicalization so difficult to reverse is that it claims the imprimatur of religion.[19] U.S. National Intelligence Director John Negroponte told the Senate Intelligence Committee in February 2006 that, 'Pakistani militant groups represent a persistent threat to regional stability and U.S. interests in South Asia and the Near-East. They also pose a potential threat to our interests worldwide'.[20]

To be sure, the entire expanse from West Asia to Southeast Asia is home to militant groups and wracked by terrorist, insurgent and separatist violence in a manner unmatched elsewhere in the world. This poses a serious challenge to international and Asian security. The radicalization of Muslims in Southeast and Central Asia, where Islamist groups such as the Jemaah Islamiyah, Mujahidin Kompak and Islamic Movement of Uzbekistan are becoming increasingly entrenched, demonstrates the ideological power of religious extremism. With the radicalization has come virulent anti-Americanism. The visceral hatred towards America has drawn sustenance from the polarizing effects of the Iraq conflict and potent symbols of abuse, such as the Abu Ghraib prison in Iraq, the Guantánamo Bay detention centre in Cuba and the secret rendition, or transfer, of suspected terrorists to countries that have engaged in torture. In addition, there has been outrage over the massacre of Iraqi men, women and children by U.S. Marines in the Iraqi village of Haditha and the killings at American camps in Afghanistan.

The debacle in Iraq, and the civil war there resulting from America's hubris, are likely to serve as a humbling lesson for future generations of U.S. leaders. In fact, by deceptively linking Iraq with Al Qaeda to justify its invasion, Washington created a self-fulfilling prophecy that now haunts it. More broadly, the U.S. invasion proved divisive in international relations, splitting the world and fracturing the global consensus to fight terror. Not only has the direction of the international war on terror been derailed, but also the global image of America has yet to fully recoup from the losses of the Bush years, according to a 2009 world-opinion poll[21] In fact, despite the spreading jihad culture, President Barack Obama, with the stroke of his pen, effectively ended Bush's global 'war' on terror as dramatically as his predecessor had initiated it.

Not calling it a war any longer but labelling it 'an enduring struggle' doesn't change the ground realities. Secular, pluralistic states, depending on their location, have come under varying pressures from the forces of terror. Vulnerability to terrorist attacks is critically linked to a state's external neighbourhood. A democracy geographically distant from the Muslim world tends to be less vulnerable to frequent terrorist strikes than a democracy proximate to Islamic states. The luxury of geography of the U.S. and Australia, for instance, contrasts starkly with the tyranny of geography of India and Israel. It is such realities that no change of lexicon can address.

Winning the war on global terror means winning the battle of ideas, for it is evil ideas that turn ordinary persons into murderers. But the battle of ideas can be won by example, not by force. Even the Cold War was won by the West not so much by military means as by spreading market capitalism to other regions that helped suck the lifeblood out of communism's international appeal, making it incapable of meeting the widespread popular yearning in societies worldwide for a better life. Similarly, the way to keep further recruits away from the lure of *jihad*, which instils and then exploits an identity of victimhood, is not so much through military action as by ideas and example that confute the *jihadist* arguments.

Combined with the rise of terrorism in Asia is the emergence of failing or renegade states pursuing nuclear ambitions at a time when popular concerns in the world have increased over terrorist groups possibly getting hold of nuclear materials for blackmail, such as a radiological 'dirty' bomb. Although nuclear weapons will continue to play a 'critical role' because they possess 'unique properties', as the 2002 U.S. Nuclear Posture Review stated, few want a world bristling with weapons of mass destruction (WMD), especially in the hands of failing or outlaw states.

In the Asian context, there are three sets of pressing concerns. The first is the potential nexus between terrorism and WMD, a concern underscored by the ease with which for years the Abdul Qadeer Khan-led network in Pakistan sold nuclear blueprints and equipment to states like Iran, North Korea and Libya, with the active participation or connivance of the Pakistani military and intelligence.[22] As a U.S.-trained nuclear scientist of Pakistani origin cautioned, 'Whitewashing Pakistan's official complicity in such activities ... will only result in rogue proliferators sprouting up everywhere'.[23] Yet the entire blame was put on one individual, Khan.

It was Libya, seeking to re-enter the international mainstream, that first disclosed the existence of the Pakistani proliferation ring, but the United States took the credit by stage-managing an event in October 2003. With the help of documents Tripoli had turned over to Washington, a German cargo ship, *BBC China*, was intercepted en route to Libya with uranium-enrichment components routed through Dubai. The exposure prompted a self-protective Pakistani military and intelligence to make A.Q. Khan the scapegoat — a charade that saw General Musharraf in early 2004 pardon Khan and then place him under house detention to help shield him from international investigators.

Following the uncovering of the Pakistani proliferation ring, the United Nations Security Council passed Resolution 1540, which obliges all states to establish domestic controls to ensure that WMD and related materials do not reach terrorists. The extent of the covert Pakistani nuclear dealings should have persuaded Islamabad's Western allies to distance themselves from the military there and invest in the only real guarantee for Pakistan's future as a stable, moderate state — its civil society. Instead, Washington went along with Musharraf's charade because it traditionally has viewed the Pakistan military as central to U.S. strategic interests in that country.

The United States invaded Iraq to eliminate WMD that were not there but allowed terrorist-haven Pakistan, with real WMD, to escape international censure for selling nuclear secrets to North Korea, Iran and Libya. By condoning the worst proliferation scandal in world history — that too involving covert nuclear trade with nations Washington had labelled 'rogue states' — a terrible precedent was set in international relations. If non-proliferation is to become a genuine global norm, and if the international non-proliferation regime is to survive and do its job, it is important to endow the anti-proliferation mission with consistency, credibility and commitment.

The second proliferation issue relates to the nuclear and missile programmes in failing or problem states — North Korea, Iran and Pakistan. The notion of an 'Islamic bomb' was actually conceived long before 9/11 by the architect of Pakistan's nuclear-weapons programme, Zulfikar Ali Bhutto, who once had vowed that his nation would 'eat grass', if necessary, to make such a bomb.[24] Ironically, it was the same A.Q. Khan who stole blueprints from a European nuclear consortium in the Netherlands in 1975 to set up Pakistan's uranium-enrichment plant at Kahuta.

The third issue in the Asian context concerns the nuclear arsenals of the big players — China, India, Russia and the United States (which extends nuclear-umbrella protection, among others, to Japan, South Korea and

Australia). The international spotlight on Iran's low enrichment of a small amount of uranium and North Korea's nuclear waywardness obscures the fact that are still 27,000 real nuclear weapons in the United States, Russia, China, France and the United Kingdom. And it is usually overlooked that currently the largest expansion of nuclear and missile armouries anywhere in the world is taking place in China. As part of a big upgrade of its arsenal, Beijing is shifting from liquid-fuelled missiles like the DF-5s and DF-4s to advanced, solid-fuelled systems like the DF-31 and DF-31A intercontinental ballistic missiles and the JL-2 submarine-launched ballistic missile.

Soaring Dragon, Rising Tiger and Assertive Godzilla

In a world of rapid change, the Asian strategic landscape is altering even faster. Given Asia's immense diversity and complex challenges, divisive elements very much dot the Asian landscape. The commercial logic of the market has helped engender profitable trade and economic cooperation between Asian states, especially as economic success in one state has helped motivate and breed similar success in another state. But politics has not been able to keep pace with the changing economics in Asia.

In the face of diversity, what Asia has achieved so far is the establishment of normal conditions for interstate investment and trade, ensuring in the process that politics does not seriously impede economics. With regionalism as embodied by the European Union and the North American Free Trade Agreement becoming a concomitant process of globalization, the question that arises is whether Asia can muster the political will to initiate integration in order to gain advantages similar to those of Europe and North America. There cannot be integration, of course, unless Asian states begin to appreciate that the policies they formulate and pursue are not exclusively a matter of domestic concern.

Broadly, in the coming years, Asian security and prosperity will be greatly influenced by the relationships between the continent's three major powers — China, India and Japan. In addition, the relationship of each of these three giants with the world's pre-eminent power, the United States, will matter considerably in the architecture of the new Asia. In an era of globalization, a power can command immense economic and political clout on a continent distant from its own shores. This is what the United States does in Asia.

Never before in history, however, have there been a strong China, a strong India and a strong Japan at the same time. This development is already creating contradictory pulls and pressures, despite deepening economic ties among these three giants who also make up Asia's largest economies. The once-great nations of India and China, with more than a third of the planet's population, are on the rise again. China's spectacular ascent, however, has helped erode Japan's identity as the global economic miracle. In the coming years, given the tangled Japan–China and India–China relationships, the competitive pride and rivalries among Asia's three biggest powers are likely to greatly influence the continent's geopolitics.

While the heated rivalry between Japan and China has deep roots, dating back to the sixteenth century, the Chinese and Indian military frontiers met for the first time in history only in 1950, when China annexed (or, as its history books say, 'liberated') Tibet, a buffer nearly the size of Western Europe. Within 12 years of becoming India's neighbour, China invaded that country, with Mao Zedong cleverly timing the aggression with the Cuban missile crisis. Since then, the dynamics of the India–China equation have evolved in a way that their nuclear rivalry, competition for influence in Asia, growing bilateral trade and festering border disputes remain centre-stage.

The intricacies of the relationships between China–India and China–Japan are evident both from the bilateral territorial or maritime disputes and the lingering emphasis on historical grievances, especially by Beijing concerning Tokyo and New Delhi vis-à-vis China. Both those relationships remain weighed down by bitter memories. The focus on the past also makes it more difficult to build mutual trust.

Before the terrorist strikes on the World Trade Center and Pentagon deepened American involvement in Asia, a Rand study had suggested that the United States pay greater attention to Asia and widen its strategic alliances there by setting up new military bases in vantage locations from Oman to Guam.[25] In recent years, U.S. policy has increasingly focused on Asia. Moreover, U.S. President Bush's missile-defence plans helped serve as an important element in crystallizing strategic alignments in Asia. The Asian line-up on U.S. missile-defence plans could be a precursor of global power alignments in the years ahead — the United States, its traditional allies and India on one side; China and its three militaristic friends, Burma, North Korea and Pakistan, on the other side; and Russia somewhere in the middle but potentially tilting towards the former.

The Asian strategic landscape is also evolving in response to the efforts of the major players to fashion new equations and expand their strategic space. After the 9/11 terrorist strikes, America used its war on terror to set up a string of new military bases stretching from the Caspian basin to the Pacific. As a consequence, the U.S. military is now present in the largest number of countries since World War II. At the same time, the U.S. preoccupation with the Iraq and Afghanistan wars has come in handy to China to expand its influence in Asia.

Seemingly encouraged by a belief that the geopolitical winds are blowing its way and that before long it will emerge as a global colossus, China is pursuing — for the first time since the Ming dynasty — security interests far from its shores, as underlined by its construction of

Pakistan's deep-water naval base and port at Gwadar, its naval activity along the Burmese coastline, its use of Sri Lanka as a strategic anchor in the Indian Ocean, and its oil-driven strategic forays into Africa. New Delhi not only confronts China along a long, disputed land frontier, but Beijing's strategy for a forward naval presence around peninsular India represents a direct challenge to Indian strategic, energy and commercial interests.

The most striking feature of Asia, with its relatively young demographics, has of course been its rapid economic growth. This is epitomized by China's unprecedented export surge that enabled it, according to its own published figures, to triple its trade surplus with the rest of the world in 2005 alone. In just over a decade, China's foreign trade grew from $289 billion to $2.56 trillion. Surging exports in particular helped lift China to an average GDP growth rate of 9.6 per cent in the quarter century before the 2008-09 global financial insis.

Moreover, Japan and China remain the world's largest creditor nations, with the latter having amassed $2.2 trillion by 2009 in the world's biggest holding of foreign-exchange reserves. Yet, despite such extraordinary liquidity, Asia faces a glaring mismatch between its huge cash mounds and limited investment opportunities. Partly as a consequence, Asia still ploughs much of its foreign-currency reserves into U.S. dollar-denominated investments, incurring a serious risk if the U.S. economy were to go downhill. Despite Asia's new vibrancy, its financial markets need to be better developed, especially the bond markets and the venture-capital markets.

In the case of India, its knowledge capabilities have been amply demonstrated by its emergence as a global information technology powerhouse. With India's open, free system aiding innovation and its knowledge industries, the country has the potential to emerge as a leader in some other advanced technologies, such as biotech and medical sciences. India is pursuing a pioneering model of modernization via democracy — a model that holds important lessons for India as much as for other developing nations. This model based on the rule of law and social justice has helped give voice, identity and opportunity to millions belonging to the traditionally deprived and disadvantaged sections of Indian society. By focusing on original designs and products, India can move rapidly from business process outsourcing (BPO) to knowledge process outsourcing (KPO).

Economically, Asia appears on the right track, with its high GDP growth rates likely to continue in the foreseeable future. Such has been the surge in Asian exports that it has unbalanced global shipping: 60 per cent of the containers from Asia to North America, and 41 per cent from Asia to Europe, came back empty in 2005, according to Drewry Shipping Consultants, a research organization and consultancy.[26] In the years ahead, Asia is expected to remain the main engine driving global economic growth, including in the world's largest economy, the United States.

Long-term Winner: India or China?

In the context of the Asian renaissance, it has become commonplace to compare the economic march of the continent's two giants, China and India, and to project future growth on the basis of their present relative advantage. The comparisons inexorably pit India's services-driven growth and institutional stability, founded on pluralism, transparency and the rule of law, against China's resolute leadership, high savings rate, good infrastructure, manufacturing forte and strong work ethics.

China's success in attracting foreign direct investment totalling a staggering $563.8 billion between 1978 and 2004 — more than 10 times what Japan drew between 1945 and 2000 — comes from a comparative advantage rooted in its present demographic asset: a vast supply of cheap labour. In contrast, India has profited from its considerable pool of skilled, English-speaking workers that have boosted its business-process, information-technology and high-tech sectors. India's multitude of software engineers and other professionals has helped secure two-third of all the information-technology work off-shored from America. Indian IT and BPO exports are set to rise to $80 billion by 2011.

The hype on China, nonetheless, remains the strongest, although closer scrutiny tells a somewhat different story. For example, Indian firms managed to deliver higher rates of return of between 80 per cent and 200 per cent than their Chinese counterparts in six major industrial sectors from 1999 to 2003.[27] While lagging far behind China in attracting foreign direct investment (FDI), India is way ahead in drawing foreign-equity investment. Indeed, it has emerged as a destination of choice for private-equity firms.

The China–India competition, first and foremost, symbolizes contrasting political ideals and represents a quiet rivalry over ideas. Ideas also define their comparative (and prospective) appeal. Can India, for example, prove that democratic politics and market economics blend nicely as a formula to make a poor country prosperous, or is the Chinese autocratic model better suited for that mission? Lacking the U.S. zeal to export democracy, India looks at democracy in practical terms, as 'the most effective means to reconcile the polyglot components of the [Indian] state emerging from the colonial past', according to Henry Kissinger. He also notes: 'India, striving neither to spread its culture nor its institutions, is thus not a comfortable partner [of the United States] for global ideological missions'.[28]

Despite such a down-to-earth Indian approach, Beijing has shown for the time being at least that while India has valid reasons to feel proud about the dividends yielded by its democracy, it is the Chinese model that can deliver superior economic dividends, as underlined by China's 9.6 per cent average annual economic growth rate over a quarter century. The Indian GDP has grown, in contrast, at an average rate of nearly 6 per cent a year since economic reforms were introduced in 1991, almost doubling the size of the Indian economy. Asian tigers like South Korea and Taiwan also achieved impressive economic growth under political autocracy, before pressure from their burgeoning middle classes made them move towards democracy.

India, which is still a decade behind China in economic reforms and reluctant to streamline its mammoth bureaucracy, remains mired by red tape that slows down business growth. In fact, given its more recent economic history — which was dominated first by colonialism, built on foreign capital, and then by socialism, built on fear of that capital — India embarked on economic reforms grudgingly, in response to a balance-of-payments crisis in 1991 and not as part of a calculated, China-style strategy. Prone to populism, India has continued to pursue reforms haltingly, without a clear vision. Yet today, private capital in India has created not only an unshakable entrepreneurial revolution but also an array of world-class companies or mini-multinationals that are busily signing mega-deals and gobbling up overseas firms. In contrast, China's corporate acquisitions abroad have been led by its state-owned behemoths.

With its many bottlenecks and layers of officialdom, India, however, remains its own worst enemy. This is apparent from the manner in which it has over the decades constrained the development of its own economic and military power. India can easily develop more rapidly if it were to break free from the fetters tying it down. While any visitor to China is struck by that country's new grand cities, express highways and top-notch tunnels and bridges, the Indian republic can hardly boast of a single world-class, imposing building it has built in its capital, with colonial-era structures still serving as seats of government. Indian cities, on the whole, present themselves as less clean, modern and orderly than cities in China, where frenzied construction activity has made the tall cranes ubiquitous.

Even now, as revealed by a World Bank study, it takes more than twice as long to start a business in India as in China — 89 days compared with 41 — or to register property, 67 days to 32, or to enforce a contract, 425 days to 241. To make matters worse, when the business is established, the study found, Indian factories suffer 17 power failures a month on average, compared with five in China.[29] Forcing policy changes through India's labyrinthine political and bureauratic processes is not easy. With India lagging behind China economically and militarily, a condescending Chinese attitude towards India has taken root. Chinese border provocations have grown.

The real advantage of China over India lies in its very opaque, tightly run system that enables the neo-Leninist regime in Beijing to set long-term policy goals and then work quietly and resolutely to achieve them, in line with what the Chinese remind visitors — that they are a patient lot. The opaqueness helps to cloak facts or plans China does not wish to bring to light. China's unwavering direction and perseverance have been highlighted by its relentless accretion of economic and military strength since Deng Xiaoping's reforms began in 1979, with even the bloody 1989 crackdown in Beijing's Tiananmen Square not interrupting that march to greater power. India's fundamental weakness arises from its revolving-door politics and weak leadership, and the ensuing difficulty to establish long-term plans or to unflinchingly pursue them. Indian foreign policy has remained largely *ad hoc*, risk-averse and prone to after-the-fact rationalization.

In general, China's ruthless pragmatism and assertiveness contrast sharply with India's sanctimonious worldview and internal political squabbling. Prone to seduction by praise, India is a nation that yearns to be loved, and feels best when its policies enjoy external affirmation. China, quite the opposite, wants to be held in respect and awe, and never muffles its view when any interest is at issue. As the only thriving democracy in a vast region stretching from Jordan to China, India can rightly be proud of its deeply rooted democratic traditions. But through its seeming inability to fashion policies as astute and farsighted as China's, or marshal the unflinching resolve that Beijing displays, India lamentably shows that democracy is not always an advantage.

Yet democracy remains India's greatest asset. According to one publication, 'As the two growing powers of Asia sort out their places in their continent and the world, India has a comparative advantage over China that it doesn't always exploit: its status as the globe's largest democracy. For a while, when China was growing economically much faster than India, this advantage wasn't so obvious; you could conclude that democracy was too messy to allow rapid development. But India's pace of growth has picked up dramatically in the past decade, and it now can offer a model to smaller Asian countries — themselves increasingly democratic — of growth and a humane government complementing each other'.[30]

Despite China's rapid strides, reports of growing peasant protests and other unrest in China do raise doubts about the long-term sustainability of the Chinese model, characterized by the pell-mell pursuit of private wealth. In 2004 alone, according to official Chinese admission, 74,000 rural 'incidents' involving some 3.7 million citizens occurred — a euphemism for 'violent protests' — prompting President Hu Jintao and Premier Wen Jiabao in 2005 to pose for photographs with peasants and to slash farm taxes in a desperate effort to contain the spreading unrest.

Yet the number of such protests in China officially rose to 87,000 in 2005. Given that the number of 'incidents' reported in 1993 was 8,700, 2005 represented a 10-fold increase. But 2005 was not an unusual year: such 'incidents' have continued to rise by about 10 per cent annually since, according to Chinese media accounts and officials. What is interesting is that with globalization precluding the effective muzzling of all channels of information by the state, China's commissars are learning, even if reluctantly, to adopt novel methods to cope with new realities, as demonstrated by Hu and Wen. More importantly, what the rising discontent suggests is that the Chinese leadership is sitting on a tinderbox of political and social unrest. Unrest is growing as rapidly as China's GDP.

For its part, India, despite its factionalized politics and raucous democracy, has continued to make steady economic strides. Through superior corporate performance, a globally competitive services industry and a rising consumption base that diminishes reliance on exports as the growth engine, India's model seemingly assures stable development and sound returns for investors. In contrast, consumption is deprioritized in China's massive investment-led, exports-oriented growth.

China's dogged focus on generating more and more exports is reflected in a factory slogan designed to inspire Chinese workers: 'One who earns money in China is a winner; one who earns money overseas is a hero'.[31] That is in keeping with what the late Chinese leader, Deng Xiaoping, said three decades ago that 'to get rich is glorious'. The exports-driven approach has prompted the United States to demand that China rely more on domestic demand and less on global trade imbalances to power its economic drive.

On the negative side, both India and China are witnessing greater income gaps between rural and urban areas as well as between provinces. Such inequalities are starker in China because of faster economic growth, as revealed by comparative inequality indicators.[32] In India, which is far from becoming a real globalization success story, there is a yawning gap between economic growth and social progress, with the country still home to the world's largest conglomeration of malnourished people. That gap has not narrowed despite the Indian state's massive pork-barrel spending largely in the form of subsidies, designed to mitigate the hardship of the poor and help create a trickledown effect of wealth.

China's income distribution now is analogous to the socially and economically corrosive income divides in Latin America, setting China apart from its three prosperous East Asian neighbours — Japan, South Korea and Taiwan. In fact, Japan, with an impressive egalitarian structure akin to Scandinavian countries, can genuinely be proud of its inspiring model of income distribution — a model that has come under strain in the face of policies of deregulation, privatization, spending cuts and tax breaks for the rich introduced by the now-ousted Liberal Democratic Party.

There is also a deep-seated China–India divide that not many recognize. India's boisterous, cut-throat politics and unruly parliamentary practices tend to advertise turbulence and conceal a deeper consensus in the system over key elements. Unknown to many, India is actually a beacon of tolerance and inner strength. China, in contrast, portrays stability, clarity and direction, with the opacity of its system helping to hide the turbulence within. Its massive repressive machine is increasingly being directed to help maintain social stability on the domestic front.

The two countries represent contrasting approaches to stability building and public-interest promotion. China enforces order from the top down, while India, by facilitating grassroots participation in governance and development, seeks to ensure that its stability is built from the bottom up. Social unrest thus is a bigger threat to China's long-term stability than to India's.

Furthermore, China puts public interest ahead of individual rights, with the regime in Beijing arrogating to itself the right to decide what is in public good. One example of that are the local regulations restricting freedom of movement within China to help keep rural migrants out of major cities. This has allowed the city landscape in Shanghai or Guangzhou not to be marred by the carbuncular sight of slums so common in Bombay or Rio de Janeiro. An influx into Chinese cities is deterred through a permit system and by denying illegal migrants access to social and educational services.

The scene in India is quite the opposite, with public interest defined by a multitude of players. The constitutional protection of individual rights in India, while ensuring public oversight over the exercise of governmental and corporate powers, has become a licence for the organized minority to hold public interest at ransom. From protests against the building of hydropower projects to local opposition to the broadening of highways, the organized few in India can block development.

But even the silent majority in India feels empowered to the extent that if any Indian government dared to impose Chinese-type controls on migration to cities, it would be swept out of office. As described by two foreign reporters, Indian citizens on the margins 'have the power to derail the best-laid plans of investors and the government with votes, protests and the courts. India desperately needs to fix its archaic infrastructure — potholed roads, rundown airports and decrepit power plants — if it wants to seriously compete with China for investment. Yet getting it done often runs counter to the interests of those just beginning to share in the new prosperity. In China…illegal squatters…are dealt with decisively and unceremoniously. One day they are there; the next they are not. Democratic India is a different story'.[33]

All told, China's overarching advantage over India is leadership, vision and a result-oriented approach. However, China's strengths also help hide its frailties. It is doubtful whether the Chinese system, with its inherent limitations, can survive cataclysmic political and financial shocks to the extent of its Indian counterpart. While the going stays good, the Chinese system will continue to draw strength and legitimacy from its ability to deliver timely and impressive dividends.

Little noticed in the clash of ideas is that, in the longer run, globalization threatens China's autocracy, not India's democracy. Whether China follows a stable or violent path to political modernization will determine its continued unity and strength. China may have arrived as a global economic powerhouse in the twenty-first century, but its record on the basic human principles of freedom, liberty and justice puts it in the Dark Ages. Also, assessments that it could overtake the United States as the largest economy by 2050 presuppose that it will have decades of peace and internal political stability — something that few rapidly rising world powers in history have enjoyed.

Clearly, the risks of grave social and political flare-ups are higher in China than in India, where the participatory processes and avenues for free expression and debate serve as a safety valve and provide a measure of stability. In most other aspects, however, China knows what it takes to become a great power. While growing realism in India has yet to overcome traditions of naïve idealism and political divisiveness, Beijing epitomizes strategic clarity and pragmatism, zealously erecting the building blocks of comprehensive national power.

China's level-headedness and subtlety in foreign policy are evident from its handling of the United States. Maintaining a constructive, mutually beneficial relationship with the United States remains central to Chinese foreign-policy interests. That objective is also critical to China's continued rapid economic growth, symbolized by the ubiquitous nature of the 'Made in China' label in the world. The export of cheap consumer goods to America indeed helps subsidize Chinese military and economic modernization. China's trade surplus with the United States grew from $28 billion in 2001 to $251 billion in 2007. Indeed, China's trade with the United States rose some 1200 per cent between 1990 and 2005, even as the Asian share of American imports slipped to 36 per cent in the same period.

At the same time, the United States now relies on Chinese surpluses and savings to finance its huge budget deficits, even as cheap Chinese-made toys, clothing, furniture and electronic goods help keep U.S. inflation down. By outsourcing lower-cost manufacturing to China and back-office work to India, the U.S. economy can concentrate on higher-value productivity. According to various estimates, about two-thirds of China's exports are produced in factories that are financed at least in part with foreign investment. It is also significant that China has become such a major creditor to America, investing as much as 70 per cent of its mammoth foreign-currency reserves in U.S. government and corporate debt.[34] Such purchases of U.S. debt help hold down U.S. interest rates, prop up the value of the dollar and finance American spending.

Although the two demographic titans, China and India, loom large in popular perceptions on where Asia is headed economically, the much-smaller Japan has remained a global economic powerhouse. Given the size of Japan's economy — its gross domestic product was just under $5 trillion in 2008 — annual Japanese growth of just 2 per cent translates into about $100 billion a year in additional output, or nearly the entire annual gross domestic product of small economies like Singapore and the Philippines. Still, given China's rapid economic strides, Japan has been readying itself for the day that it is eclipsed economically by its neighbour.

In December 2005, China said it had found a statistical error, which, upon correction, put the size of the Chinese economy 17 per cent, or $285 billion, larger than previously determined. The 'discovery' of previously unaccounted-for economic production equivalent to the size of Austria's or Indonesia's economy, helped China's economy, in one stroke, to leapfrog over Britain, France and Italy and become the world's fourth largest. In fact, the revision was equivalent to the combined annual output of Argentina, Venezuela and Ecuador.[35] Then at the beginning of 2009, China overtook Germany to become the world's third largest economy after revising its figures for output growth. China's economy now is nearly three times larger than India's. Even in land size, China is three times bigger than India. In fact, China is close to surpassing Japan as the world's number two economy.

The world already courts Beijing and takes Tokyo less importantly. The ugly truth is that a country's international standing is tied to the reach of the weapons in its armoury. It is revealing that countries armed with intercontinental ballistic missiles (ICBMs) are all veto-holding permanent members of the Security Council, while the aspirants for additional permanent seats (such as Brazil, Germany, India, Japan and South Africa) strikingly lack such military reach. If Britain and France were stripped of their submarine-launched ballistic missiles, they would cease to look important powers.

India and Japan cannot fail to notice that China's global clout flows from the combination of military muscle, strategic ambition to be 'a world power second to none' and an economy that has come up so fast that few economists and pundits could foresee the rise. These strengths of China spur fear and uncertainty among its neighbours, on one side, as well as offer opportunity and profit, on the other. The opportunity part is evident from the efforts of its neighbours and other trading partners to expand their access to the Chinese market, which has become a major driver of Asian and global growth.

Beijing, in turn, has been employing its buying power to promote its security and foreign-policy interests. It has a record of using high-visibility commercial deals to garner leverage or punish other governments. In the largest-ever Chinese shopping extravaganza, a trade team from Beijing went on a coast-to-coast buying spree in the United States in April 2006, committing to purchase $16.2 billion worth of aircraft, agricultural products, auto parts, tele-communications gear and computer software — deals that were intended to deflect tensions over China's gargantuan trade surplus with America, accounting for more than one-quarter of the overall U.S. trade deficit.

China, despite a smaller economy, overtook Japan as the country with the largest foreign-currency reserves in the world. That gives Beijing more power to influence global interest rates. China's foreign-exchange reserves went from a mere $11.09 billion in 1990 to $853.6 billion by early 2006 to overtake Japan as the country with the world's largest foreign-currency holdings. But by the end of 2008, China more than doubled its foreign-exchange reserves to over $2 trillion. Aided by the low value of yuan, which keeps its goods cheap, China's huge trade surpluses are swelling its coffers.

The trade surpluses are all set to continue in the coming years as China pursues an economic model that favours export-driven growth over domestic consumer-led growth. Between 1995-2005, for example, China, by its own admission, racked up a whopping $350 billion through such surpluses.[36] Despite demonstrating its trading clout worldwide, China's own financial system is fraught with risks, as underlined by the estimated $500 billion in bad debt that is holding back its banks. The state has tolerated a lot of bad debt as a sort of welfare payout to keep workers employed in loss-making enterprises and hold unrest under control.

While the wealth in India is with private entrepreneurs, it is largely with the state in China. Indeed, the differing approaches of China and India go beyond their political and economic systems and practices: they are rooted in the fact that the two represent contrasting cultures and civilizations, with little in common between them other than shared values on family, education and individual enterprise. Culturally and in terms of their worldview, India and China are as disparate as any two societies can be.

The Demographic Factor

Internationally, demographics will drive economic growth. Economies with burgeoning young populations clearly have a leg up in the economic-growth race, as nations saddled with aging citizens like Japan and several in Europe struggle to grow at rates above zero. In fact, Japan's population began shrinking in 2005, according to two separate official Japanese reports. Such has been the steady aging of the Japanese society that the proportion of people in the age group 65 and above in Japan reached the world's highest at 21 per cent in 2005, surpassing Italy's 20 per cent. Government statistics also revealed that Japan now has the world's lowest percentage of people under the age of 15; they constitute only 13.6 per cent of its population. The year 2005 also marked the first time that the number of natural deaths surpassed the number of babies born since 1899, when the compilation of statistics first began in Japan.

Japan's fertility rate — the average number of children born to a woman over a lifetime — was 1.37 in 2008 after having dropped to a record low of 1.29 in 2005. In comparison, the fertility rate is 2.12 in the United States and 1.84 in Britain. Japan's present population of 127.6 million could shrink by a third within 50 years if current trends continue. That would lead to a smaller workforce and to a serious impact on Japan's economy, besides constricting its social-security resources.[37] Already one in five Japanese is 65 or older. In fact, Japanese women continue to have the highest life expectancy in the world, living an average of 85.49 years, while Japanese men live an average of 78.53 years.

Japan's declining-population problem, however, is not as acute as the one faced by Russia, whose population could shrink from the present level of 140 million to less than 100 million by 2050 unless financial incentives and subsidies to encourage women to have more children succeed in arresting the fall. Russian women at present have more abortions than births, while the average age of death for a Russian male has declined to 58.9 years — nearly two decades below that of an American man. While Russia's Slavic population has been dwindling at the rate of 700,000 a year, its Muslim minority has been growing by leaps and bounds. If this trend were to persist, Russia could well become a Muslim-majority state in the decades ahead.

On the other hand, India's population could outstrip China's by 2040. While China's population will age by then, a vast majority of India's population will still be of working age. In that sense, India is better placed demographically for long-term economic growth.[38]

Asia, as a whole, faces an unusual demographic challenge — a gender imbalance with far-reaching social and political ramifications. While women outnumber men in Europe by 7 per cent and in North America by 3.4 per cent, Asia has too many men who cannot find wives and who thus could fan jingoistic nationalism as well as aggravate social problems, including crime, prostitution and sex tourism.

The misuse of modern diagnostic technology to identify female foetuses for abortion has aided the traditional pick for sons in ethnic Chinese societies (in China, Taiwan and Singapore) as well as in South Korea and parts of northern India. 'Understanding the effect of the testosterone overload may be most important in China', according to one analyst, who has warned: 'A Beijing power struggle between cautious old technocrats and aggressive young nationalists may be decided by mobs of rootless young men, demanding uniforms, rifles and a chance to liberate Taiwan'.[39]

While by 2020 as many as 40 million marriageable-age men in mainland China may have to make do without wives, China at the same time is projected to grey fast because of the policy instituted in 1979 that put a one-child cap on urban families and allowed a rural family to have only two kids. China has come a long way since the Mao era when sex was officially a matter of doing one's reproductive duty for the state. After the communist takeover in 1949, Mao encouraged high birth rates to expand the labour force and build a new country. But after his death, a rethink in Beijing led to a policy to restrict the booming population growth.

Now China confronts very different population-related challenges. Its population is beginning to age 'at a much lower-income level (and thus at a much earlier stage of economic development) than industrial countries. Today, China is still relatively poor, but its median age is not far from the international average', according to a February 2006 report from the Deutsche Bank's research department. The report also points out: 'Other countries have reached a similar age bracket as China's today of between 32–34 years at a much higher income per capita and thus at a later stage in their economic development.'[40]

All these factors imply three possible consequences. One, China is likely to grow old before it becomes rich. Two, China's pension system faces a demographic time bomb, with the Deutsche Bank report citing an International Monetary Fund assessment that the transition to a more sustainable pension system is likely to cost Beijing $100 billion, plus local-government expenses. And three, a shrinking labour force in the looming demographic scenario could seriously damage China's economic prospects, prodding wary foreign investors to diversify their portfolios away from the emergent risks in China. However, China's population problem, in comparison to Russia's or Japan's, is less pressing and potentially reversible through a change in official policy that lifts the cap.

Although India's population-growth rate has been on the decline since reaching a peak of 2.5 per cent in 1981, the current rate still translates into India adding a Netherlands to its populace every year. While a chart of Japan's projected population picture looks like a pyramid standing on its head, with large numbers of retirees supported by a narrow workforce base, India's population projections underscore a broad, sturdy base.

Yet India, too, faces a demographic challenge, but of a very different kind, as its pool of skilled workers is set to reach its natural limit. Without reforms in its education system to improve quality and skills, including through the deregulation of higher education, India could face a shortfall of well-qualified professionals in many fields. For example, it now is already confronting a shortfall of business-process workers and IT engineers, as had been warned by a 2005 NASSCOM–McKinsey Report.[41] That is because only 25 per cent of Indian technical graduates and 10 per cent to 15 per cent of general college graduates are suitable for employment in the offshore IT and BPO industries, respectively. Yet, the Indian government is doing the opposite of what the emerging challenge demands — further burdening the higher-education system with caste-based quotas.

At present, as profits flatten in the West, companies continue to pivot to India, China and other Asian nations with young demographics. For corporate leaders around the world, emerging industrial powers like China and India are sources not only of low-cost production and cheap labour but also of substantial growth opportunities. Finding and serving new customers in the developing world, not merely cutting costs, constitute the focus of corporations in the new phase of global expansion. At the same time, access to brainpower in countries like

India and China has become essential for Western firms to build up their research and development and become more competitive. This relationship benefits the West as much as it does Asia.

Challenge of Effective Governance

Demographics alone cannot determine interstate issues of power and strength. Which country becomes (or stays) a great power will be decided largely by the quality of its statecraft and its ability to develop and exploit 'hard power', economic and military. That is where the India–China gulf and the Japan–China gulf become wide, not merely because India and Japan are politically open and the third power is politically closed. Unlike China, Japan or India, fundamentally, has yet to develop a clearly thought-out strategy and the grit to become a true world power in its own right.

A country's power and standing are shaped by positive attributes, such as leadership quality, strategic vision, good governance, pursuit of growth-boosting policies, rigorous education standards, political stability and internal cohesion. Negative determinants, such as deficient governance, a high level of corruption, environmental and other man-made problems, and wide social and economic disparities, act as a drag on a country's pursuit of goals.

Political corruption poses a corrosive and intractable problem for China and India. It clearly risks undermining the vitality of Indian democracy, as pointed up by the World Bank's 2006 suspension of $800 million in loans to the Indian health sector because of corruption in procurement. On that score, the opaque, autocratic system in China does not fare much better either, with increasing evidence linking those holding the reins of power in Beijing with endemic, big-bucks corruption. President Hu, who has recommended a list of do's and don't's, or 'eight glories and eight shames', to Communist Party members, has emphasized 'anti-corruption and the building of a clean government' as 'an important strategic mission'.

In fact, India and China, in different ways, demonstrate how power is the supreme corrupter. The more corrupt a system, the greater its corrupting power. The greater the concentration of decision making, the bigger the abuse. It is not an accident that the most corrupt sectors in China happen to be all state monopolies, like financial services, infrastructure and energy. The same is the story in India. A corrupt system quickly corrupts those who enter it, turning them into prisoners of greed. The ideals, commitments and goals with which well-meaning individuals go into a corrupting system dissipate rapidly.

Metastasizing corruption is a major challenge staring Asia as a whole in the face. The Berlin-based Transparency International, as part of its annual survey of corruption (which it defines as the abuse of public office for private gain), publishes an index of countries ranked from the least corrupt to the most corrupt, on a scale of 10 to 0, with 10 representing no corruption and 0 signifying total sleaze and bribery. Its annual *Corruption Perceptions Index* brings out the growing problem of corruption in Asia, bestowing the continent with the dubious distinction of having one of the world's two most corrupt countries. The 2008 index lists Singapore, with a score of 9.2, as the least corrupt state in Asia, and Burma (with a score of only 1.3) as the most corrupt nation in the world after Somalia.[42]

Of the three largest Asian economies, Japan by far is the least corrupt, with a score of 7.3, according to that index. The strong traditions of 'honour' and personal integrity in Japan have been a great help in containing the level of corruption. China and India, with fairly close scores of 3.6 and 3.4 respectively, are way down in the list.

Among the most corrupt states in Asia, besides Burma, are Afghanistan (with a score of 1.5), followed by Uzbekistan (1.8), Laos (2.0) and Bangladesh (2.1). The growing tolerance of corruption in Asia is exemplified by China's official statistic that only 2.9 per cent of the 170,850 Communist Party officials and members implicated in corruption scandals in 2004 were prosecuted in that country. Chinese Premier Wen, addressing the 2006 annual meeting of the National People's Congress, acknowledged that China's rise has been accompanied by a 'high concentration of all kinds of acute problems', including official corruption that 'violated the rights of the people'. In Vietnam, after the uncovering of a trail of mansions, mistresses, luxury cars and protection money led to the ouster of the transport minister and the jailing of his deputy in the spring of 2006, the leader of the ruling Communist Party, Nong Duc Manh, warned that corruption 'threatens the survival of our system'.

Corruption is an evil that eats into the vitals of a society. That the poorest states of Asia like Bangladesh and Burma are also among the most corrupt only shows that corruption is both a cause of poverty as well as a hindrance to the amelioration of the conditions of the impoverished people. Corruption undermines economic growth and social progress, undercuts the trust and confidence of citizens in the fairness and impartiality of public administration, impedes good governance, erodes the rule of law, distorts competitive conditions in business transactions, discourages domestic and foreign investment, fosters a 'black-market' economy and raises serious moral and political concerns. In sum, corruption obstructs a nation from realizing its goals.

The only way corruption can be fought is through integrity in public service; improved governance; measures and systems to ensure fiscal transparency; strengthened anti-bribery enforcement; governmental accountability; and active public involvement. No anti-corruption drive can work if those who are the source of the problem hold the key to the campaign's effective implementation. The independence of investigative and judicial bodies is a prerequisite to strengthening the rule of law and developing an anti-corruption culture in politics and business. Proactive strategies to promote citizens' participation in anti-corruption efforts can be a great aid.

Rapid economic growth in Asia has also created, unfortunately, greater social inequity. Asia is more unequal than ever before, as shown by the United Nations Development Programme's annual *Human Development Reports*, underscoring the need for governments to adopt progressive tax and social policies. The *Human Development Reports* measure inequality on the basis of the 'gini index' instead of the 'gini coefficient'. A gini-index value of 0 represents perfect equality and a value of 100 perfect inequality. In the 2009 *Report*, there are no nations close to either end of the scale. The United States, the spearhead of capitalism, measures 40.8 on the gini index, reflecting the vast social and economic disparities in its society, despite the American economic paradigm serving now as the sole model in the world in the absence of any credible alternative.

What the index brings out is that, with perhaps the sole exception of Japan, Asian states are becoming increasingly inequitable in terms of distribution of income. Such states even include the three Asian nations still under communist rule — China, Vietnam and Laos. These three one-party states, where income inequalities were narrow not long ago, now measure 41.5, 37.8 and 32.6, respectively, on the gini index.

Even the tiny city-state of Singapore is pretty unequal, registering 42.5 on the index. With a score of 36.8, India, surprisingly, comes out better than China, Vietnam and Singapore.[43] Yet the spreading Maoist rural insurgency in the poorest districts of India at a time when the country is politically more resilient and economically booming is a testament to the costs of growing inequalities. The ragtag bands of rebels wish to supplant Indian parliamentary democracy with a proletariat dictatorship inspired by Mao's Little Red Book, despite Maoist China's own embrace of market capitalism. In fact, Indian Prime Minister Manmohan Singh went to the extent of declaring Maoist violence as the 'single biggest security challenge ever faced by our country'. The high incidence of malnutrition among children in some Indian states, particularly Bihar, Uttar Pradesh and Madhya Pradesh, illustrates why New Delhi needs to focus on inclusive growth.

More striking are the level of disparities in Singapore. Given Singapore's claim to having the highest standard of living in Southeast Asia, the extent of inequalities is appalling in a teeny, one party-dominated state where the younger generation aspires for greater social and political freedoms.

Japan's gini-index value is 24.9, about the same as the values of Scandinavian countries — Denmark (24.7), Sweden (25.0), Norway (25.8) and Finland (26.9). Nothing can better illustrate Japan's world-class egalitarian structure than this UNDP finding: the bottom 20 per cent of the Japanese population consumes 15.4 per cent of GDP, and the top 20 per cent consumes 35.7 per cent of GDP. In comparison to Japan, the disparities in most other Asian states are really stark.

China's social stability, for example, faces a serious threat from the widening income gaps in the country, particularly between rural and urban populations and between the residents of the eastern coastal belt and the interior provinces. With less than 1 per cent of households holding more than 60 per cent of China's wealth, income inequality is estimated to have shot up by at least 50 per cent since the late 1970s, 'making China one of the most unequal societies in Asia'.[44]

Even in egalitarian Japan, a new trail of conspicuous consumption is creating glaring lifestyle differences in a nation of nearly 128 million people that once prided itself as a one-class society. From a stratified pre-war society, post-war Japan transformed itself into a classless nation where companies offered lifetime employment and the government practised a form of paternalistic capitalism. To help reverse the dramatic fall in Japan's economic fortunes since 1990, the 2001-2006 government of Prime Minister Junichiro Koizumi embarked on painful economic reforms carrying significant social costs, while many Japanese firms began abandoning lifetime employment and linking promotions to performance, not seniority.

Clearly, one of Japan's most remarkable accomplishments — egalitarianism — now faces the threat of erosion. Tokyo's Roppongi Hills district, for instance, has come to symbolize Japan's new mega-rich, even as the number of Japanese households receiving welfare payments rose sharply in a five-year period — from 751,000 in fiscal 2000–01 to almost 1.4 million in 2005–06. Official statistics also show that the percentage of Japanese households with no savings virtually doubled to 23.8 per cent in the same period — the highest figure since the early 1960s.

In addition to the rise of corruption and greater disparities within states, a third consequence of the rapid economic growth in Asia has been environmental degradation. Again, other than Japan, the other Asian states are doing poorly in reconciling development with environmental protection. For example, ever-rising sand squalls not only blanket Beijing and other northern Chinese cities, but also threaten to speed up the spread of barren wasteland to the heart of China. The desert's advance from the arid northwest has been aided by government-led irrigated farming that has diverted water resources from the region's ecological lifeline — the Shiyang River and its offshoots — and thereby left other land open to desertification. Respect for the environment and better management of natural resources are notions still not embraced actively by governments in Asia.

Asia is already facing a fresh-water crisis, with several hundred million Asians lacking ready access to drinking water. The geopolitical importance of Tibet, whose forcible absorption brought the new Chinese state to the borders of India, can be seen from the fact that almost all the great Asian rivers originate there. If the demand for water in Asia continues to grow at the current rate, the interstate and intrastate disputes over water resources could potentially turn into conflicts in the years ahead.

Deforestation, overgrazing, poor management of river basins and inefficient irrigation systems have aggravated fresh-water scarcity, with contamination also limiting access to clean water. The Aral Sea in Central Asia serves as a stark example of how pollution can degrade water sources. Such is the inefficient water use that it takes 1000 tons of water in China to produce just one ton of wheat.

To fight poverty, disease and pollution, Asia needs both to augment its water supplies through better distribution and management of resources and to improve its sanitation services. After all, clean water is the key to good health. However, the growing use of subterranean supplies of groundwater in China, India and elsewhere due to inadequate availability of surface water threatens to accelerate environmental degradation.

Modernizing economies like China and India, with their growing demands for resources, including energy and water, are bound to add pressure to the global ecosystems. Their growth trajectories will impact on efforts to slow down environmental degradation and global climate change.

According to government figures put out by the Xinhua news agency of China, the drinking-water supply of 300 million Chinese — nearly a quarter of the country's population — is laced with harmful chemicals; nine of 10 Chinese cities suffer from polluted water; and more than 100 Chinese cities already face severe water shortages.[45] Such information jibes with the estimate of China's State Environment Protection Agency in 2005 that 70 per cent of the water in five of the country's seven major river systems is too contaminated for human use. Pollution of rivers is also a major problem in India.

China has already emerged as the world's largest net emitter of greenhouse gases, overtaking the United States. China, in per capita terms, however, remains far behind the U.S., which, with just 4.5 per cent of the world's population, discharges nearly a quarter — 24 per cent — of all emissions of carbon dioxide, the main greenhouse gas linked to global warming.[46] According to the U.S. Environmental Protection Agency, about 6.6 tons of greenhouse gases are emitted per person in America, placing that country No. 1 in the world in per capita emissions, with Japan ranking No. 13. China and India rank much lower, with the latter not even among the top 100 per capita emitters of greenhouse gases.

Even so, India and China face major environmental problems in terms of air pollution, contamination of water, waste mismanagement, and the destruction of forests, mangroves and other natural habitats. When the tsunami, a disaster of epic proportions struck southern Asia on December 26, 2004, it wreaked destruction with a vengeance on beaches that had been cleared of mangroves for development. In a different context, researchers from the U.S. Department of Energy have reported in the *Geophysical Research Letters* that China's skies have darkened over the past 50 years, possibly due to haze resulting from a ninefold increase in fossil-fuel emissions, and that the amount of solar radiation measured at more than 500 stations in China actually fell between 1954 and 2001 despite a decrease in cloud cover.[47]

Nothing better illustrates the formidable challenges Asia faces to evolve effective governance than the annual *Failed States Index* (FSI) prepared by the independent, Washington-based group, The Fund for Peace. The index, first unveiled in 2005, focuses on the comparative vulnerabilities and weaknesses of various countries carrying the risk of state failure. Employing a conflict-assessment methodology that examines internal conflict and decay, the index is based on the capacities of core state institutions to mitigate adverse trends spurring state instability.

The 2009 index ranks 177 states in order of their vulnerability to violent conflict and societal dysfunction on the basis of 12 specific social, economic, political and military indicators, including refugee flows, rising demographic pressures, factionalized elites, 'legacy of vengeance-seeking group grievance', deteriorating public services, existence of a security apparatus that operates as a state within a state, and criminalization or delegitimization of the state.[48] Norway, with a score of 18.3, ranks as the most stable state and Somalia, with a count of 114.7, figures as the most dysfunctional state.

Japan is the only Asian country to feature among the index's 15 most stable states in the world. Interestingly, China and Russia, despite their strong leadership, run a significant risk of state decay. The index ranks China No. 57 and Russia No. 71 in the world in terms of vulnerability to state failure. In contrast, India, with its No. 87 ranking, is presented as a relatively more stable state, notwithstanding its weak leadership and political squabbling.

Yet grave symptoms of state failure are most visible in the neighbourhood around India — a region that bristles with six failing states, underscoring the lurking dangers to Indian security. Pakistan, with a high score of 103.1, is ranked as the 10th most dysfunctional state in the world.[49] According to the 2009 index, Pakistan and Afghanistan (ranked No. 7) are even more unstable than the Stalinist, isolated state of North Korea, which is placed No. 17. The other failing states in southern Asia are Burma, ranked No. 13 in the world, Bangladesh, No. 19, Sri Lanka, No. 22, and Nepal, No. 25. The more dysfunctional a state the lesser its ability to provide basic security and public services to its citizens and retain a monopoly on the use of force.

Evolving Strategic Balance

The high GDP growth rates and deepening interstate trade and investment in Asia have not helped settle political differences and disputes. China is India's and Japan's largest trading partner, but that has not stopped Beijing and New Delhi, and Beijing and Tokyo, from sharpening their political rhetoric against each other. Taiwan is the largest single investor in China, but that has not influenced the latter to abandon military plans for a full-scale invasion of the island. If anything, the lingering political disputes have underscored the need for a stable strategic balance in Asia.

Rapid economic growth, not surprisingly, has yielded more money to Asian states to import weapons. A 2005 report of the U.S. Congressional Research Service actually put Asian nations at the top of the global list of arms importers. The report revealed that Asia accounted for nearly 50 per cent of the total value of new arms-transfer agreements with developing countries from 2001 through 2004. That worked out to a total of $34.9 billion in current dollars.[50] In other words, Asia has overtaken the Middle East as the biggest conventional weapons importer. It is also not a surprise that the largest importers of weapons in Asia are India and China, both of which value a modern military as vital for expanding power projection force capability.

Again, there is an important difference between China and India. China produces many weapons at home and even exports arms in significant quantities, especially to India's other neighbours — Pakistan, Burma, Bangladesh, Iran and Nepal. Such is the secrecy surrounding Chinese arms exports that Beijing rarely confirms sales of weapons and military equipment abroad. India, on the other hand, spends billions of dollars annually to import conventional arms, some of questionable value, while it neglects to build its own armament-production base and even underfunds its nuclear-weapons and missile programmes.

According to the same CRS study, India has been such a major importer of weapons that it ordered arms worth $15.7 billion just between 1997 and 2004. That accounted for 10.3 per cent of all arms purchases by the developing world. India now has emerged as the world's largest arms importer since 2004. It spent $6.2 billion on new arms deals in 2008. The Indian government budgeted a paltry $160 million for missile development, production and infrastructure and $425 million for nuclear research and development in fiscal 2005–06, but paid, for example, $1.8 billion to Britain for 66 already-obsolescent Hawk jet trainers.

India has become such a big market for foreign arms makers that the U.S. is eyeing a significant share of the $100 billion New Delhi has earmarked for military modernization over the next decade. India pays through its nose for weapons the militaries of the exporting states don't value anymore. Yet India naïvely equates a state's arms sales to it as strategic 'cooperation' or 'partnership'. There is little reflection on why, despite its world-power pretensions, India remains the only large-size country in the world to import most of its conventional weaponry.

In contrast, China's accumulating military capabilities arise largely from indigenous research and production and are aimed at determinedly shifting the balance of military power in Asia in its favour. The rising Chinese military might threatens Japan, India and Taiwan, in particular, and opens the way to constricting U.S. strategic options in Asia in the years ahead.

As part of a calculated strategy to project power far beyond its frontiers and to strengthen its deterrent capabilities, China has placed missile prowess at the centre of its force modernization. It is developing a range of land-attack and anti-ship cruise missiles, long-range surface-to-air missiles and anti-radiation missiles.[51] India, quite the reverse, has found it difficult to break out of its subcontinental straitjacket because its weaponry remains subcontinental in range.

It was only with the Agni-class missiles and the 1998 overt nuclearization that India gained greater strategic space and a higher international profile. Years later, however, India's nuclear and missile capabilities remain regional in range. Although it has Asia's oldest nuclear programme, launched in 1948, India has fallen way behind China in nuclear-weapons capability. According to a 2006 assessment by a former U.S. president, China possesses 400 nuclear weapons and 'India and Pakistan 40 each'.[52] While China developed its first intercontinental ballistic missile, the 12,000-kilometre DF-5, when it was still poor and backward in the 1970s, India has yet to embark on an ICBM programme.

China now spends far more on its military than any other country in Asia. While China's official defence budget in 2009 was approximately $71 billion, the Pentagon estimated it to be two times higher. America's own defence spending is many times larger, totalling $655 billion in 2009. In comparison, Russia's defence budget was $50 billion in 2009. In fact, the United States alone accounts for nearly half — 45 per cent — of the total global military spending, with the United Kingdom, France, China and Japan each making up 4 to 5 per cent of the world total.[53] Compared to the United States, Japan appropriated $53.3 billion and India $29 billion for defence in fiscal 2009. The 14.9 per cent rise in military outlays announced by Beijing in 2009, despite the economic slowdown, was very much in line with its unbroken double-digit increases in defence spending for the past two decades and more.

Two other facets of the fast-altering Asian strategic landscape are the political resurgence of Japan, especially in reaction to China's growing strength and assertiveness, and an ongoing fundamental revision of the U.S. military posture. The defence posture of Japan, which has nearly 240,000 military personnel, is itself undergoing a subtle change. Such a change is taking place in spite of the military proscription in Article 9 of Japan's U.S.-imposed Constitution.

Article 9 of the pacifist Constitution, which came into effect in May 1947, reads: 'Aspiring sincerely to an international peace based on justice and order, the Japanese people forever renounce war as a sovereign right of the nation and the threat or use of force as a mean of settling international disputes.' It goes on to state: 'In order to accomplish the aim of the preceding paragraph, land, sea, and air forces, as well as other war potential, will never be maintained. The right of belligerency of the state will not be recognized.'

For its part, the United States is beginning to reposition its forces and reframe its policies in the Asia–Pacific region. That includes strengthening the operational control of the U.S. Pacific Command, beefing up forces in the U.S. territory of Guam, tightening the U.S. military alliance with Japan and integrating American and Japanese capabilities, and streamlining the U.S. military presence in South Korea. More U.S. forces are being shifted to Asia, including submarines and aircraft carriers. The U.S. relationship with Beijing, while characterized by booming trade and growing engagement, appears stuck somewhere between shaky stability and unsettled tension, with public disputes centred on trade, human rights, military spending, intellectual property and energy. Without the bases in Japan, the United States would be hard placed to project power in East Asia. In fact, America is realigning its military posture in Japan so as to step up interoperability with Japanese forces and enhance U.S. capability to tackle military contingencies even if they were to occur far from Japan's shores.

Japan, a high defence spender maintaining Asia's most powerful non-nuclear navy, seems set to re-emerge as a 'normal', or even a great, military power. It appears determined to shore up the maritime basis of its security.

Although China's rise and assertiveness have compelled Tokyo to reinvigorate its military ties with Washington under the framework of the 1960 Security Treaty, Japan seems headed, at least in the long run, towards greater independence on security matters.

One early signal of that has been Tokyo's expressed intent to slash its host-nation financial support to U.S. forces stationed in Japan. Since the 1952 San Francisco Peace Treaty with Tokyo, U.S. forces have been stationed at bases in Japan. But in recent years issues related to those bases and local demands for their relocation have acted as a spur to Japanese nationalism. Such issues have been particularly observable in the southern island of Okinawa, which had remained under U.S. administration for two additional decades after America ended its occupation of the Japanese mainland. The creeping sentiment against U.S. military presence was exemplified in March 2006 when 87 per cent of the voters in a referendum in the western Japanese city of Iwakuni rejected a plan to host additional American warplanes at the U.S. Marine Corps air station there.[54]

Tokyo, going far beyond its financial obligations under the Japan–U.S. status-of-forces agreement (SOFA), has over the years gradually assumed all expenses for utilities and building-maintenance costs for U.S. troops stationed on its territory. While the United States had to pay the Philippines for many years about $200 million in annual base-leasing fees, the reverse has been true in Japan, where the U.S. military receives a huge host-nation support package from the Japanese government for maintaining bases that constitute a major plank of America's global power-projection strategy. The generous host-nation support, making up about 8 per cent of Japan's defence budget, covers a broad range of items, from expenses for maintaining facilities to utility bills for American troops and their dependents and salaries for Japanese base workers. In addition, Tokyo also provides large federal subsidies to Okinawa for hosting U.S. bases.

Such host-country support has permitted the United States to keep forces in Japan on the cheap — a privilege Washington, not surprisingly, wishes to preserve, despite the nationalistic and local passions aroused by the presence of U.S. troops and bases on Japanese territory. In fact, without access to bases in Japan, the U.S. military will have to withdraw to distant Guam — a move that would further weaken America's naval mobility after the loss of its bases in the Philippines. Yet, in the years ahead, the political rise of Japan is bound to complicate America's desire to preserve its military presence in Japan largely at present levels. Protests by Okinawans have already prompted the United States to agree to relocate the headquarters of its 3rd Marine Expeditionary Force to Guam. Through grants, investments and loans, Tokyo is picking up $6.09 billion of the estimated $10.27 billion tab to relocate 8000 troops of the 3rd Marine Expeditionary Force and about 9000 of their dependents to Guam. About 6 per cent of Okinawa's area now occupied by U.S. military facilities will move back to Japan.

At the same time, Japan is determined not to kowtow to a China eager to supplant the United States as the main player in Asia. India, too, is unlikely to subordinate its interests to a dominance-seeking China. For its part, the United States values any countervailing weight to China but focuses its policy and strategy on promoting its own interests. It would resist getting directly drawn into Sino–Japanese or Sino–Indian disputes. The United States attaches importance to its forward military presence in Japan primarily for advancing its own security and prosperity, not to get drawn into a potential Sino–Japanese clash in the East China Sea that may compel it — against its interest — to extend military support to Tokyo.

Strategic competition between the major Asian states may jibe with U.S. interests, but not strategic conflict. The

Sino–Japanese rivalry and the heated, unresolved issues troubling the India–China relationship play into America's long-standing strategy to maintain a balance of power in Asia. But U.S. interests would not want any competition between Asian powers to descend into confrontation. America's own political, diplomatic and economic ties with China are too intertwined for either side to pursue confrontation.

Clearly, the centre of gravity of world affairs is moving to Asia, and all the major actors on the international stage are defining new roles for themselves in that vast continent. As these powers, including China, India and Japan, seek to carve out new, larger roles for themselves or forge fresh equations between and among themselves, the stage has been set for greater cooperation and competition in Asia. It is only á matter of time before the Group of Eight (G-8) nations is expanded to formally include China and India. The Group of Twenty (G-20) has already emerged as the premier economic forum. Also, no reform of the United Nations Security Council can be complete without adding India and Japan as its permanent members. As a 2006 BBC poll revealed, there is nearly universal support for radical UN reforms, including the inclusion of permanent new members to the Security Council, with most international respondents favouring adding India, Japan, Germany and Brazil.[55]

Asia, through its dynamism and uncertainty, is all set to mould the future course of globalization. Few can doubt the Asian renaissance. By the same token, few can fail to notice the daunting challenges Asia faces.

Notes and References

1. George W. Bush, *State of the Union Address 2006* (Washington, D.C.: White House, February 1, 2006).
2. White House, *The National Security Strategy of the United States of America* (Washington, D.C.: White House, March 2006).

3. Lawrence Freedman, 'The Changing Forms of Military Conflict', *Survival*, Vol. 40, No. 4 (Winter 1998–99), pp. 39–56.

4. For a discussion of how terrorism challenges have evolved internationally over the past quarter century, see Christopher C. Harmon, *Terrorism Today* (London and Portland, Oregon: Frank Cass, 2000); Harvey W. Kushner (ed.), *The Future of Terrorism: Violence in the New Millennium* (Thousand Oaks, California: Sage Publications, 1998); Bruce Hoffman, *Inside Terrorism* (New York: Columbia University Press, 1998); Peter Taylor, *States of Terror: Democracy and Political Violence* (London: BBC Books, 1993); Stansfield Turner, *Terrorism and Democracy* (Boston: Houghton Mifflin, 1991); Richard Clutterbuck, *Terrorism and Guerrilla Warfare: Forecasts and Remedies* (London: Routledge, 1990); Bard O'Neill, *Insurgency and Terrorism: Inside Modern Revolutionary Warfare* (Washington, D.C.: Brassey's, 1990); Juliet Lodge (ed.), *The Threat of Terrorism* (Boulder, Colorado: Westview, 1988); Walter Laqueur, *The Age of Terrorism*, 2nd edn (Boston: Little Brown, 1987); Terrell E. Arnold and Neil C. Livingstone, *Fighting Back: Winning the War Against Terrorism* (Lexington, Massachusetts: Lexington Books, 1986); and Claire Sterling, *The Terror Network* (New York: Charles Scribner's, 1983).

5. Donald Kagan, *On the Origins of War* (New Haven, Connecticut: Yale University Press, 1998).

6. Nobel Laureate Sir V.S. Naipaul in interview with Adam Shatz, 'Questions for V.S. Naipaul on His Contentious Relationship to Islam', *New York Times*, October 28, 2001.

7. While the knowledge gap often translates into an income gap, this is not the case with the oil-exporting Muslim states. For a discussion on this topic, see Avinash Persaud, 'The Knowledge Gap', *Foreign Affairs*, Vol. 80, No. 2 (March/April 2001), pp. 107–17.

8. Cited in John M. Broder, 'The Saturday Profile: For Muslim Who Says Violence Destroys Islam, Violent Threats', *New York Times*, March 11, 2006.

9. Curt Gasteyger, *Security in the 21st Century: Trends and Perspectives*, PSIS Occasional Paper Number 1 (Geneva: Programme for Strategic and International Security Studies, 1999), pp. 15–16.

10. Mortimer B. Zuckerman, 'The Times of Our Lives', *U.S. News & World Report*, December 27, 1999.

11. Stephen D. Krasner, 'Sovereignty', *Foreign Policy*, No. 122 (January/February 2001), pp. 20–29.

12. Christoph Bertram, 'Interregnum', *Foreign Policy*, No. 119 (Summer 2000), pp. 44–46.

13. Michael T. Klare, 'The New Geography of Conflict', *Foreign Affairs*, Vol. 80, No. 3 (May/June 2001), pp. 49–61.

14. U.S. Department of State, *Patterns of Global Terrorism – 2000* (Washington, D.C.: Office of the Coordinator for Counterterrorism, Department of State, April 2001).

15. U.S. Department of State, 'South Asia Overview' in *Patterns of Global Terrorism – 2003* (Washington, D.C.: Office of the Coordinator for Counterterrorism, Department of State, April 2004).
http://www.state.gov/s/ct/rls/pgtrpt/2003/31600.htm

16. Steven Hadley, press briefing, New Delhi, March 2, 2006. Text at:
http://www.whitehouse.gov/news/releases/2006/03/20060302-14.html

17. See Brahma Chellaney, 'A Chance to Reshape Pakistan', *Far Eastern Economic Review*, Vol. 168, No. 11 (December 2005), pp. 47–50.

18. According to one account, barely 30 per cent of the military aid reached the Afghan guerrillas. Anthony Cordesman and Abraham Wagner, *The Lessons of Modern War*, Vol. 3 (Boulder, Colorado: Westview, 1991), p. 20.

19. Jessica Stern, 'Pakistan's Jihad Culture', *Foreign Affairs*, Vol. 79, No. 6 (November–December 2000), pp. 115–26; Ahmed Rashid, 'Pakistan: Trouble Ahead, Trouble Behind', *Current History* (April 1996), pp. 158–64; Mansoor Ijaz, 'Stop Pakistan's Fall into Nuclear-Armed Failure', *International Herald Tribune*, May 4, 2000, p. 8; and Barry Bearak, 'In Pakistan, A Shaky Ally', *New York Times*, October 2, 2001, p. 1.

20. John Negroponte, statement to the U.S. Senate Intelligence Committee, February 2, 2006, released by the Department of State.

21. 2009 Pew Global Attitudes Survey, Chapter I: 'Views of the U.S. and American Foreign Policy', (Washington, D.C.: Pew Research Centre, July 23, 2009).

22. See, for example, David E. Sanger and William J. Broad, 'From Rogue Nuclear Programmes, Web of Trail Leads to Pakistan', *New York Times*, January 4, 2004; David Rohde,

'Nuclear Inquiry Skips Pakistani Army', *New York Times*, January 30, 2004; and William J. Broad and David E. Sanger, 'Pakistani's Nuclear Black Market Seen as Offering Deepest Secrets of Building Bomb', *New York Times*, March 21, 2005.

23. Mansoor Ijaz, 'Not All of Pakistan's Nuclear Scientists Were Rogues', *Christian Science Monitor*, February 11, 2004.

24. On January 20, 1972, about 300 Pakistani nuclear physicists and engineers from around the world met at a secret conclave in Multan, Pakistan, called by Prime Minister Zulfikar Ali Bhutto to launch a covert Pakistani bomb programme. In 1977, after being deposed in a military coup led by General Mohammad Zia-ul Haq, Bhutto addressed posterity in the following words from his death cell in a Rawalpindi prison, where he would be hanged two years later: 'We know that Israel and South Africa have full nuclear capability. The Christian, Jewish and Hindu civilizations have this capability. The communist powers also possess it. Only the Islamic civilization was without it, but that position was about to change.'

25. Zalmay Khalilzad, David Orletsky, Jonathan Pollack, Kevin Pollpeter, Angel Rabasa, David Shlapak, Abram Shulsky and Ashley Tellis, *The United States and Asia: Toward a New U.S. Strategy and Force Posture* (Santa Monica, California: Rand, 2001).

26. Thomas Fuller, 'Vessels Sailing to Asia Empty', *International Herald Tribune*, January 30, 2006.

27. Cited in Minxin Pei, 'The Dark Side of China's Rise', *Foreign Policy* (March/April 2006).

28. Henry A. Kissinger, 'Anatomy of a Partnership', *Tribune* Media Services, March 10, 2006.

29. Cited in Dan Bilefsky and Anand Giridharadas, 'China–India Rivalry: Seesaw of Strengths', *International Herald Tribune*, January 24, 2006.

30. 'India, Out of Step', editorial, *Washington Post*, February 27, 2006, p. A14.

31. David Barboza, 'Some Assembly Needed: China as Asia Factory', *New York Times*, February 9, 2006.

32. See, for example, UNDP's inequality measures at: http://hdr.undp.org/statistics/data/indicators.cfm?x=148&y=2&z=1

33. John Larkin and Eric Bellman, 'Growth Hits Roadblock', *Wall Street Journal*, March 17, 2006.

34. Peter S. Goodman, 'Foreign Currency Piles Up in China', *Washington Post*, January 17, 2006, p. D1 and David Lague, 'China Sees Foreign Cash Pile as Possible Peril', *International Herald Tribune*, January 17, 2006.

35. William Pesek Jr., 'Size Matters and China Just Got Much Bigger', *Bloomberg News*, December 21, 2005.

36. China's trade surpluses are with the United States and Europe. With the rest of the world, it actually has a trade deficit. See David Barboza, 'Trade Surplus Tripled in '05, China Says', *New York Times*, January 12, 2006.

37. 'Carrying on with Fewer People', editorial, *Japan Times*, December 30, 2005.

38. Nicholas D. Kristof, 'They're Rounding the First Turn! And the Favourite Is...', *New York Times*, January 17, 2006.

39. Martin Walker, 'The Geopolitics of Sexual Frustration', *Foreign Policy* (March–April 2006).

40. A synopsis of the report, 'Deutsche Bank: China Pensions Face Crisis', available at: http://news.monstersandcritics.com/business/article_1130899.php/Deutsche_Bank_China_pensions_face_crisis

41. Summary of the joint report released in December 2005 by India's private-sector trade association, NASSCOM, and McKinsey & Co., available at: http://www.nasscom.org/artdisplay.asp?Art_id=4782

42. Transparency International, *Corruption Perceptions Index 2008*, available at: http://ww1.transparency.org/cpi/2008/cpi2008_infocus.html

43. The full gini-index table measuring inequality in income or distribution is available at: http://hdr.undp.org/

44. Minxin Pei, 'The Dark Side of China's Rise', *Foreign Policy* (March/April 2006).

45. Cited in Richard McGregor and Fiona Harvey, 'Environmental Disaster Strains China's Social Fabric', *Financial Times*, January 26, 2006.

46. The World Bank, *Little Green Data Book 2006* (Washington, D.C.: The World Bank, 2006).

47. Yun Qian, Dale P. Kaiser, L. Ruby Leung and Ming Xu, 'More Frequent Cloud-Free Sky and Less Surface Solar Radiation

in China from 1955 to 2000', *Geophysical Research Letters* (Vol. 33, No.1, L01812), January 11, 2006.

48. The *Failed States Index* 2009 of The Fund for Peace is available at:
    http://www.fundforpeace.org/web/
    It is also available at:
    www.ForeignPolicy.com

49. In the country profile on Pakistan accompanying the *Failed States Index*, The Fund for Peace pointed out that the shadowy Pakistani Inter-Services Intelligence agency (ISI) has ties to the Taliban. It also stated: 'The remote regions of the country are almost entirely beyond the control of the government, and the areas the government does control are plagued by deeply divided factional politics. Political violence remains commonplace as suicide bombings continue in even the most populous and secure cities.'

50. Richard Grimmett, *Conventional Arms Transfers to Developing Nations, 1997–2004* (Washington, D.C.: Congressional Research Service, August 29, 2005).

51. Seth G. Jones and F. Stephen Larrabee, 'Let's Avoid Another Trans-Atlantic Feud', *International Herald Tribune*, January 13, 2006.

52. Jimmy Carter, 'A Dangerous Deal with India', *Washington Post*, March 29, 2006, p. A19. In the op-ed, Carter wrote that, 'So far India has only rudimentary technology for uranium enrichment or plutonium reprocessing...'

53. Stockholm International Peace Research Institute, *SIPRI Yearbook 2008: Armament, Disarmament and International Security* (Stockholm: SIPRI, 2008).

54. AFP, 'Majority Says No to US Base Plan in Japan's Iwakuni Referendum', March 12, 2006.

55. http://www.bbc.co.uk/pressoffice/pressreleases/stories/ 2005/03_march/21/un.shtml
    According to the 2005 Nobel Peace Prize winner, Mohamed ElBaradei, the UN Security Council has too often failed to act swiftly and effectively to contain international crises and, therefore, needs reforming. 'Too often, the Security Council's engagement is inadequate, selective or after the fact', Elbaradei, the director-general of the International Atomic Energy Agency, said in a March 25, 2006, speech at Karlsruhe, Germany. Reuters despatch, March 25, 2006.

2

Why Asia Is Dissimilar to Europe

EVEN AS ASIA'S IMPORTANCE CONTINUES TO RISE IN economic and political terms, the continent remains at the crossroads, with the shape of its future security order uncertain. Several factors are contributing to this uncertainty. Indeed, it will not be easy for Asia to emulate Europe and forge an economic union or even build reliable security architecture to promote peace and stability. Unlike Europe, Asia has yet to define a common identity. Despite recurrent references to 'the Asian way', the meaning of that expression remains fuzzy even in Asia.

The reality is that Asia is attempting not only to catch up with Europe economically, but also to buy up European companies. China Inc. and India Inc. — following in the footsteps of Japan Inc. — have made a quiet push for corporate acquisitions in other parts of the world, including in Europe. For example, in 2008, the Tata Group, among the largest of India's industrial conglomerates, acquired British luxury icons, Jaguar and Land Rover, from Ford for $2.3 billion. Europe, however, appears ill at ease whenever it sees Asian firms attempting to take over any of its industrial icons. Economic nationalism in France has prompted legislation to help foil hostile takeover of French companies in sectors deemed as strategic to the economy.

Concern over foreign takeovers has not only helped fuel European arguments for national ownership couched in the outdated language of protectionism, but also promoted in some quarters a longing for globalization à la carte.

The protectionists' claim that corporate nationality matters was best exemplified by the European disparagement of Mittal Steel's 2006 hostile bid for rival Arcelor as a corporate clash of civilizations, with European officials and media casting its owner, the Indian-born Lakshmi Niwas Mittal, as 'the barbarian at Europe's gates'.[1] Arcelor's chief executive derisively labelled the Netherlands-based Mittal Steel as a 'company of Indians' and proclaimed that his firm, based in the Lilliputian duchy of Luxembourg, was 'perfume' to Mittal's 'eau de cologne'. And to torpedo Mittal Steel's bid, Arcelor's directors unsuccessfully brought in Russian oligarch Aleksei Mordashov, who they declared was, at least, 'a true European'. Until Mittal Steel managed to seal a $38.3-bilion takeover of Arcelor to create the world's biggest steel-making company, newspapers in India depicted Arcelor's hostility and racial slight as the 'Mittal Barricade'.

Similar nationalist considerations led India's United Breweries to lose its 2006 battle to acquire French Champagne maker Taittinger. United Breweries, seeking to establish an international footprint, faced a strong French reaction to its Indian roots. Although a US buyout group, Starwood Capital, was seeking to sell its ownership of Taittinger, growers in the Champagne region, who deliver grapes to the company, threatened to halt supply if the firm fell into Indian hands. Taittinger was finally sold to Crédit Agricole du Nord Est, a French bank that bowed to local pressure and raised its bid by more than 15 per cent to triumph over its Indian competitor. The ugly face of protectionism, tinged somewhat with racism, also was apparent from the political tempest in the United States over the acquisition of Peninsular & Oriental Steam Navigation Company by Dubai Ports World, which is owned by the emirate of Dubai. Although Dubai Ports World was to take control of freight terminals at ports in 18 countries, including more than half of India's container shipping operations, there was a public outcry over the deal only in the United States. The congressional rejection of the deal sent out a chilling message that, despite all the U.S. rhetoric about free trade and investment, Washington is basically xenophobic about foreign ownership of its assets, especially when the buyer happens to be from outside the circle of Western industrial democracies. A second message it sent out is that the Arab world, in its own interest, should seek to connect more with Asia than with the West.

Asia, given its rising importance in trade and capital flows, is decidedly reawakening, and Asian multinationals are now on the prowl for acquisitions in Europe and North America. Yet, despite its renewed vibrancy and renaissance arming it with growing international clout, Asia is still far from embracing European-style benchmarks on good governance, social equity, public transparency and accountability, common rules of origin for trade and respect for the environment.

The gulf between Europe and Asia is wide on many an issue. Take gender equality as an example. The world's second-largest economy, Japan, ranked 57th in the United Nations Development Programme's 'Gender Empowerment Measure' in 2009, the lowest position among all the developed nations. According to this index — based both on the male-to-female ratio among lawmakers, professionals, technicians and managers and on income disparities by gender — Sweden rates as the world's most women-friendly nation, followed by Norway, Finland and Denmark. Because of inadequate data, India was not ranked in this index, but other Asian states did not measure up to European standards.[2]

A Divided Asia

Asia is a long way from embracing pan-Asianism. In fact, Asia remains deeply divided, with its major powers at loggerheads. The heated rivalry between China and India and the underlying dissonance between China and Japan have emerged as major destabilizing elements in Asia. Asia may be coalescing economically, as shown by the deepening interstate trade, but strategically it is going in the other direction. China's meteoric rise is dividing, not uniting, Asia, as states seek to hedge against or balance Chinese power. A rules-based regional order appears distant.

The grand concept of an East Asian Community has begun to wither before any tangible progress on such community building could be registered. Similarly, moves triggered by the 1997 Asian currency crisis to create an Asian Monetary Fund have not progressed beyond the Chiang Mai Initiative on currency swaps, thus falling far short of the need to construct a permanent and stable institutional mechanism to avert serious risks like a region-wide financial crisis. In general, the Asian financial markets remain not adequately developed, especially the bond and venture-capital markets. Such are the challenges to promoting greater financial cooperation that an Asia Monetary Fund or a European-style common currency seems decades away.

The proliferation of free-trade areas in Asia is creating overlapping free-trade agreements (FTAs), with the consequent need to streamline them and simplify their rules, including the rules of origin. IntraAsian flows of investment, information and technology also need to be improved. Rather than routinely pump a large portion of its national savings and trade surpluses into U.S. government and corporate debt, Asia could supplant America as the world's largest borrower of capital and importer of goods and services if it were to channel capital flows inward and help spur greater Asian development, trade and consumption.

Despite its impressive strides, Asia confronts a wide range of problems, such as economic divides, divergent historical perceptions, interstate disputes over territories and delineation of exclusive economic zones (EEZs), ethnic and sectarian strife, and cultural conflict. It lacks the European-type institutional means to tackle these and other transnational challenges, including pandemics like avian influenza and HIV/AIDS, environmental degradation, energy-related competition, natural disasters like tsunami, floods, hurricanes and earthquakes, illicit trade in drugs and human beings, and management of regional currency-crisis risks. The twenty-first-century ease and speed of transport and exchange have made some of these challenges more pressing.

In the eighteenth and nineteenth centuries, it was Europe's attempts to ensure security for itself and its aggressive search for colonies that affected the rest of the world. Today, of all the continents, it is Asia that is beginning to have the greatest bearing on international relations and international security. First, all major world players are active in Asia. Second, several areas or interstate relationships in Asia carry high risk potential. Such troubled areas or relationships are spread across the entire continent. They include the Spratlys, Taiwan, Kashmir, the Pakistan–Afghanistan terrorism epicentre, Central Asia and the Korean Peninsula.

The disputes in the South China Sea, covering an area of 800,000 square kilometres, alone involve eight nations, with three of them claiming the entire region. The strategic vacuum in the early years after the Cold War led to coastal states asserting their claims on the islands in the South China Sea. Another dimension of the present Asian strategic landscape is that Japan is involved in territorial, maritime or historical disputes with three other players in Asia — China, Russia and South Korea.

The reality is that Asia is fundamentally dissimilar to Europe, a fact that can be overlooked only at the cost of a realistic assessment of the Asian situation and its challenges and opportunities. While Europe has several major middle powers, principally Britain, France, Germany and Italy, Asia has one rapidly rising power at its centre whose growing weight and assertiveness are casting an increasingly large shadow over much of the continent. China's dramatic rise has been accentuated by the decline of Russia and Japan's economic slump since the early 1990s, although now the Japanese economy may be turning the corner with the aid of its two principal engines of growth — consumer spending and business investment.[3]

The European Union is the outcome of an equilibrium that has come into being between and among the middle powers in Europe. Asia, however, is still far from evolving equilibrium among its important states. In fact, the present situation in Asia can be characterized as a case of power disequilibrium. In other words, Asia, unlike Europe, has still to resolve the issue of hegemony. While there is neither a hegemon in Europe nor a state there aspiring to be one, the same cannot be incontrovertibly said about Asia.

In Asia, in fact, there is as yet no security architecture in place nor are efforts under way to create a structural framework of security. Additionally, the regional consultation mechanisms in Asia are weak, if not non-existent. Those two realities make Asia's security situation less than stable and expose the continent to important risks of sudden and unexpected volatility. This is apparent from the recrudescence of Sino-Indian border tensions and revival of the Japan-China historical rivalry.

Any strategic assessment has to recognize that the existing interstate arrangements in Asia are highly varied and potentially unpredictable. On the one side are states in Asia like India that are untied to bilateral or multilateral alliance commitments in either the military or economic sphere, a posture that has ensured for them maximum freedom in terms of options but also has its drawbacks. On the other side are states with close military and commercial partnerships with the United States as well as militaristic states like Burma, North Korea and Pakistan which can be described as allies or quasi-allies of China. Then there are states that fall in the middle category.

The embryonic or weak nature of regional mechanisms for consultation and cooperation in Asia has been manifest from the time of the failure to evolve a prudent response both to the 1997–98 Asian financial crisis and to China's 1999 encroachment on the Mischief Reef Island near the Philippines. The 1997–98 crisis exacted a toll on the vitality and dynamism of the Association of South-East Asian Nations, or ASEAN. Since then, however, ASEAN has recouped and expanded, incorporating all the 10 states in Southeast Asia. The expansion, at the same time, has made ASEAN unwieldy, with the momentum for further integration being stalled. Yet, it is also true that from the time it was formed in 1967 with the political mission to fight the menace of a proselytizing communism and help build regional peace and stability, ASEAN has evolved remarkably as a dynamic institution.

The ASEAN states straddle vital shipping lanes and their region is beset by interstate problems within and by great-power competition for influence. In fact, major Asian powers like China, Japan and India regard Southeast Asia as an extension of their security perimeter. Moreover, Southeast Asia, with its different political systems and dissimilar levels of economic development, has deep internal fault lines, raising the spectre that if things are not managed satisfactorily, the region could potentially slide into a situation where it becomes the 'Balkans of the East'.[4] In general, Southeast Asia faces the choice of either integrating more closely or becoming an arena for interstate squabbles and great-power competition, as outside powers seek to expand their spheres of influence. In plain terms, the choice is to integrate or vegetate.

Although an extremely useful body, ASEAN is plagued by many problems that have helped dampen the high expectations that were aroused when the ASEAN Regional Forum (ARF) was formed. The ARF, for its part, has played a useful role in promoting dialogue and understanding. It deserves credit for focusing regional attention and stimulating dialogue on the tangle of overlapping sovereignty claims in the South China Sea and thereby keeping the gunboats quiet. But, lamentably, it has remained more of a 'talk shop' than an action group. Yet, despite its limited role, it is seen as an idea worth replicating elsewhere.

This aspect is apparent from the push at the Track II level to establish an ARF-style Northeast Asian Regional Forum to help deepen economic interdependence, reduce political mistrust and aid security in a volatile yet vibrant region where the interests of several major powers intersect. Such a forum would have to include two key players — the United States and Russia — that do not find a place in the proposed East Asian Community. As three scholars have put it, 'In some ways, Northeast Asia today evokes Europe at the turn of the twentieth century, when rising regional powers, territorial conflicts and troubled bilateral relations were about to set the continent on the road to 50 years of catastrophic violence. That's why a Northeast Asia Regional Forum needs to be established'.[5] However, far from any tangible progress being achieved on building multilateral mechanisms in Northeast Asia, there have been important setbacks to the promotion of regionalism there.

Traditionally, a web of bilateral alliances has helped underpin deterrence, peace and stability in Asia. Such a hub-and-spoke architecture of bilateral alliances indeed has compensated for infirm or non-existent regional-security mechanisms and thereby served as a key stabilizer. The changing security dynamics and new challenges, however, have sharpened the need for multilateral security architecture in Asia. Such a framework of security and cooperation can be developed only on the building blocks of the existing and emerging regional mechanisms.

The regional institutions of varying width and depth include ASEAN, the 21-member Asia-Pacific Economic Cooperation (APEC) forum, ARF, the ASEAN Plus Three (a grouping that brings in China, Japan and South Korea), the Asia–Europe Meeting (or ASEM, which brings together 10 Asian nations and 15 European states, as well as the president of the European Commission), the East Asia Summit, and the now-stalled Six-Party Talks on North Korea (involing North Korea, South Korea, China, Japan, Russia and the United States). The main shortcoming of several of these mechanisms is that they have been set up on the simplistic assumption that the way to tackle complex issues and build multilateral cooperation is to merely provide a venue where regional and international leaders can meet and talk. The realities in Asia demand a more rigorous and thorough approach.

Given the intractable nature of some of the interstate disputes as well as the intensifying political rivalries in Asia, some of the existing mechanisms, in order to help initiate forward-looking steps, could seek to overcome their drawbacks by focusing first on the non-traditional security challenges. Such challenges centre on maritime security, environment, human security, refugee flows, currency-related issues and pandemics like the swine flu and avian flu. Blooming collaboration on non-traditional security challenges is likely to serve as a major building block to the fostering of cooperation on more complex political issues. A wider Asian security framework, however, appears still distant, even though such architecture could serve the collective interest of Asian states and enhance Asia's importance to the rest of the world.

Homogeny and Hegemony

Efforts at building political homogeny in Asia constantly run into the unresolved question of hegemony. Without exorcizing the threat of hegemony, there can be no movement towards homogeny in Asia. In fact, as history testifies, attempts at hegemony normally trigger countervailing pressures, which at times can be very disruptive.

In that light, the Indian proposal for setting up an Asian energy grid, for example, will remain what it is — a grandiose idea. Yet it is true that Asia faces major energy-related challenges that carry the risk of escalating from the present competition over scarce resources to actual conflict among major states. As a one-stop shop offering investment, aid, trade, skilled workers, weapons and diplomatic protection through its United Nations Security Council veto power, China — the world's fastest-growing energy consumer — has signed up international deals for securing new supplies of oil and other critical resources, often from problem states in Africa, the Persian Gulf region, Asia and Latin America. That approach has only spurred concern in other energy-importing states. A prudent response to the energy-related challenges lies in developing a coordinated, long-lasting approach and strategy that minimizes competition and puts the accent on collective benefit.

Even in the financial and trade realms, it is proving difficult in Asia to go beyond free-trade agreements to a European-style integration process. Asia has some of the wealthiest states in the world, like Japan and Singapore, and also some of the poorest, such as North Korea and Afghanistan. Tiny Brunei, Bhutan and the Maldives have to deal with giants like China, India and Indonesia. Interestingly, Asia has countries with the highest and lowest population densities in the world — Singapore and Mongolia, respectively.

In a continent with economies as diverse and outlying as China and Singapore, South Korea and India, and Japan and Vietnam, Europe hardly appears as a role model, especially at a time when competitive nationalism is getting sharper in Asia. Before the yuan overshadows the yen, Japan, for instance, wishes to reinforce its role as the pivot of financial mechanisms in Asia. Beijing, on the other hand, with its authoritarian political corporatism, increasingly tries to assert itself as the prime mover in the new, emerging Asia.

The power politics behind the efforts to fashion an East Asian Community (EAC) — the economic or trade equivalent of the European Union and the North American Free Trade Agreement (NAFTA) — has exemplified how the absence of multilateral Asian security architecture poses a growing problem, especially at a time when rivalries between the major Asian powers are intensifying. Yet the holding of the first East Asia Summit (EAS) was simplistically seen by some as opening the path to the formation of an Asian Community along the model of the European Community.

As one analyst has put it succinctly and correctly, 'In the absence of a thaw in Sino–Japanese and Sino–Indian relations or great-power cooperation, the EAC is unlikely to take off because multilateralism is a multiplayer game. If anything, the first EAS may well have had the opposite effect, intensifying old rivalries. If such rivalry continues, there is every risk that the community-building exercise would be fatally compromised. At best, the EAS will be just another "talk shop" like the APEC or the ARF where leaders meet, declarations are made, but little community-building is achieved'.[6]

Realizing the vision of an EAC remains a long-haul endeavour, even though that idea dates back to a 1991 Malaysian proposal for an East Asian Economic Caucus (EAEC). The original EAEC proposal of then Malaysian Prime Minister Mahathir Mohamad ran into immediate

American opposition as well as into other misgivings. Years later, with the blessing of an increasingly assertive China, the idea was revived at the 2004 ASEAN Plus Three meeting by Mahathir's successor, Abdullah Badawi.

China was quick to bless the resurrection of an old idea because it saw in the proposed EAC an opportunity — along the lines of the Shanghai Cooperation Organization (SCO) — to expand its influence by excluding America and serving as the lead force. Beijing's barely disguised motivation behind its overflowing enthusiasm for an EAC, however, provoked a countermove by others, principally Japan, to checkmate its intent to lead the EAC. Those countersteps culminated in the admission of India, Australia and New Zealand to the EAS.

The inaugural EAS meeting in Kuala Lumpur in late 2005, in fact, ended up as an important setback to the Chinese diplomatic strategy in Asia. According to one observer, 'instead of confirming China's position as prime mover in the new emerging Asia, the summit emphasized the misgivings that other nations have about its potential and ambitions'.[7] The intraAsian rivalries and historical grievances also stood out at the inaugural EAS, with the Chinese and Korean leaders declining to hold bilateral or trilateral talks with the Japanese prime minister.

Without the countervailing presence of the United States in the EAS, several Asian countries have perforce joined hands to doggedly frustrate China's design to lead the proposed East Asian Community. In fact, out of the 16 EAS members, five (Australia, Japan, the Philippines, South Korea and Thailand) are military allies of the United States. Additionally, several other EAS states have close strategic ties with America, including India, which is building a global strategic partnership with the United States.

Such a configuration of forces clearly influenced the outcome of the inaugural EAS. That summit meeting rebuffed China's effort to divide EAS's participating members into two groups — core states and the 'outliers' — in order to keep out India, Australia and New Zealand from the proposed East Asian Community. The meeting also spurned China's offer to host the second EAS.

The net outcome of China's diplomatic manoeuvring to gain a dominant role in the planned EAC was to strengthen the hand of ASEAN at Beijing's own expense. ASEAN managed to perch itself on the driver's seat and gain the right to host future EAS meetings annually, in tandem with its own ASEAN summit. All in all, an Asian Community or even a narrowly defined East Asian Community now looks no closer to realization.

In contrast to the painfully sluggish progress on the development of Asian security and economic mechanisms, Europe rose from the ashes of World War II to gradually build the institutions that stand it in good stead today. The relative stability and prosperity of Europe are a tribute to the institution building of the past. Europe has come a long way, particularly since the 1992 Maastricht Treaty that led to the creation of the European Union, even as the momentum for greater integration has slowed in the face of the expansion of the EU. The slackening of the momentum was mirrored in the 2005 French and Dutch rejection of the European constitution.

The European Union now wields considerable supranational authority over its members, which have ceded to it control over key aspects of their policies. Monetary union has further expanded EU's authority, with the advent of the euro having political ramifications worldwide. By breaking the U.S. hegemony in the international monetary system, where the dollar had overshadowed all other national currencies for long, the euro has helped make that system bipolar.

Unlike Asia, Europe had one clear advantage in institution building: many West European states were members of the U.S.-led military alliance, the North Atlantic

Treaty Organization (NATO), and enjoyed relative security. The financial and economic institutions in Europe were built on the bedrock of security provided by NATO.

That security did come with considerable risks during the Cold War years. For instance, West Germany, a frontline state, demanded and got special military arrangements that would have put it directly in harm's way, if things had gone wrong. Those arrangements included a 'layer-cake' deployment of foreign and German forces along its eastern frontiers, and special nuclear procedures that limited political decision making in the event of armed attack and introduced military automatism. Yet collective defence through NATO and the enhanced security it brought helped engender an environment conducive to rapid economic modernization in Europe and to intraEuropean cooperation.

The volatile security situation in Asia, on the other hand, remains a key dampener to institution building both in the political and economic realms. A NATO-type security alliance in Asia is unthinkable because of the unresolved question of hegemony. NATO was fashioned as an archetypal asymmetric alliance led by an outside hegemon, which took on the responsibility to defend smaller powers and, in return, gained substantial leverage over them. Most successful military alliances in history have been asymmetric. Smaller states or powers seek such alliances because they can combine their own resources with those of the alliance partners to more cost-effectively secure their territories and populations.

In Asia, an outside hegemon can have bilateral military arrangements with individual states, as the United States has with several Asian nations. Such bilateral military ties can also serve as the bedrock of an economic partnership, as between the United States and Japan. But America is hardly in a position to lead a continent where at least one state (China) aspires to be its peer competitor. This was evident from China's effort at the first EAS to create an

East Asian version of the SCO in order to help constrict U.S. strategic leeway and influence. It also was no coincidence that China's first-ever joint war games with Russia were officially held under the SCO auspices in August 2005. China's unbridled geopolitical ambition, paradoxically, helps reinforce the importance of the United States to Asia, because it drives some states closer to Washington.

Shadows of History

Asia and Europe are strikingly different in how they deal with history. In Asia, unassuaged historical grievances or the use of history as a political instrument have helped spur resurgent nationalism and interstate rivalries. That, in turn, has sharpened rival territorial or maritime claims and constricted diplomatic space for building accommodation and reconciliation.

In contrast, Europe has done a much better job in coming to terms with its past. Ironically, throughout much of history, it was Asia that had a more liberal and assimilative culture than Europe. With its ancient polytheistic or pantheistic religions and pluralistic norms, Asia had more tolerant and integrative traditions compared to Europe's conservative, dogmatic Christian past. Historically, the placidly pacifist Hindus and Jains, complacent Buddhists, agnostic Confucians and ingenious Shinto disciples imbued Asia with liberalism and pluralism. Yet Asia now finds it difficult to overcome its more recent history.

Nothing can better illustrate the contrast between Europe and Asia on the issue of history than the very different ways Germany and Japan handle their brutal militaristic past. Japan, for instance, does not have the museums, archives, memorials and exhibitions that Germany houses to graphically document its military atrocities before and during World War II. While Germany has patched up with its neighbours in the framework of the European Union, Japan's continuing political tensions with China and South Korea have kept alive its record of the 1930s and 1940s, setting limits on its political influence. And although patriotism is no longer a dirty word in Germany, as it was for more than four decades after World War II, the German display of national pride — unlike in Japan — is still generally free of nationalistic or chauvinistic undertones.

Indeed, Japanese public discourse has never properly come to terms with Japan's culpability in such horrible events as the military's forced sexual enslavement of many young Korean women, the biological-weapon experiments conducted on some hapless prisoners of war, and the civilian massacre in the Chinese city of Nanjing. However, it is also true that in contrast to the Chinese and Koreans, many Taiwanese look at Japan's colonial-era history in benevolent terms.[8] When Taiwan was its colony from 1895 to 1945, Japan helped build that island's infrastructure. Not only do older Taiwanese love to speak in Japanese, the official language of their youth, but also Taipei has preserved and declared as national treasures the island's imperial-era structures, including the Presidential Office Building.

South Korea and China, on the other hand, have eliminated the last vestiges of Japanese colonial rule. At the other end of the spectrum is India, an unusual example even in comparison to Taiwan. The Indian republic continues to transact much of its key business from British colonial edifices. The president is ensconced in the British Viceroy's palace. Parliament sits in a colonial structure, as do the prime minister and the foreign, defence, finance and interior ministers. The civil services still service the nation on colonial-era principles. Several major criminal and civil laws in force date back to the colonial period.

In Asia, history is still used by some states to instil among citizens an abiding and overweening sense of grievance and victimization. For example, China and Japan use Nanjing and Hiroshima-Nagasaki respectively as national symbols of crimes by outsiders against them. To Germans, in contrast, Auschwitz symbolizes Germany's genocide against the innocent. Japan's status as the only victim of nuclear attack in history has not only helped infuse anti-nuclear sentiment in its national consciousness, but also reinforced an identity of victimhood. In fact, it is because of the way history is used to whitewash or justify the past that the Yasukuni Shrine in Tokyo has emerged at the centre of Sino–Japanese and Korean–Japanese controversies. The shadows of history have fostered very negative public opinions about a rival state. A global-opinion poll has shown that while traditional European rivals, Germany and France, rate each another more positively than they rate their own country, only 28 per cent of Japanese have a positive opinion of China and even fewer Chinese (21 per cent) have a favourable view of Japan.[9]

Yasukuni, a Shinto shrine, honours Japan's 2.5 million military dead, including the 14 individuals judged to be Class A war criminals by the Allied powers that won World War II. It was only in 1978 that the 14, who had been convicted and executed by the military tribunal set up by the U.S.-led Allied powers, were enshrined at Yasukuni built by the pre-war Japanese government. It is because of these 14 that a prime ministerial visit to the shrine ignites passions in China and South Korea. To these countries, the shrine is a symbol of Japanese militarism, with its adjoining museum promoting the view that Japan waged aggression in Asia to liberate it from European colonial rule but was tricked into war by the United States. The history issue has been made more problematic by Japan's reluctance to take a national view on the 14. Did the 14 start the war or commit atrocities? Or are they guilty of losing or prolonging a losing war? The post-war Japan has been loath to publicly debate and settle such questions. Instead, patriotism has been employed as an ideological tool in recent times to complete the biggest overhaul of state education since the U.S. occupation authorities drew up the 1947 Fundamental Law of Education.

Distortion of history persists across much of Asia. Take the case of China, which is seeking to assertively fashion a central role for itself in international relations in order to ostensibly make up for the 110 years of national humiliation it suffered up to 1949. While China harps on Japan's past, its own selective memory is evident from its school textbooks, which black out the Chinese invasion of Tibet (1950), the aggression against India (1962) and the attack on Vietnam (1979). Chinese children certainly do not learn that Mao Zedong's record was worse than Hitler's. As a famous new biography of Mao states, this neo-emperor 'was responsible for well over 70 million deaths in peacetime, more than any other twentieth-century leader'.[10]

Chinese textbooks conceal or make light of the post-1949 disasters that occurred under communist rule, such as the mass starvation and death during the so-called 'Great Leap Forward' during the 1950s and the large-scale state atrocities during the 'Great Proletarian Cultural Revolution' in the 1960s and 1970s. Such was Mao's Machiavellian personality that in 1957 he encouraged intellectuals and others during his 'Let a Hundred Flowers Bloom' campaign to speak up, only to ensnare them for persecution. Millions died or were persecuted during the decade-long Cultural Revolution, as Mao worship reached fever pitch. Triggered by Mao's May 16, 1966, directive that the party be purged of capitalist infiltrators, the so-called revolution ended with Mao's death on September 9, 1976, with the 'Gang of Four' being made the principal scapegoats. Although the party admitted in 1981 that the revolution was a 'disaster' wrought by Mao, public discussion on the events of that period remains barred.

To help instil patriotic feelings, Chinese textbooks also distort the Boxer Uprising of 1900, presenting it as a nationalistic uprising when in reality it was a brutal xenophobic campaign that left thousands dead in orchestrated attacks on Westerners and on Chinese who had converted to Christianity. So deeply ingrained is the politicization of history in China that authorities in early 2006 shut down *Bing Dian* (Freezing Point), the weekly supplement of the *China Youth Daily*, for carrying an article by a respected Chinese historian that criticized the falsification of history in a textbook for secondary schools.[11]

While embellishing China's past, the country's propaganda machine and tightly controlled education system stress the indignities China suffered at the hands of foreign powers from the mid-nineteenth century through World War II, especially the period between 1937 and 1945 when Japanese atrocities occurred. The indignities inflicted by Western imperialists were also terrible, symbolized by China's forced import of opium in return for Chinese goods as well as by the legendary sign that appeared in a park near one of the European compounds in Shanghai: 'No Dogs or Chinamen.'

Such indignities and the subsequent Japanese military atrocities laid the foundation of the Maoist ideology of ultranationalism. Even today, they continue to serve as justification for the Chinese Communist Party's continued peddling of historical fictions and its claimed legitimacy to hold power. The result is that an entire generation of 'angry youth has emerged with one-sided views of the world that are often laughably ignorant and frighteningly arrogant'.[12] The past has also come handy to keep alive the threat of foreign intervention and rationalize President Hu Jintao's 'smokeless war' against liberal elements supported from outside.

Asia's Political Diversity

In addition to the ancient fractures that it needs to bridge, Asia lacks the political symmetry and cohesion that Europe had when it fashioned a community of nations. Democracy may have become the political norm in Europe, but that can hardly be said about Asia. While the community in Europe was built among democracies, the political systems in Asia are so varied and some even so opaque that it is not going to be easy to build the key requirement for close cooperation — trust. Asia indeed is a reminder of the challenge democracies face in seeking to form a community with autocracies. An EU-style community building demands minimal political and economic compatibility among its members, which Asia does not possess.

In Asia, the world's largest democracy, for instance, is located right next to the world's largest autocracy, with the two sharing a long, disputed frontier. At the same time, these two states, India and China, are the most populous nations on earth, with their tangled relationship central to the future stability and prosperity of Asia. As a matter of fact, India shares more political values with Europe than with next-door China, from which it was always separated by a large buffer until Tibet's fall in 1950 brought Chinese troops to India's frontiers for the first time in history.

Several states in Asia — from Kazakhstan to Singapore — are characterized by the insidious domination of one party. In prosperous Singapore, for instance, the opposition to the long-ruling People's Action Party (PAP) has been kept largely symbolic through the erection of major organizational and legal hurdles. Singapore's prime architect and PAP founder, Lee Kuan Yew — once labelled 'the Little Hitler of Southeast Asia' by a U.S. columnist — ushered in a form of soft authoritarianism. After opposition lawyer J.B. Jeyaretnam won a by-election and ended the PAP's total political monopoly in 1981, the PAP leadership wreaked such vengeance on Jeyaretnam that he became bankrupt and was banished from Parliament.

Under Lee's elder son, current Prime Minister Lee Hsien Loong, the protest vote, however, has grown louder, with the PAP winning only 66.6 per cent of the votes in the 2006 general election, compared with 75.3 per cent in 2001. Yet the Singaporean Parliament still has only two opposition members, just like it did following the 2001 election. Such is the PAP's pervasive hold that its leadership also controls the huge, cash-rich state-owned enterprises, with Lee Kuan Yew's daughter-in-law, Ho Ching, in charge of the giant state investment fund, Temasek Holdings, and his younger son, Lee Hsien Yang, chief of Civil Aviation Authority of Singapore (CAAS). Lee Kuan Yew, now holding the reverential title of 'minister mentor', is himself chairman and his elder son vice-chairman of the Government Investment Corporation. Had Singapore not made itself indispensable to the regional interests of the United States and multinational companies, it would have invited intense international scrutiny of its political and media controls and restrictive freedoms.

When strongman Deng Xiaoping started economic reforms in China, he sent, at the invitation of Lee Kuan Yew, Chinese officials to Singapore in small teams to study the intricacies of market-oriented policies. Having mastered capitalist practices so well that China can now provide useful lessons on market techniques to others, the Chinese leadership today might have liked to look at Singapore again to see whether in the years ahead Beijing could emulate its political system, step by step. But Beijing's mass privatization of housing, for example, dents its ability to engineer limited political pluralism in the style of Singapore, where public housing, multiseat constituencies and state control over a large part of the economy have been used by the PAP to maintain its grip on the levers of power.

A shift from hard authoritarianism to soft authoritarianism, in any case, cannot get for China the kind of international acceptability Singapore has enjoyed. Not only is Singapore a tiny city-state, but it also represents no threat to others. By contrast, China presents itself as a large empire with even larger imperial ambitions. As one U.S. newspaper put it editorially, 'There was a time when Americans worried about China because it was Communist. But times change, and today the reason to worry about China is that it is capitalist — in an especially unrestrained, unprincipled way'.[13]

Divergent political systems in Asia make the development of common political standards not possible. That, in turn, makes the task of community building in Asia more onerous. How can we expect the development of economic and political transparency that a community necessitates when some states in Asia at present do not have an independent judiciary, or free media, or even the rule of law? As shown by the World Press Freedom Index by the Paris-based international rights group, Reporters Without Borders, a number of Asian countries are among the worst suppressors of freedom. In the 173-nation list, North Korea ranked virtually at the very bottom, Burma 170th, Vietnam 168th, China 167th, Sri Lanka 165th, Laos 164th, Pakistan 152th, Singapore 144th and the Philippines 139th.[14]

Without democracy expanding to several formerly communist-ruled states of Eastern Europe, the EU would not have been able to absorb them as new members. Asia, to the contrary, remains home to several citadels of authoritarian rule that stretch from Central Asia to Southeast Asia to Northeast Asia, including scofflaw states like North Korea and Burma. Some of the autocracies in Asia are engaged in covert actions in breach of international law, including the export of terrorism, narcotics and nuclear materials. For example, India, the world's back office for information technology, has to contend with Pakistan, the back office for IT of a different type — international terrorism.

The political diversity in Asia is extraordinary. According to a study by Freedom House, a U.S.-based non-governmental organization, 16 of Asia's 39 countries are free, 12 are partly free and 11 are not free, with Chinese-ruled Tibet being one of the two worst-rated territories in the world. Asia has 'some of the world's most repressive regimes'.[15] While the UN Special Rapporteur on Torture, Dr Manfred Nowak, has been investigating what he called a 'consistent and systematic pattern of torture related to ethnic minorities [in China], particularly Tibetans and Uighurs', the U.S. government, in its international religious freedom report, has cited Beijing's suppression of even innocuous activities such as 'venerating the Dalai Lama'.[16] In Uzbekistan — another egregious example of human-rights violations — authoritarian President Islam A. Karimov has been challenged by the Islamic Movement of Uzbekistan, an underground militant group that has declared a holy war against him.

More broadly, the powerful Internet poses a bigger threat to repressive governments in Asia than pro-democracy protests on the streets, if they are allowed at all. Seeking to fight fire with fire, some authoritarian regimes have, however, clamped down on the Internet, closing blogger sites and employing sophisticated filtering software to block Web sites that carry references to 'subversive' words. Yet another development is the advent of online cartoon cops, along with some 30,000 'Internet police', at the frontline of China's battle to counter the threat posed by the information revolution. For instance, 'Jingjing' and 'Chacha', the animated online icons, have been designed in the southern Chinese boomtown of Shenzhen to patrol news and discussion Web sites and thereby deter subversive activity.

In some cases, Western companies have aided the Internet controls of repressive regimes by providing devices or software. As exemplified by Google, even self-censorship has been undertaken by such firms. Visitors from China to the uncensored Web address www.google.com get redirected to the self-censored www.google.cn site by Google, whose company motto ironically is, 'Don't be evil'. Such is the level of self-censorship that a search, for example, of 'Tiananmen Square' on google.cn and google.com showed 1,240 listings on the former and 1.6 million listings on the latter.[17] At Tiananmen Square, thousands were killed or detained or went missing on June 4, 1989, when Chinese troops backed by tanks broke up student-led rallies for democracy. The rival Yahoo faced severe criticism from human-rights groups for providing information in 2005 that helped the Chinese government to trace and jail a journalist, Shi Tao. Autocrats may find common ground with Internet companies but not with democratic values.

In an effort to control what people read and write on the Web, authoritarian regimes in Asia employ a bureaucracy of censors and, in the case of China, one of the world's most technologically sophisticated systems of filters. Yet the Web poses difficult challenges to the efforts of autocrats to control news and shape public opinion. Chinese President Hu Jintao has presided over a severe crackdown on the state media, bringing newspapers, magazines and television stations under tighter control. But that has only helped make cyberspace — tougher for the state to effectively censor — a more attractive terrain for the dissemination of dissenting messages. The Web allows citizens with shared concerns to meet, exchange ideas and plan activities without their autocratic regime's knowledge or approval, despite governmental use of filtering systems to scan e-mail and text messages for banned words. Podcasting and other newer technologies are making it more difficult for official censors to effectively carry out their tasks.

At the same time, the Internet has not served as a harbinger of democracy in China, as then U.S. President Bill Clinton somewhat naïvely thought it would when he consciously went out to promote closer economic engagement with Beijing. Clinton had believed that closer economic cooperation would help loosen China's instruments of authoritarian control. If anything, China has proven that a country can blend control, coercion and patronage to stymie the politically liberalizing elements of market forces, especially when the state still has a hold over large parts of the economy. Through discreet but tough controls, Beijing pursues a policy of *wai song, nei jin* — relaxed on the outside, vigilant internally.

A marketplace of goods and services will not necessarily allow a marketplace of ideas in a country suffering under a dictatorial yoke. In China, for example, the combination of autocratic politics and the state's dominant economic role has spurred a potent but perilous form of crony capitalism. With the governing elites in China converting their 'political power into economic wealth and privilege at the expense of equity and efficiency', a corrupting 'marriage between unchecked power and illicit wealth' has been cemented.[18] Such a marriage only makes the process of democratization more difficult to initiate. Vested interests, with a stake in not altering a system rich in economic spoils, are ever ready to invest even more in the instruments of popular control and coercion.

To survive, autocrats will, of course, do whatever they can, including getting a handle on any new, potentially 'subversive' technology. Autocrats don't want to be left behind by the global information revolution; nor do they wish to be swept away by it. It is thus not a surprise that an authoritarian government like the one in China has periodically blocked its citizens' access even to Wikipedia, the online encyclopaedia that anyone can edit. China sees even the plain, non-political Wikipedia, now one of the Web's most popular knowledge sources, as a threat to its control of information. With search engines like Google often turning up Wikipedia entries at the top of their results, more people in the world access Wikipedia than *Encyclopaedia Britannica*.

Some autocrats have learned the hard way that an instrument of technology, even if sanctioned by them, can turn into a double-edged knife. That is because ham-fisted methods of control or manipulation are not easy to sustain in the new era of globalization. For instance, the officially orchestrated anti-Japanese protest marches in April 2005 in China began going out of control, forcing authorities to clamp down, due to one unforeseen reason — the large numbers of messages for support sent out by demonstrators to others via the Internet and mobile phones.

Having instigated the demonstrations, the Chinese government had to unobtrusively clamp down on the protests in order to protect its own interests. It must have realized the danger that the demonstrators, having tasted popular power, could turn against it. As a matter of fact, anti-Japanese protests in China's history have usually recoiled on the government of the day. A student-led demonstration on May 4, 1919, to protest a decision by the World War I Allied powers allowing Japan to take over Germany's colonial possessions in China led to widespread Chinese protests against Western colonialism. That movement and subsequent uprisings, in 1931, 1937 and as recently as 1987, turned against the national government, because protestors viewed it as too weak or corrupt to stand up for national interests.

In general, the central challenge confronting autocrats in any political system that emerged from the barrels of guns relates to their legitimacy to retain the reins of power. In China and Vietnam, for instance, the communist leadership trumpets rapid economic growth and other capitalist accomplishments to claim political legitimacy. Having ideologically forsaken even the pretence of egalitarianism, ruling communist parties in Asia are distinguished by the single-minded pursuit of money and materialism. Yet, as world history shows, materialist progress tends to sharpen problems of legitimacy for authoritarian regimes.

The legitimacy challenge, with the accompanying insecurity, motivates autocrats of all hues to regulate their citizens' access to information about what is going on in their own nation or in the world at large. It is not just Google, Yahoo and Microsoft that are implicitly helping to prop up the Chinese Communist Party's dictatorship, for example. 'So are most of the world's multinational companies — as well as you (and me)', as one analyst has put it. 'We all support the dictatorship of the CCP by trading with China, by investing in China, by taking holidays in China and by buying Chinese goods and services'.[19]

Indeed, it was the U.S. government, driven by commercial greed, which granted Beijing permanent normal trade status in 2000, an action that paved the way for China to join the World Trade Organization and allowed U.S. firms to do business more easily with the regime in Beijing. China's WTO membership actually undercut U.S. leverage to compel change in Chinese trade practices so as to help shrink the massive U.S.–China trade imbalance. As a WTO member, Beijing now enjoys protection against the use of unilateral sanctions by the United States, which earlier could readily threaten to slap tariffs on Chinese imports in an effort either to force Beijing to reduce the unfair advantage its exporters enjoy against U.S. manufacturers or to stem its rampant intellectual-property piracy.

Despite personal and political freedoms expanding in the world, some of the worst abuses continue to occur in Asia, with little indication that autocratic governments there are willing to end repression and loosen their vice-like grip on power. A white paper issued by Beijing, for example, rationalized the denial of freedoms to the Chinese people by claiming that, 'China's democracy is a people's democracy under the leadership of the Communist Party of China. The CPC leadership is the fundamental guarantee that the Chinese people will be masters in managing the affairs of their own country'. Beijing has even denied Hong Kong the free elections that were promised when Chinese sovereignty over it was restored.

In fact, Beijing sees a threat to its unity from democracy, and is determined to block any attempt to kindle a Ukrainian-style 'orange revolution' or a Georgian-type 'rose revolution' on its territory. Its fears were reinforced by the effects of the so-called 'tulip revolution' in Kyrgyzstan, with which it shares a 1000-kilometre-long frontier. Street protests in Kyrgyzstan after supposedly rigged parliamentary elections there in early 2005 prompted President Askar Akayev to flee the country.

Such 'colour revolutions', more broadly, have had the effect of instilling greater caution among authoritarian regimes and prompting autocrats to search for possible countermeasures to foreign-inspired democratization initiatives. Uzbekistan's Karimov responded by ordering U.S. military forces out of his country and entering into a new security agreement with Russia. Asian autocrats, in general, have introduced greater vigil or restrictions on inflow of foreign funds and on non-governmental organizations and foreign media personnel. To deter a Kyrgyzstan-type eruption, elections now tend to come with precautions. Many observers from foreign governments and international organizations were invited, for example, to the December 2005 Kazakhstan election, which returned President Nursultan Nazerbayev to a new seven-year term with 91 per cent of the vote. Yet that election did not meet international standards.

Democracy is certainly not the cure-all for political problems, but it does aid stability, instil moderation and promote equity in society. Democratic states are more likely to govern responsibly and less likely to go to war with one another. After all, democracies are predisposed to cooperation and conciliation. In contrast to the mature democracies in Western Europe, however, most democracies in Asia are weak or dysfunctional. In fact, Asia is a reminder that democracy means far more than the holding of free and fair elections. Elections might help empower citizens but they do not necessarily translate into able governance. Basic governance remains a challenge in many a democracy.

There is no dearth of examples of nascent or dysfunctional democracies in Asia being hobbled by political impasses. From the forced resignation of Thai Prime Minister Thaksin Shinawatra to the political gridlock and periodic coup rumours under Philippine President Gloria Arroyo, from the Nepalese divide between the Maoists and other political parties to Taiwan President Ma Ying-jeou's confrontation with the opposition Democratic Progressive Party (DPP), Asia illustrates the need to build state capacity and healthy institutions to make democracy more meaningful.

The spread of Islamic extremism and corruption in Bangladesh, for instance, is a symptom of a not-uncommon deeper malaise — dysfunctional democracy. Similarly, in the Philippines, political paralysis, a politicized military and state failure in the south have turned Mindanao into a training ground and refuge for Southeast Asian *jihadists*, such as from the dreaded Jemaah Islamiyah, linked to the 2002 and 2005 Bali bombings and the 2003, 2004 and 2009 Jakarta attacks. Fragile or dysfunctional democracies that lack the institutional capacity to inspiringly act, or deliver results, or even maintain law and order can actually engender political or civil conflict.

Even in a deeply rooted and vibrant democracy like India, public accountability and oversight need to be improved. A striking reminder was provided by the vaunted U.S–Indian nuclear deal, signed in July 2005. While the deal faced rigorous public examination in the United States, with New Delhi itself spending more than $2 million of Indian taxpayer money to lobby American lawmakers to support the accord, Prime Minister Manmohan Singh neither needed the approval of the Indian Parliament nor was he answerable to the public for a deal that centred on India's main strategic asset — its nuclear deterrent. It is a tribute to the vitality of U.S. democracy that the White House was called upon to demonstrate beyond a reasonable doubt that the deal carried significant national-security advantages for the United States not attainable through other means. It is precisely due to the anaemic checks and balances in the Indian system that a nominated prime minister, who came to office without winning a single popular election in his career, escaped legislative scrutiny of his action at home even as he anxiously awaited the outcome of the vetting process in the U.S. Congress.

Given the varied political systems in Asia — from 'guided democracy' run through meritocracy in Singapore to limited democracy without the military being under civilian oversight in terrorist-haven Pakistan — some Asian leaders have tried to sidestep the need for building strong democratic norms and practices by suggesting that prudent policies driven by market logic could serve as a substitute. For example, Singapore's senior minister, Goh Chok Tong, has contended that 'good governance — by which I mean predictable and honest legal systems, protection of intellectual property, rational property and labour laws, pro-business policies on international trade and investments and sound social policies, among other things — is not necessarily linked to any particular type of political system.... The logic of the market is coldly relentless. The market will punish, bypass and eventually marginalize states that do not meet its exacting standards'.[20]

Goh's argument flies in the face of the 1989 thesis that Francis Fukuyama published in the journal, *The National Interest*, as a young policy geek working at the State Department — a thesis that catapulted him into intellectual stardom. Fukuyama had self-righteously contended: 'What we may be witnessing is not just the end of the Cold War, or the passing of a particular period of post-war history, but the end of history as such: that is, the end point of mankind's ideological evolution and the universalization of Western liberal democracy as the final form of human government.'[21] The Asia of the twenty-first century demonstrates that Western liberal democratic values and practices are anything but universal. And that the strategy to use market forces to open up closed political systems has not worked in some prominent cases.

Yet, sound democratic traditions, a liberal and secular ethos, a free media, a developed civil society and checks on insularity and nationalism are essential elements for any regional community building. A totalitarian or authoritarian state that denies its citizens fundamental rights and disdains transparent, accountable governance can hardly help build a rules-based regional community. Despite its authoritarian politics, however, China claims to be the natural leader in Asia. There is also a resurgence of ugly nationalism in several major Asian states, including Japan, China and South Korea, helping to turn the spotlight once again on gaping historical wounds. A growing public sentiment against foreign capital in South Korea, for instance, has fanned the 'chill wind' of xenophobia.[22] ASEAN, despite facing the 'integrate or vegetate' choice, finds itself politically too disparate to be a force for anything beyond trade. India, even with its democratic and secular credentials, is too weighed down by its interminable domestic problems to proactively seek regional community building.

The trend in Europe, on the other hand, has been quite the reverse. EU members have sought to blunt their national identities for the sake of the Union, even if the process to temper identities is far from perfect or far from complete. The EU no doubt faces its own set of challenges, including those relating to further integration. Even enlargement beyond a 27-nation EU with the admission of Bulgaria and Romania is proving unpopular with European voters. That has only made a root-and-branch reform of the Union's decision-making processes and mechanisms imperative. The EU needs the requisite legal and financial means to promote greater integration even as it seeks to build greater democratic accountability towards its member-states. Yet, the fact is that while maintaining its cultural and linguistic vibrancy, Europe has undertaken the most extensive exercise in regional integration in the world, creating a single market and a single currency.

Despite the weighty challenges that stare Asia in the face, the rationale for creating an Asian Union remains as compelling as it was for the establishment of the European Union. This rationale is underscored by the rising levels of trade, investment, tourism and other exchanges between Asian states. However, in the absence of tangible forward movement on community building or multilateral accords, the emphasis has turned to creating larger and more ambitious free-trade areas in Asia, as showcased by the China–ASEAN, Japan-ASEAN and India-ASEAN agreements. Examples of bilateral free-trade agreements in the works include Japan–India and China–India accords. The most ambitious proposal is Japan's idea of a vast free-trade zone in Asia (excluding Taiwan) to rival the EU and NAFTA markets.

In general, FTAs have become so common that they are beginning to appear more political than economic. In addition, they create webs of copious special favours and country-of-origin rules that become a bureaucratic maze, haunting businesses. They remain a poor substitute for the need to build wider multilateral cooperation and concord in Asia. In fact, bilateral and subregional trade deals without common rules of origin and effective governance devices only turn attention away from identifying and promoting pan-Asian interests. The EU, despite its membership enlargement making it more heterogeneous and less raring to go for greater integration, has continued to serve as an example to Asians of how incremental, sector-by-sector economic integration can help establish political cooperation founded on a community of values across a continent.

Notes and References

1. Anand Giridharadas, 'Mittal Views the Takeover of Arcelor as "Inevitable"', *International Herald Tribune*, February 21, 2006.
2. See Table K in the 2009 Human Development Indicators at: http://hdr.undp.org.
3. 'Japan Emerges From Worst Post-War Recession', Bloomberg, August 17, 2009.
4. Julius Caeser Parrenas, 'Washington Could Help Southeast Asia Get Itself Together', *International Herald Tribune*, May 15, 2001.
5. Ian Bremmer, Choi Sung-Hong and Yoriko Kawaguchi, 'Northeast Asia: Defusing a Dangerous Region', *International Herald Tribune*, December 30, 2005.
6. Mohan Malik, 'The East Asia Summit: More Discord than Accord — Is the New East Asian Community (EAC) the First Step towards a United Region, or an Irritant to Old Rivalries?', *YaleGlobal*, December 20, 2005.
7. Philip Bowring, 'An Asian Union? Not Yet', *International Herald Tribune*, December 16, 2005.
8. Anthony Faiola, 'Japan–Taiwan Ties Blossom As Regional Rivalry Grows: Tokyo, Wary of China, Tilts toward Taipei', *Washington Post*, March 24, 2006, p. A14.
9. According to the poll, while 72 per cent of the German respondents have a positive view of France, only 65 per cent hold favourable feelings about Germany. Similarly, 89 per cent of the French view Germany positively but only 68 per cent see their own country in a favourable light. Pew Global Attitudes Project, Chapter I: 'America's Image and U.S. Foreign Policy', *America's Image Slips, But Allies Share U.S. Concerns over Iran, Hamas* (Washington, D.C.: Pew Research Centre, June 13, 2006).
10. Jung Chang and Jon Halliday, *Mao: The Unknown Story* (London: Jonathan Cape, 2005), p. 1. One major disclosure in this biography is Joseph Stalin's powerful role in Mao's rise.

11. Frank Ching, 'China Swaps Historical Facts for Fiction', *Japan Times*, February 8, 2006.

12. Fei-Ling Wang, 'Heading Off Fears of a Resurgent China', *International Herald Tribune*, April 11, 2006.

13. 'Murder Made in China', *The Boston Globe*, July 4, 2006.

14. World Press Freedom Index 2008 by Reporters Without Borders at:
    http://www.rsf.org/

15. See Freedom House, *Freedom in the World* (Washington, D.C.: Freedom House, 2009).

16. U.S. Department of State, Bureau of Democracy, Human Rights and Labour, *Seventh Annual International Religious Freedom Report* (Washington, D.C.: Department of State, November, 2005).

17. Search comparison done on September 27, 2009.
    http://www.google.cn/search?hl=zh-CN&source=hp&q=tiananmen+square&btnG=Google +搜索&aq=f&oq=
    http://www.google.com/search?q=tiananmen+square&rls=com.microsoft:en-US&ie=UTF-8&oe=UTF-8&startIndex=&startPage=0

18. Minxin Pei, 'The Dark Side of China's Rise', *Foreign Policy* (March/April 2006).

19. David Wall, 'A Yen to Help a Dictatorship', *Japan Times*, February 12, 2006.

20. Goh Chok Tong, 'Towards an East Asian Renaissance', address at the Opening Session of the 4th Asia–Pacific Roundtable, February 6, 2006, Singapore, text at:
    http://www.globalfoundation.org.au/documents/4APRTOpeningAddressbySM.pdf

21. Francis Fukuyama, 'The End of History?' *The National Interest* (Summer 1989). At that time, Fukuyama was deputy director of the State Department's policy planning staff.

22. Kim Wan-soon and Lee You-il, 'The Chill Wind of Korean Xenophobia', *Far Eastern Economic Review*, Vol. 168, No. 11 (December 2005), pp. 41–46.

3

Asian Geopolitics of Energy

TODAY ENERGY AND SECURITY ARE INSEPARABLE. AS ASIA demonstrates, energy is getting increasingly intertwined with geopolitics. With competition for the world's oil and gas resources heating up, a twenty-first-century version of an energy-related Great Game looms large on the horizon. Like the Great Game played out over the mid-to-late nineteenth century, foreign powers are competing for influence. But the contemporary competition is for access to vast, untapped oil and natural-gas reserves.

In the Great Game that took place in Central Asia, there were principally two players — czarist Russia and the British Indian Empire, each of which sought to win over the local sultans and emirs through various inducements. Ironically, the British spy who coined the phrase, 'Great Game', Captain Arthur Conolly, was captured along with another British agent in 1842 by the emir of Bukhara, a city now in southern Uzbekistan. The two were forced to dig their graves and then beheaded. But it was Rudyard Kipling who made the term popular through his novel, *Kim*, which is the story of an orphan boy groomed by the British secret service to go 'far and far into the North, playing the Great Game'.

In the emerging version of the Great Game, however, there are several players. They include China, Russia, the United States, Iran, Turkey, Japan and India. In the name of waging a global war on terror, the United States, for example, has set up new military bases stretching across the oil-rich Caspian Sea basin and Central Asia, even as it has consolidated its strategic interests in the main oil-exporting region of West Asia. Russia has used its oil and gas exports to revive its fortunes, succeeding in becoming an important geopolitical player again. Such is its rapidly rising, energy-driven wealth that, in nominal terms, its GDP rose from less than $200 billion in 1999 to $1.29 trillion in 2007, according to a CIA estimate. The oil-price decline in 2008-09, however, came as a warning against being a largely petro-state.

Washington has sought to inject its own geopolitical interests in the Asian energy competition by playing pipeline politics. It has discouraged India from sourcing gas from Iran and instead promoted an alternative gas pipeline from Turkmenistan to India via Afghanistan and Pakistan. Similarly, to the annoyance of Russia (which regards Central Asia as part of its backyard), America has prodded Kazakhstan's autocrat, Nursultan Nazarbayev, to ship oil through the U.S.-backed Baku–Tbilisi–Ceyhan pipeline that terminates at Turkey's Mediterranean coast.[1]

China, which has viewed with alarm the creation after September 11, 2001 of U.S. military bases in Central Asia, has built its own pipeline to bring oil from Kazakhstan and is seeking two pipelines from Russia that would eventually supply it with 60 to 80 billion cubic metres of gas a year. These ventures are a lynchpin in China's goal to diversify its imports away from the volatile Middle East, the source of more than half of Chinese overseas purchases. Overland pipelines will help reduce China's reliance on shipping lanes policed by the United States and its allies. In contrast, energy-poor India or Japan does not have a similar option. Lacking geographical contiguity with Central Asia and Iran, India will remain largely dependent on oil imports by sea from the Middle East.

China, with the world's most resource-hungry economy, fears that in the event of a strategic confrontation, its economy could be held hostage by hostile naval forces through the interdiction of its oil imports. That same concern has prompted Beijing to build its long-hoped-for strategic oil reserve, also intended to help cushion any unforeseen event in the world's volatile energy markets. Such is China's concern over its energy vulnerability that two Chinese academics have warned in a published article that Beijing might be willing to go to war to defend its interests. According to these academics, 'If confronted with serious threats to its energy security, it will mobilize all its economic, political and military resources to ensure a secure energy supply, or to interfere in the energy-supply chains of the United States and its allies like Japan in key chokepoints such as the South China Sea, the Strait of Malacca or even the Taiwan Strait'.[2]

Owing to its tireless efforts to secure oil and gas resources internationally, China has emerged as a major player in the global geopolitics of energy. This is manifest from the deals it has signed with rogue regimes for new supplies of oil, gas and other key resources. It has employed arms sales to gain access to raw materials, unmindful that its weapon exports would only fuel intrastate conflicts and human-rights violations. As a consequence, according to an Amnesty International report, China is fast emerging as one of the world's biggest and the most opaque arms exporters, neither revealing any information about its arms sales nor submitting data to the United Nations Register on Conventional Arms.[3]

China's covetous hunt for oil in Africa, for example, has presented it as the new colonial power in that region and led to the China–Africa trade jumping from $10 billion in 2000 to $107 billion in 2008. Similarly in Latin America — rich in metal and energy resources — Beijing's increasingly cosy ties with repressive regimes have been accompanied by a ten-fold rise between 2001 and 2008 in its trade with a region that traditionally has been within the U.S. sphere of influence.

Along with the emergent Great Game has come the phenomenon of resource nationalism in oil-rich countries that feel empowered by soaring oil revenues. In the decade after the fall of the Berlin Wall, oil-exporting states competed for capital inflows in an era of low energy prices, granting Western companies favourable terms to bring in new technology and expand their production. But with higher oil prices resulting in overflowing coffers, the same states started embracing resource nationalism. This has encouraged the rewriting of the rules of foreign investment, the giving of preferential treatment to national companies, the imposition of higher taxes and royalties, the renegotiation of projects that were drawn up when oil and gas prices were low, or even the retaking of control (as illustrated by Russia and Bolivia) of oil or gas fields.

Today, Western oil companies are facing growing competition from Asian giants like China National Petroleum Corporation (CNPC), China National Offshore Oil Corporation (CNOOC) Limited, India's Oil and Natural Gas Corporation (ONGC) and Malaysia's Petronas. This is a big change from the situation after World War II when the so-called 'Seven Sisters' — five U.S. companies, one British and one Anglo-Dutch — monopolized global oil production, refining and distribution and set international prices. It was the stranglehold of a small cartel on the world markets that prompted four Arab states, Iran and Venezuela in 1960 to establish the Organization of the Petroleum Exporting Countries (OPEC), an association that subsequently expanded and become more organized. The recrudescence of resource nationalism — centred on securing a larger share of windfall profits for the state —

has come at a time of lofty prices and a frenetic scramble for resources around the world, with companies bidding record amounts for new exploration or production rights or even to acquire a minority stake in a venture. China has come to epitomize the rush for resources.

Sharpening Energy Competition

Spiralling demand in China, India and elsewhere has driven global energy prices up to record levels, making the prospect of sharpening interstate competition over scarce resources look real. Global energy demand, particularly for oil and natural gas, is projected to increase sharply in the coming years — from 75 million barrels per day in 2004 to 120 million barrels in 2025. With Asia alone expected to consume 80 per cent of the added 45 million barrels, Beijing has embarked on an ambitious naval modernization programme.[4]

As energy is now inextricably tied to security, the protection of the world's main oil arteries has become a priority. Much of the global oil-export supply passes through two constricted passageways — the piracy-plagued Strait of Malacca, which is barely 2.5 kilometres wide at its narrowest point between Indonesia and Singapore, and the 89-kilometre-wide Strait of Hormuz between Iran and Oman. More than 50,000 ships pass through the Malacca Strait alone each year. To safeguard these and other critical passageways (including the Bab el-Mandab Passage between Yemen and the Horn of Africa, the Suez Canal and the Bosporus and Turkish Straits), stepped-up patrolling and port defences have been introduced. The nightmare scenario 'remains a maritime 9/11, the hijacking of an oil or gas tanker by terrorists who turn it into a floating bomb that could devastate a major port city'.[5]

In general, energy-importing states are deeply concerned about their vulnerability and thus keen to find ways to safeguard supplies. Large importers recognize that their energy dependency on specific exporting states may be a drag on their foreign policy. It is much harder for large oil importers to boldly assert their concerns and interests vis-à-vis supplier states. In the 1980s and 1990s, Saudi Arabia, for example, pursued a wink-and-nod approach towards Islamic extremism and terrorism, bankrolling *jihad* as part of its aggressive export of the medieval theology of Wahhabism, which is named after the revivalist movement founded by Muhammad Ibn'Abd al-Wahhab in 1744. Its target countries, such as India, could do little to mount diplomatic pressure on it because of their dependence on Saudi oil supplies.

Today, energy concerns are a key element in the ongoing profound and potentially far-reaching transformation of the Asian security environment. In the face of emergent threats that are more diverse, complex and amorphous than those in the past, the security agenda in Asia is undergoing a fundamental change. Attitudinal shifts are being followed by policy shifts. Nowhere is this change more striking than in the case of issues related to energy security.

Asia's high GDP growth rates have indeed set off a scramble among its principal economies to secure energy resources. The major Asian countries are searching for newer sources of energy overseas to feed their fast-growing economies. Asia is now a key propellant of the global energy competition.

It is important, however, to recognize that Asia's energy consumption is still low by the standards of the developed world. The United States, with 4.5 per cent of the world's population, remains by far the largest consumer of oil, devouring almost a quarter of the total global supply. While this is a testament to its continuing consumption of a vastly outsized share of global resources, America now has to contend with the demands of a rising Asia in the global energy markets. It is thus not a surprise that, in response, the United States has actively sought to shape the geopolitics of energy in Asia, including the routes of pipelines. It is more geopolitics than the promotion of regional interdependence and cooperation that has influenced decisions on establishing the 'pipelines of power'.

Demand for oil has been particularly shooting up in China and India, in keeping with their emergence as major economic players. Although their per capita consumption of resources remains small by Western standards, a booming China and India, through their ravenous demands for natural resources, spurred a surge in oil and commodity prices in the world up to 2008. Per capita oil consumption in China and India at present is just 1/15th and 1/30th that in the United States.[6] Yet, the huge new thirst for oil in China, India and other fast-growing Asian economies not only drove up petroleum prices between 2004 and 2008, but it is also set to exacerbate the global-energy challenges. The challenges indeed have been conspicuously underlined by China's own aggressive energy-assets acquisition drive.

At a time when the assertive pursuit of national interests has globally begun to replace ideology, idealism and morality in international relations, there is a danger that interstate conflict in Asia could in the coming years be driven by competition not so much over political influence as over scarce resources. Nothing better illustrates the dangers of resource wars than the emerging strategic landscape in Asia, where high economic growth rates have fuelled concern and competition over raw materials and energy resources.

Energy has become critical to the continued economic expansion in Asia, and the spectre of inadequate energy supply has intensified geopolitical rivalries in the oil-rich Central Asia, Caspian Sea basin, West Asia and East China Sea. Africa's oil wealth is increasing that continent's strategic importance, with China, India and other major oil-importing nations paying greater attention to Africa and vying to buy up available African energy assets.

Not only is there mounting pressure on the present global oil reserves due to rising consumption, but there is also a shortage of refining capacity to meet the worldwide demand. Unless that shortage is addressed and the supply situation eased, prices will climb again sharply after the decline from the second half of 2008. Interestingly, Japan's declining population means it will have much-sought-after spare capacity to refine crude oil into gasoline and other products for sale to other Asian countries, particularly its neighbours, China and South Korea.

China versus India and Japan

As the demand for oil and natural gas has soared in Asia, some major Asian countries have time after time been pitted against each other in bidding wars for energy assets. China's state-run oil behemoths have been in the lead in such contests, trouncing their Asian rivals. Indian firms have not hesitated to join the bidding wars. Yet they have lost out to their Chinese counterparts in Angola, Iran, Ecuador, Kazakhstan and elsewhere.

A cash-rich China has shown time and again through its nimbleness that it can outmanoeuvre India in competitive energy dealings. Beijing's edge in global commercial negotiations and transactions also comes from its ability to wield political clout of a type that India and Japan cannot muster. As a veto-carrying permanent member of the United Nations Security Council, China can help shield unpopular or renegade regimes from punitive UN action, including sanctions. Moreover, through its emphasis on developing intercontinental-range weaponry, China has been successful in projecting power far beyond its frontiers. Many of the energy-exporting nations are problem states, and they see in China an assertive, ambitious, clear-eyed power that can help protect them from international opprobrium and chastisement.

Yet, some in India have imaginatively proposed cooperation with China on energy. Before he was removed as India's petroleum minister in January 2006, Mani Shankar Aiyar had floated one grand idea after another, including an Asian energy grid. During a visit to Beijing at the beginning of 2006, Aiyar also reached an accord-in-principle that, where possible, the two countries would cooperate in bidding for third-country assets.

The reality, however, is that as a larger and more aggressive player willing to take major risks and with a track record of greater success, China has little to gain from such cooperation with India. With their deeper pockets and ruthless tactics, the state-run Chinese companies are loath to share their commercial plans with Indian peers. That explains why all the energy-cooperation suggestions have come from India. The Indian cooing is music to Chinese ears but incongruous to Chinese commercial interests.

There has been only one joint Indian–Chinese acquisition to which Beijing consented because it involved a state — Syria — that the administration of U.S. President George W. Bush had been seeking to isolate. As the 2006 U.S. national-security strategy report warned, 'Any government that chooses to be an ally of terror, such as Syria or Iran, has chosen to be an enemy of freedom, justice, and peace. The world must hold those regimes to account'.[7] At the end of 2005, China's CNPC tied up with India's ONGC to pick up PetroCanada's 37 per cent stake in the old, past-the-prime oil and gas fields in al-Furat, Syria, for $573 million. By joining hands with America's emerging global strategic partner, India, Beijing deftly deflected any U.S. criticism of the move. It was India that faced U.S. heat over the acquisition, carried out through a joint Sino–Indian venture named Himalaya Energy Syria

Ltd. In a bid to stall that acquisition, Washington submitted a protest *démarche* to New Delhi.

The two Asian giants, China and India, which make up more than a third of the global population, are competing quietly but fiercely to source energy supplies from overseas. With India already importing more than 75 per cent of its oil and China importing about 40 per cent, their need for imports will only grow in the coming years, fuelling their competition for energy resources. India's annual oil-import bill has swelled to more than $75 billion, putting a massive burden on the national exchequer. The larger Asian energy competition is also underlined by the fact that Japan, South Korea and Taiwan import all their oil.

India, however, cannot be a real match to China in the global-energy competition and will continue to lose out in direct bidding wars until it evolves an integrated energy policy tied to its foreign policy. It also needs to take steps to make its state-run oil companies internationally competitive with China's behemoths. If India were to blend its economic and political strategies to create synergy and leverage, it would certainly position itself more advantageously to handle the sharpening Asian geopolitics on energy resources.

Given the global trend towards greater deregulation and privatization in the energy sector, India would do well to adapt its energy-security strategy to the international market conditions. A governmental role is not easy in energy acquisitions and resource development unless it is an authoritarian state with a clear mission. China's government pursues commercial interests abroad just the way the board of a large multinational company hunts for international opportunities. In such a setting, state-owned firms become vital.

Whetting China's aggressive drive is the fact that, in less than 15 years, that country has gone from being a net energy exporter to becoming the world's second-largest energy consumer. India, already fifth in global petroleum demand, is set to replace South Korea as the world's fourth-largest energy consumer, after America, China and Japan.[8] India's oil imports are expected to rise from 2.65 million barrels a day at present to about 4 million barrels a day by 2020.[9]

Slaking the Chinese, Japanese, Indian and Korean thirst will roil oil markets. At the same time, growing dependency on energy imports from politically unpredictable states is likely to further tempt China and India in particular to try and reduce their vulnerabilities to energy disruption by acquiring energy assets overseas.

Separately, China has battled with Japan for several years now over the rights to Russian oil — to the delight of Moscow, which is eager to reap the full strategic benefits of its energy resources, its main source of leverage today. Tokyo and Beijing manoeuvred hard for the best routing of the 4100-kilometre East Siberian–Pacific pipeline, especially because not enough oil may exist in Siberian fields to satisfy both Japanese and Chinese demands. Japan pressed for the East Siberian pipeline to ship crude oil to the Russian Pacific port of Nakhodka, where Japanese tankers could come and carry much of it away. An oil pipeline to Nakhodka would open Russian exports to the global markets, while a pipeline to China would bind Moscow to a single buyer.

Having received a $6-billion pledge from Japan to fund a major share of the project, Russia gave assurances that the oil pipeline eventually would be built to Nakhodka. But, to keep Beijing happy too, it also announced a south-bound branch, although it may not have enough oil to feed both pipelines. Tokyo has also been interested in liquefied natural gas (LNG) production on Russia's Sakhalin Island.

Russia, clearly, is in dire need of foreign investments in new oil and gas projects in order to ensure that its production does not fall below current levels. Japan, China, India and Europe can provide investments to upgrade Russia's rundown oil and gas infrastructure and help in the long-term development of Russian exploration. China, the largest buyer of Russian weapons, including fighter-jets, warships and missiles, has been keen to make major investments in Russia's energy infrastructure.

Beijing, for its part, views potential oil and gas finds in the South and East China Seas as justifying its hard-line stance over territorial and maritime disputes there. For instance, China wants the boundary of its Exclusive Economic Zone (EEZ) to stretch to the very edge of the continental shelf. This shelf, however, extends almost to Okinawa and covers Taiwan. Japan, in contrast, insists on the boundary being the median line between the two countries.

When Chinese platforms began drilling for gas inside the Chinese side of the median line, seeking to mine into a field that is also within Japan's claimed EEZ, Tokyo in reprisal allowed a Japanese company to test drill into the same field, but on Japan's side of the median line.[10] The hotly disputed oil and gas fields in the East China Sea — named Chunxiao, Duanqiao and Tianwaitian by China, and Shirakaba, Kusunoki and Kashi by Japan — straddle the median line, which Beijing refuses to recognize as the EEZ-demarcation boundary.

Another example of China's assertiveness was its 1992 'Law on the Territorial Waters and Their Contiguous Areas', which claimed four-fifths of the South China Sea and underscored Beijing's creeping jurisdiction claims. Through an inclusive, horseshoe-shaped baseline in its maps, Beijing has signalled its intent to assert control over the South China Sea as its 'historic waters', in case large quantities of oil and gas are found there. In a 1951 case between Britain and Norway, the International Court of Justice had pronounced: 'By "historic waters" are usually meant waters which are treated as internal waters but which would not have that character were it not for the existence of an historic title.' Having already declared the

Paracel Islands to be part of its historic waters despite the absence of an historic title, China wields the threat of doing the same to the Spratlys to the south, in order to deny freedom of navigation and overflight rights to others.

Commodity Diplomacy

The growing demand in Asia is not only for oil and gas but also for other primary commodities needed to feed industry. As a consequence, world commodity prices are now at historically high levels. Such spiralling demand, in turn, has given rise to a new commodity diplomacy, as exemplified by China's drive to stock up on supplies of iron ore, copper, aluminium, nickel and other foreign-origin resources. Employing the lure of development aid, Beijing has been signing important resource agreements with commodity-producing states. According to one observer, 'As China's hunger for energy and primary commodities has grown, so too has the adventurism of its state-owned oil and extractive companies'.[11]

Emulating Japan and the United States in the earlier decades, China is underpinning its commodity outreach through financial muscle by offering soft loans to primary-commodity producers. Through such aid diplomacy, China has won access to key resources — from gold in Bolivia, to coal in Indonesia, to nickel in the Philippines and Burma, to oil in Ecuador and Indonesia, to copper in Chile, and to gas in Burma again. China is already the world's largest consumer of iron ore, aluminium, steel, copper and cement. With Chinese commodity companies scouring the globe for resource assets, 'resource-rich countries such as Australia, Canada, Indonesia, Peru and Russia were, circa 2003, among the top 10 country-destinations for China's offshore investment'.[12]

In fact, China's large and growing imports of natural resources have helped spur an economic boom in resource-wealthy countries. Australia is a prime example, with its economical miracle being revitalized by China today after having been set in motion by Japan a generation or two ago. Once regarded with distrust, China has gained recognition and respectability in Australia, despite Canberra's special relationship and close military ties with Washington. Exports of iron ore, alumina, uranium and liquefied natural gas to China have helped boost the Australian economy. Indeed, Chinese companies, in a bid to buy legal security of supply, have begun to invest billions of dollars in Australia to help secure their access to raw materials.

The new Sino–Australian cosiness is exemplified by Canberra's agreement to sell uranium for power generation to an autocratic state still modernizing its nuclear arsenal and maintaining an opaque nuclear posture. Canberra overlooked concerns that the deal could result in the diversion of more resources for China's nuclear-weapons programme. Commercial benefits, clearly, took precedence over security concerns. Such is the commercial significance of the deal that the shares of Australian uranium miners and explorers have boomed. An infusion of Chinese investments will open the way for more uranium deposits to be found and mined in Australia.

The spread of Chinese influence to Down Under was further exemplified when the Mandarin-speaking Australian Prime Minister Kevin Rudd, in one of his first actions after assuming office, pulled the plug on the Quadrilateral Initiative — a nascent initiative founded on the concept of democratic peace. In fact, such is Canberra's sensitivity to Chinese concerns that the previous Foreign Minister, Alexander Downer, had publicly declared, 'We don't support a policy of containment of China'.[13]

Australia prefers to balance its relationship with Tokyo and Beijing, and loves to cite the fact that its largest trading partner (China) is no longer the same as its main security anchor (the U.S.). But there is nothing unique about this situation. It is a testament to Beijing's rising global economic clout that China now is also Japan's and India's largest trade partner. While permitting China to slake its thirst for Australian mineral and energy resources, Australia has been reluctant to make up its mind whether, as an Indian Ocean as well as a Pacific Ocean power, it should grant India similar access, including to its uranium store. India has agreed to segregate its nuclear programme into civil and military components, but in China there is neither civil–military separation nor rigorous inspections by the International Atomic Energy Agency to verifiably ensure that Australian uranium is being used for commercial nuclear power reactors, and not for weapons purposes. Beijing has accepted largely symbolic inspections under its 'voluntary safeguards' accord with the Vienna-based IAEA.

Australia doesn't have a single nuclear power plant of its own, yet it holds 38 per cent of the known global uranium reserves, although at present it meets only 22 per cent of the world demand, partly because of state restrictions on exploration and mining. Only one of Australia's seven major states and territories has been willing to approve new uranium mines. Yet Australian uranium production, limited to four mines so far, is set for more expansive extraction. The Melbourne-based BHP Billiton has unveiled a $5 billion expansion of its already-large Olympic Dam mine that alone would double Australia's uranium exports. As global demand threatens to outstrip supply, uranium prices have soared since 2003, beating all but one of the 19 commodities in the Reuters/ Jefferies CRB Index. Only the price of sugar rose higher. With global uranium supplies from dismantled nuclear weapons in Russia diminishing at a time when some nations have unveiled plans for new reactors, spot uranium prices have come under pressure.

As the global competition for procurement of minerals increases, China's state-run companies are going to the source to ensure adequate supply of iron ore, coal and other commodities through the acquisition of foreign mines.[14] Burma has allowed China to invest in several of its large mines in return for Beijing's help in the development of hydropower, with electricity from one such Chinese-assisted project being supplied to the newly established Burmese capital, Nay Phi Daw (or 'Royal City'), located just outside the lumber town of Pyinmana, 370 kilometres north of Rangoon. According to a report by Macquarie Bank, Australia's leading investment bank, China in 2010 will account for 30 per cent of the world's consumption of aluminium, copper, iron ore and nickel, up from 15 per cent in 2000 and just 7 per cent in 1990.[15]

The scramble to secure primary commodities has opened a wider debate as to whether producing countries should protect certain scarce commodities as strategic resources. China, a major steel consumer, has substantial reserves of iron ore, yet it has banned exports of this commodity. It actually encourages its own steel producers to import iron ore. China, in fact, has emerged as the largest importer of iron ore, accounting for a third of all global imports.[16] India, in contrast, remains a major exporter of iron ore, although China has, according to various accounts, iron-ore deposits more than two-and-half times that of India. Indeed, iron ore makes up more than half of India's total exports to China.

About 96 per cent of the world's iron ore is produced in 15 countries, with Australia, Brazil, the United States, Russia, China and India being among the largest producers.[17] About 98 per cent of the iron ore produced goes into steel production. China's conscious decision to conserve its iron-ore resources and go in for rising imports has led to a record surge in the global price of iron ore since 2005. China could account for nearly half of the world steel output in 2015, making its iron-ore import requirements the key determinant of global prices.

India's estimated iron-ore reserves of 18 billion metric tons will last between 30 and 50 years, if India were to boost its per capita iron-ore consumption from the present 30 kilograms to the developed world's 300- to 400-kilogram level. China, on the other hand, has total iron-ore reserves of 472 billion metric tons in its seven largest mining areas, although the average content of iron in Chinese deposits is low at 32.1 per cent.[18] Given India's comparatively limited reserves, the deal between the Indian state of Orissa and South Korea's POSCO steel maker ignited a debate in India on the advisability of a captive lease agreement involving national mineral wealth. In returning for making a large $12-billion investment to manufacture steel in Orissa, the South Korean company secured a commitment from the state government that it would be free to export 30 per cent of its iron-ore supply. Indian industrialist Ratan Tata had argued that if China, with much-larger deposits, could treat iron ore as a strategic resource, India ought to do the same.

While buying up metals overseas, China now supplies, according to one estimate, about 95 per cent of the world's consumption of rare earths — a precious group of minerals vital to high-technology industry, such as miniaturized electronics, computer disk drives, display screens, missile guidance, pollution-control catalysts and advanced materials.[19] In a calculated way, Beijing has cornered the international market for these strategic minerals, which include cerium, neodymium, lanthanum, yttrium and dysprosium. It first quietly made some major foreign investments to get hold of important processing and manufacturing technologies for rare earths, which it mines in Inner Mongolia. China's new monopoly and its 2009 threat to halt exports of rare minerals have raised international concern and prompted a search for alternative sources.

Securing Long-term Supplies

The scramble for resources among Asian states has raised a fundamental question: Does energy or resource security demand legal ownership of far-flung assets? Can a nation embark on a path to energy stability by acquiring untapped oil and gas assets in distant lands?

China certainly thinks so. For a country that even internally is becoming more money-driven by the day, its avaricious acquisition of energy assets in pariah or problem states has attracted unwanted global attention. Its energy-driven ties with Sudan, Iran, Venezuela, Burma, Chad and other problem states have raised international suspicions that it is consciously employing its buying power to mould a strategic circle of influence, even if it undermines multilateral efforts to discipline problem states. In Burma, for example, massive Chinese aid has propped up a military regime that not only rejected the outcome of the 1990 national election, but also has jailed or forced into silence or exile the majority of the 392 members of Aung San Suu Kyi's National League for Democracy elected to Parliament then. As one observer has put it starkly, 'Just as the United States today is reaping the consequences of cynical or manipulative behaviour in the past, in places like Iran and in parts of Latin America, China will be judged in the future based on the actions of today'.[20]

Indeed, a U.S. national-security strategy report has warned China against 'old ways of thinking and acting' in its competition for energy resources. China's rulers, according to this report, are 'expanding trade, but acting as if they can somehow "lock up" energy supplies around the world or seek to direct markets rather than opening them up — as if they can follow a mercantilism borrowed from a discredited era'.[21] Until China makes 'the right strategic choices for its people', the strategy statement menacingly added, the United States will 'hedge against other possibilities'. The expressed concerns of China's neighbours, however, are more muted.

One example of the Chinese drive to 'lock up' energy supplies was the success of the China National Petroleum Corp. (CNPC) to acquire for $4.18 billion a Canadian oil company with large oil reserves in Kazakhstan — PetroKazakhstan Inc. CNPC is China's largest state-owned oil and gas company and accounts for 95 per cent of the country's natural gas market and 40 per cent of its oil products market. CNPC beat out a competing bid by a joint venture between ONGC Videsh Ltd., the international arm of India's state-owned Oil and Natural Gas Corporation Ltd., and an investment company owned by London-based steel billionaire Lakshmi Niwas Mittal, one of the world's wealthiest men.

Another example was CNPC's purchase of a 40 per cent stake in Sudan's government-led oil consortium, Greater Nile Petroleum, with Beijing underpinning its commercial interests in that pariah state through the correlated sale of 34 new fighter-jets to the Sudanese military that has been battling rebels around the southern oilfields.[22] Subsequently, China shipped more than 200 military trucks to Sudan. The Greater Nile stake makes CNPC the single largest shareholder in that consortium, which owns oil fields, a pipeline, a large refinery and a port. By 2006, Sudan — accused of committing genocide in its arid western region of Darfur — accounted for almost 7 per cent of China's oil imports, or about 235,000-plus barrels a day.

Now, China is buying nearly 60 per cent of Sudan's oil production. Ever since an uprising against the Sudanese government by two rebel groups in February 2003 triggered the Darfur violence, leaving more than 200,000 villagers dead and driving two million others from their homes, an opportunistic China turned its face away from the crisis and kept reciting its familiar hollow principles — that it respects all other cultures, that it believes in the peaceful resolution of crises and that it opposes interference in the internal affairs of other nations. Amidst the escalating violence, Beijing had no compunction in selling arms, seizing oil-investment opportunities and lending political support to Sudan, turning that country into its largest overseas oil-production base. That points to more than a passive disinclination on Beijing's part to blend commerce with morality and responsibility.

China has aggressively pursued energy (and metal) interests in other African states as well, including Angola, Nigeria, Equatorial Guinea, Chad, Gabon, Republic of Congo, Zimbabwe and Ethiopia. Angola, supplying 16 per cent of China's total oil imports, has received Chinese loan commitments totalling at least $3 billion as well as Chinese engineers and workers to develop additional offshore oil wells. It is hardly a surprise that China is now Angola's biggest aid donor. In Nigeria, Africa's largest oil producer, China is increasing its investments in oil-and-gas fields and exploration.

With China's annual oil imports now soaring at a rate of 33 per cent, or three times India's, Chinese officials have taken pride in outbidding others, even if it jacks up prices of foreign assets to artificial levels. What matters to China is not price but ownership and reliability. Beijing also has been unflustered about its cosy ties with pariah states. Pushy energy acquisitions, coupled with aggressive arms sales, have drawn international attention to the unsavoury fact that China happens to be the best friend of scofflaw states.[23] As one scholar has written, 'Chinese cooperation with disreputable regimes...reflects Beijing's interest in securing access to oil in the same manner that U.S. cooperation with two of the world's worst violators of human rights — Saudi Arabia and Pakistan — reflects Washington's need to meet energy and anti-terrorism interests'.[24] Chinese military aid directly contributed to the 2009 bloodbath in strategically located Sri Lanka.

Although the popular perception is that Chinese and Indian energy companies are engaged in fierce bidding wars to acquire overseas assets, the reality is that Chinese firms have beaten Indian competition wherever it has arisen. The only exception was the Akpo deepwater oil field in Nigeria, where India's ONGC won the right to buy South Atlantic Petroleum's 45 per cent stake in that field. The irony, however, is that the Indian government blocked the state-owned ONGC from picking up that stake on grounds that the $2-billion investment entailed unacceptable risks as the Nigerian majority stakeholder was a dubious, politically manipulated shell company. But no sooner had the Indians backed out from the deal than the state-run China National Offshore Oil Corp. (CNOOC) Ltd., China's largest offshore oil producer, signed a deal on January 9, 2006, to pay $2.27 billion for the same 45 per cent stake in the Akpo offshore field, turning a blind eye to the ethical issues. CNOOC also bought 35 per cent of an exploration licence for $60 million in Nigeria's Niger Delta.

Unlike China's purchase of oil assets in Africa, the acquisition of PetroKazakhstan has fitted well with the development of its own energy infrastructure. After having turned its back on Central Asia for more than a century, China has consciously sought to source a significant share of its oil and gas imports from that region as a hedge against the potential disruption or blockade of its supplies by sea from the Persian Gulf. Beijing has been seeking — at considerable cost — to reduce its vulnerability to an interdiction of its Middle Eastern oil-supply line, in case of a conflict over Taiwan.

The heavy cost Beijing has been willing to pay is manifest from the way CNPC outbid the Indian competition by jacking up its PetroKazakhstan offer through a second bid and then, having tasted success, its subsequent resale of a third of PetroKazakhstan to KazMunaiGaz, the state oil company and industry regulator in Kazakhstan. The resale is at such discount that KazMunaiGaz is to pay CNPC for the 33 per cent stake through future revenues.[25] The transfer of one-third stake to KazMunaiGaz was designed to help mitigate the risks associated with the PetroKazakhstan acquisition in a country where political arbitrariness on ownership issues is not uncommon.

The PetroKazakhstan oil will flow through the 988-kilometre pipeline that Beijing has constructed from Atasu, Kazakhstan, to Alashankou, China, through some of the world's most inhospitable territory. Hailed by China as the 'new silk route', the pipeline was built by China at a cost of $700 million. Yet the pipeline's commercial viability will remain dubious without the addition of the yet-to-be-supplied Russian crude oil from Siberia. According to one observer, 'Even though most Kazakhs view China with a mixture of fear and suspicion, Nazarbayev approved the Chinese pipeline because it offered an extra oil export route to reduce his landlocked country's dependence on Russia, Azerbaijan and Turkey. Eventually, a sixth of Kazakhstan's total production could flow to China'.[26]

PetroKazakhstan was the largest foreign purchase ever by a Chinese company. The acquisition of PetroKazakhstan, which was the former Soviet Union's largest independent oil company, came after the failed $18.5-billion Chinese bid for the California-based oil major, Unocal Corp., by CNOOC Ltd. That bid in mid-2005, in sending out an unmistakable message that Beijing was willing to do anything for bigger oil stakes, triggered a U.S. congressional furore and raised an ugly spectre of the 'China threat'. The Unocal fiasco was the second occasion in 2005 when a Chinese state-owned company's takeover bid was derailed by nationalistic concerns in the host country over strategic assets coming under the control of a communist state. Earlier that year, a bid by China Minmetals to buy the Canadian mining giant, Noranda, was foiled.

PetroKazakhstan may be an attractive holding, but some of China's foreign-energy acquisitions carry high risks. Multinationals hesitate to bid for risky assets in pariah or problem states, but the bureaucrats running Chinese firms are ready to gamble with taxpayers' money. Despite their massive cash holdings, leading-edge exploration and production tools, and well-developed financial and managerial expertise, global oil companies are more conservative than China's energy behemoths in scouting for such acquisitions. Exxon Mobil's revenues, for example, now exceed the total economic output of Saudi Arabia or Indonesia.

China appears to treat oil as vital blood to run its fast-expanding, energy-hungry economy. With coffers overflowing from burgeoning exports, Beijing doesn't mind overpaying for overseas energy assets as long as it can beat the competition. The competition from Indian firms, clearly, has forced its oil behemoths to pay a lot more for acquisitions, such as PetroKazakhstan or the Akpo offshore field in Nigeria.

Eager to play the new Great Game on energy, India has tried to make its state-owned oil companies emulate China's example, though with far more limited success. For instance, India invested $750 million to pick up the 25 per cent stake of Canada's Talisman Energy in Sudan's Greater Nile Oil Project. Another example came up in 2005 when the Indian Oil Corporation (IOC) reached an agreement with Iran's Petropars company to develop a gas block in the Iranian South Pars gas field. India's biggest investment overseas remains the 2001 deal acquiring a 20 per cent stake in Russia's Sakhalin-1 oil-and-gas fields for $2.7 billion when international oil prices were hovering around $18 a barrel. While China astutely began making overseas investments in energy in the 1990s when the price of oil was relatively low, Indian firms by amd large have sought to acquire overvalued assets after oil prices started soaring to a historic high.

It is questionable whether energy 'security' can be built by chasing an antiquated idea that legal ownership of foreign assets, especially in problem or pariah states, is a better bet than buying oil on the world markets. It could prove a profligate waste of capital if, emulating Kremlin's example on Yukos, the pariah or problem nations were to reassert control over their assets. Many states, in any case, have scant respect for contracts. Some do not even have property rights. It has long been forgotten that some Arab states expropriated oilfields owned by U.S. companies.

Making large oil and gas investments in states that are unreliable or unstable is not energy security but energy insecurity. Japan, a long-time economic superstar and one of the world's largest oil importers, has been wise not to join the bidding wars for overseas energy assets. The safest approach, and also the simplest, is to buy oil and gas on the world markets, rather than to try and produce hydrocarbons in politically unpredictable states. It is an illusion that security lies in legal ownership of oil and gas fields abroad, or in legal permission to extract from them. The host country can block production at any time. Moreover, oil shipments to specifically targeted consumers can be blockaded on the high seas, in the event of a conflict.

This concern is further underscored by the fact that much of the world's oil is produced in volatile regions, such as the Persian Gulf, Caspian Sea basin, Central Asia and West Africa. The Persian Gulf region, which alone contains two-thirds of the world's known reserves, is becoming even more critical to international oil supply as some fields in the West dry up.

Until 2002, the world had 7 million barrels a day of spare oil production capacity. But now, there is little spare production capacity left in the world, and a drop in oil output from one OPEC member-state can no longer be absorbed by the rest of that cartel. Moreover, production has stagnated wherever a state has reasserted control over its oil industry. Such examples include Iran and Russia. Because global oil supplies remain pretty tight, with little cushion between supply and demand, supply disruptions — even if small — can make prices shoot up, as happened after the 2005 hurricanes in the Gulf of Mexico.

This arms even capricious supplier states with geopolitical leverage. By effecting selected export cuts, a major producing state can jack up global oil prices and hold other economies hostage. The adroit use of the 'oil weapon' could help a state build leverage, wrest concessions and swell its coffers through extra revenue from higher oil prices. For example, tensions between Iran and the United States, especially in the period since September 2005, have aided oil-price volatility and brought billions of dollars more to Tehran in oil revenue.

Iran, the second-largest oil producer in OPEC, has some 10 per cent of the world's proven oil reserves. Iran also has the world's second-biggest reserves of natural gas, whose demand is climbing in response to pollution and global-warming issues. But theocratic Iran is a potential hotspot of international conflict, underlined by its defiance of the UN Security Council and the United States. With its vantage location, Iran is in a position to disrupt oil exports by other Persian Gulf countries; even a temporary disruption will trigger a spike in insurance rates and oil prices. Iran's attitude towards the UN is reflected in the famous old taunt of its current supreme leader and ultimate authority, Ayatollah Ali Khamenei, that the international body is 'a paper factory issuing worthless and ineffective orders'.

More fundamentally, in response to the growing pressures on oil supplies, international trade in natural gas has been evolving fast, with Asian states becoming major gas consumers. Demand for natural gas in Asia has grown the fastest in the world, with the appeal of gas reinforced by the fact that it is generally cleaner-burning than other fossil fuels.

With improvements in technology bringing significant reductions in costs of cooling and condensing natural gas to a liquid form so that it can be transported in ships, a large global market for liquefied natural gas (LNG) has emerged. Russia is the top global supplier with the largest natural-gas reserves, estimated to total 1700 trillion cubic feet of the fuel, or 27 per cent of the world's total. 'Just two other countries rival Russia in natural-gas reserves, Iran, with 971 trillion cubic feet, and Qatar, with 910 trillion cubic feet'.[27] Actually, Iran and Qatar share a giant gas field that straddles the Gulf.

Yet, the sanctions and the diplomatic campaign against Iran by the United States — a country largely self-reliant in gas — impede the flow of foreign investments and technology to build costly new liquefaction and tanker installations to export the Persian Gulf gas to other regions. U.S. energy-related sanctions clearly limit Iran's access to high-end technology for its LNG development plans. By hindering the development of Iran's LNG-export potential, Washington has sought to deny valuable foreign-exchange earnings to the clerical regime in Tehran. Lacking the liquefaction technology, Iran must rely on foreign companies to build its LNG infrastructure through multibillion-dollar investments.[28] Yet, by ratcheting up tensions with Tehran and driving up oil and gas prices, Washington has helped bring billions of dollars of additional energy-export revenues to Iranian coffers.

A Regional Energy Grid

In energy-poor southern Asia, a constraining factor on the energy front remains the baleful geopolitics. So large are the energy requirements in southern Asia that multiple interstate energy pipelines can commercially thrive. Therefore, it is not a question whether India should choose a gas pipeline from Turkmenistan or one from Iran, because both can co-exist and help to meet the projected long-term gas demand of 50 billion cubic metres in India and Pakistan. Yet a choice is being politically dictated from outside.

Iran has bountiful reserves in its gigantic South Pars field from where it can sell gas to its neighbours to the east by the proposed $7-billion overland pipeline to India via Pakistan. In contrast, there are questions over the size of the reserves in Turkmenistan's Dauletabad gas field, from where the United States has favoured the construction of a pipeline to India via war-ravaged Afghanistan and sinking Pakistan.

The Asian Development Bank, which has been brokering the $3.3-billion, 1600-kilometre-long Turkmenistan–to–India pipeline project since 2002, revised its estimate in 2005 on the size of the untapped gas reserves at Dauletabad. According to its new estimate, the Dauletabad field has gross reserves of only 1.4 trillion cubic metres (tcm) of gas, out of the proven Turkmenistan reserves of about 2.0 tcm. That means that Dauletabad will be able to supply enough gas to India and Pakistan only for the first few years.[29]

Commercially, therefore, the pipeline from Turkmenistan would make better sense if it were built only up to Pakistan. But Pakistan can ill-afford to buy gas without the indirect Indian subsidy that would accrue when a gas pipeline from Turkmenistan or Iran extends to India.

The hundreds of millions of dollars that would come Pakistan's way annually from royalties and transit and maintenance fees on the supply of gas to India would help subsidize the Pakistani consumption of gas. That explains why despite periodic claims by Pakistani officials, from now-ousted military ruler General Pervez Musharraf to President Asif Ali Zardari, that a pipeline project would be commercially viable even without India's participation, Islamabad has not concluded a bilateral deal with either Iran or Turkmenistan.

While craving a benefit worth hundreds of millions of dollars annually in piping gas to India, Pakistan, however, refuses to establish even normal trading ties with New Delhi. Pakistan would greatly aid its own interests by establishing normal trading ties with India. Such ties would significantly assist Pakistan's own economy and help attract foreign direct investment to that country. The case of war-scarred Sri Lanka is illustrative of the major benefits accruing to a small economy from closer bilateral economic cooperation with large India. Sri Lanka more than doubled its exports to India in less than four years after bringing a free-trade agreement with India into force.[30] Pakistan's India policy, however, is shaped not by pragmatists but by army generals still in uniform.

The military regime in Islamabad refuses to reciprocate India's action years ago in granting the most-favoured-nation (MFN) status to Pakistan. It even declines to grant India the obligatory trade access to its market under the South Asian Free-Trade Area (SAFTA) accord. Yet such is the attraction of the double promise that any India-bound pipeline holds — a major foreign-exchange earner for Islamabad that will also help subsidize Pakistani gas imports — that Pakistan has been willing to give pipeline-related 'international guarantees', notwithstanding its record of covert actions in breach of international law including the export of terrorism to India and the sale of nuclear secrets to Iran, Libya and North Korea.

The United States, for its part, has sought to forestall the Iran–to–India pipeline by warning New Delhi about its Iran–Libya Sanctions Act (ILSA) and the threat of potential sanctions that law holds against foreign firms participating in any such project. Iran already is subject to energy sector-related sanctions under ILSA, a U.S. law with extraterritorial application to third-country firms. The strident U.S. opposition to the proposed Iran–to–India pipeline has visibly queered the pitch. In fact, with the Bush administration ratcheting up tensions with Iran, the pipeline project has turned into a geopolitical nightmare for New Delhi, which has faced intense U.S. pressure to side with Washington's international campaign against Tehran.

Any pipeline project involves large investments and at least a five-year completion period. If interstate energy cooperation is to take off, the more sensible, commercially viable energy projects need to be separated from the not-so-practicable or fanciful ones. Where energy supplies can be sourced through the direct bilateral route, that opportunity should not be missed. A planned gas pipeline from Burma's western coast, for example, can help invigorate economic development in India's northeast and turn that restive region into New Delhi's gateway to ASEAN.

If a pipeline from the Burmese gas fields can be extended to Calcutta through Bangladesh, it will not only become commercially more attractive but also serve as a useful political tool to overcome the present Bangladeshi hostility against exporting Bangladesh's own gas to India. Given Bangladesh's vantage location, it can be the bridge between the subcontinent and Southeast Asia. Bangladesh's ability to play such a role, however, is connected with its readiness to participate in, and benefit from, regional-integration processes. Close economic cooperation between Bangladesh and India, and Bangladesh and Burma, can help transform Bangladesh into a thriving economy, with Dhaka using its large gas reserves as an engine of economic growth. Not only can Bangladesh earn hundreds of millions of dollars annually by selling gas to India, but it can also employ its gas resources to produce electricity for export.

Yet Bangladesh remains an appalling example of a country that does not mind undermining its own interests in order to thwart regional economic and energy cooperation. Bangladesh, by most estimates, has substantial natural-gas reserves to become a major gas producer and exporter to the large Indian market next door. After its state-run oil and gas company, Petrobangla, put net proven reserves at 15.3 trillion cubic feet (tcf) in mid-2004, the U.S. Geological Survey estimated that

Bangladesh additionally holds 32.1 tcf of undiscovered gas.[31] However, Dhaka's surprising refusal to sell gas to India — ostensibly until it has reliably assessed its reserves and dealt with questions of domestic supply — has already led Unocal Corp., the largest investor in the Bangladeshi gas sector, to put its export plans on hold. The continuing political obstacles also prompted two other international oil majors, Shell and ChevronTexaco, to sell their natural-gas assets in Bangladesh to Britain's Cairn Energy PLC and Canada's Niko Resources, respectively, in 2003.

Politics, not economics, has guided Bangladesh's short-sighted policy against exporting gas to India. Such has been Dhaka's willingness to undercut its own economic interests that the Asian Development Bank publicly pleaded in vain with the Bangladeshi government in mid-2006 to put aside its political objections and approve a massive, $3-billion proposal of India's Tata Group for investments in fertilizer, steel and infrastructure sectors. In fact, the politics has become only more intense and prickly in the face of mounting Indian complaints about the unchecked influx of Bangladeshi refugees and the use of Bangladeshi territory by those engaged in subversion in India, including Pakistani intelligence operatives and insurgent groups from India's northeast. In 2005, India handed to Dhaka a list specifying the location of 172 Indian insurgent-group sanctuaries inside Bangladesh and the names of 307 Indian rebels sheltered there.

For India, the ethnic expansion of Bangladesh beyond its political borders not only sets up enduring transborder links but it also makes New Delhi's already-complex task of border management more onerous. As brought out by Indian census figures, Indian districts bordering Bangladesh have become Bangladeshi-majority areas. It is perhaps the first time in modern history that a country has expanded its ethnic frontiers without expanding its political borders. In contrast, Han China's demographic onslaught on Inner Mongolia, Xinjiang and Tibet was a consequence of the expansion of its political frontiers.

Economically, Bangladesh cannot indefinitely persist with its reluctance to commercially tap its gas reserves for export because of the mounting costs of such a defiant stance. Although one of the world's poorest and most densely populated nations relying on foreign aid and remittances from its overseas workers, Bangladesh is losing hundreds of millions of dollars every year by refusing to sell its gas to the only customer it presently has — India. Additionally, it can earn up to $200 million annually in transit and maintenance fees by allowing the construction through its territory of the proposed 905-kilometre pipeline to transport natural gas from Burma to India. Yet it has made its approval to this tri-nation pipeline contingent on far-reaching Indian concessions unrelated to the project.

Rather than undermine its financial and political interests, Bangladesh has the choice to chart a better future for its large, growing population and stem the flow of Bangladeshis seeking better employment opportunities in India. The worst choice for Bangladesh, a country that could give 'birth to the next Islamist revolution',[32] is to continue to export surplus labour to India while not taking steps to generate employment at home by exporting gas to India and employing the revenues from such sales for economic development.

With India bringing into force a free-trade agreement (FTA) with Thailand after such accords with Sri Lanka and Nepal and concluding a Comprehensive Economic Cooperation Agreement (CECA) with Singapore and an FTA with ASEAN, Bangladesh cannot keep itself isolated from the regional-cooperation trends. India is also pursuing a multifaceted engagement with Burma and participating in the Asian Highway project through the trilateral highway that will connect Calcutta to Bangkok via Burma. Additionally, India is constructing a road link to connect its Mizoram state with Mandalay and aiding Burma's modernization of the Mandalay–Rangoon railroad.

Given Bangladesh's unique geography as a country surrounded by the Indian landmass on three sides, India is a national obsession there, and any issue relating to its bigger neighbour becomes an emotive one, clouding rational thinking. Bangladesh noticeably suffers from the small-country syndrome, although it is the world's seventh most populous country, having overtaken Russia. Its 139,910-square-kilometre land area makes it 50 per cent bigger than Hungary. Because India cannot prosper or feel secure without co-opting Bangladesh, New Delhi needs to become an important stakeholder in that country's economic well-being. A positive shift in Bangladesh's geopolitical thinking, especially on energy-related issues, is also crucial to the success of India's 'Look East' policy.

A Burma–Bangladesh–India energy partnership can help revitalize the eastern subcontinent economically. Bangladesh's own gas reserves can serve as the locomotive of economic change. Daewoo International, the South Korean company that is the largest investor in a Burmese gas site, has reported that its discovered Shwe field just off Burma's west coast could produce up to 3.56 trillion cubic feet of gas annually.[33] Two Indian energy firms, ONGC Videsh Ltd. and Gas Authority of India Ltd. (GAIL), own a total of 30 per cent stake in that Burmese field, A-1, and in the adjacent A-3 block.

Yet, with Bangladesh adding extraneous demands to permitting an Indo–Burmese pipeline through its territory, Burma took India unawares by signing a memorandum of understanding with PetroChina in early 2006 to supply gas to China from the A-1 field over a 30-year period. To New Delhi's acute embarrassment, the Burmese decision came no sooner than India announced that it had reached accord with Beijing to jointly cooperate on securing oil resources overseas, so as to prevent the Sino–Indian competition from continuing to drive up the price of such assets. The memorandum of understanding was followed by a connected $84-million soft loan from Beijing and the start of work on laying a 2380-kilometre pipeline from the Burmese gas site at Kyaukphyu to Ruili, in China's Yunnan province.[34]

In the meantime, the mythical Iran–to–India gas pipeline has kept getting longer, with the Indian petroleum minister in 2005 fancifully suggesting its extension to China through the northeastern Indian corridor. Islamabad and Beijing, for their part, are intent on building an energy pipeline to western China from Pakistan's Chinese-built Gwadar port as a way to reduce the time and distance for transporting oil to China from the Gulf states. Built in parallel to the rail-and-road links to connect Gwadar to the People's Republic of China via the Karakoram Highway, a similar second pipeline could potentially carry Iranian gas to western China.

Iranian natural gas is particularly attractive for nearby India. Yet, given the overt political manner Tehran has sought to leverage its energy exports, India has legitimate concerns about becoming too reliant on imported gas from Iran. Tehran first held out veiled threats against India after the latter voted against it at the governing board meetings of the International Atomic Energy Agency (IAEA) in September 2005 and February 2006. It even threatened to abrogate its $22-billion deal to sell 5 million tons of LNG annually to India for 25 years from 2009 from its Pars fields, which are largely under the operation of Royal Dutch/Shell, Total and Repsol YPF.[35] As part of the LNG deal, the Indian Oil Corporation had reached a memorandum of understanding with the National Iranian Oil Company's subsidiary, Petropars, to develop a gas block in South Pars and build a liquefaction plant to sell LNG to India and other countries.

Iran later reneged on the gas price set in the 2005 contract, which, by specifying a ceiling of $31 per barrel for Brent crude, had capped the LNG price at $3.1375 per million British thermal units. Although the contract contained no provision for ratification by either country, Tehran conveyed to New Delhi in May 2006 that its Supreme Economic Council had not ratified the arrangement and, therefore, demanded renegotiation of parts of the deal. It principally sought higher LNG payments from New Delhi to reflect the surge in global gas prices. Another issue was the quality of gas to be exported. While Tehran wished to sell India only lean gas, stripped of ethane and propane, New Delhi wanted rich gas. The deal thus unravelled

Against this background, Iran can hardly advertise itself as a stable energy supplier. In fact, it has been forgotten that after the *mullahs* seized power in Iran during the 1979 Islamic revolution, they nationalized the oilfields, giving New Delhi a pittance for the Indian stake in the Amoco-led consortium that owned two Iranian oilfields. The Iranian refusal to honour the gas price set in the 2005 contract is the political price India has had to pay for casting its vote against Tehran at the IAEA. In deference to the U.S. line, India did not seek at the IAEA to even link the Iran case with the Pakistani proliferation ring that supplied nuclear know-how and uranium-enrichment centrifuges to Tehran in the period between 1987 and 2002.

There are also unresolved issues relating to the proposed Iran–to–India pipeline, especially on how to mitigate the strategic effects of India entering into a dependent relationship with Pakistan, which will be able to control the flow of gas to India. Such one-sided Indian dependency will arm Pakistan with immense strategic leverage. No gas-storage capacity on the Indian side will be able to cope with a major supply disruption, intentional or otherwise, that shuts down power, fertilizer and other dependent plants and has a cascading economic effect. By employing the threat of supply disruption as a tool in its repertoire of policy options, Pakistan would be able to hold India's economy hostage in a crisis.

India has been unable to persuade Islamabad to enter into reciprocal dependency through trade and energy, including by possibly buying Indian electricity from gas-fired power plants or hydropower projects like the Baglihar Dam in Kashmir. If a short-lived Russia–Ukraine squabble over natural-gas pricing could send a tremor through Europe at the beginning of 2006, the implications of India entering into a one-sided dependency can hardly be overlooked by New Delhi. And if that squabble led European energy companies to open talks with Qatar, Angola and Nigeria as part of a new, diversified strategy to buy LNG, why wouldn't India seek similar flexibility on energy imports?

The establishment of a regional energy grid in southern Asia will probably have to wait until Afghanistan becomes free of regional warlords, Pakistan's Baluchistan province is pacified, Bangladesh begins to export its own gas, and Iran and Burma are reintegrated into the international mainstream. Politically and geographically, Pakistan and Bangladesh remain barriers to India's desire to promote market-favourable exploitation of energy deposits in the region.

An energy grid in southern Asia also cannot come into being before normal trade becomes the norm between Pakistan and India and a regionally integrated market begins to take shape. Bad economics plus bad politics do not equal energy cooperation and integration. While every country has a right to focus on national interest, keeping the demons of nationalism unleashed can only harm self-interest.

A regional energy network has to emerge on the building blocks of greater economic cooperation in southern Asia and a shared interest in viable energy policies, secure sea lanes and a stable energy environment. Creating a matrix of preferential trade agreements between regional actors, and encouraging greater deregulation and privatization in the energy sector of each state, will boost the commercial and political chances of bilateral and trilateral energy cooperation, if not the establishment of a regional energy network.

Clean-Coal Technology

In Asia, the sharpening interstate competition over oil and gas tends to shroud from public view the reliance of major states on other fuels. In China and India, coal will remain for the foreseeable future the dominant fuel for generating electricity. That is no different from the situation in the United States, where the largest share of the electricity market belongs to the coal industry, with more than 600 coal-fired electric plants in operation and another 140 planned to be built. Coal makes up 64 per cent of China's primary energy consumption, with that country being the largest producer and consumer of coal in the world.

Despite the growing public interest in alternatives like wind and solar power or ethanol, coal will play an even bigger role in the future. The reason for that is simple: not only does coal remain attractively priced, but also global reserves of coal far exceed those of oil or natural gas. For example, the United States — the world's second-largest producer of coal after China — has enough coal reserves to last at least two centuries at its current use rates. Coal in the ground in Illinois state alone contains more energy than all of Saudi Arabia's oil reserves. More than 1000 new coal-fired power plants are expected to come up across the world in the next decade.

Technological innovations such as scrubbers are helping to turn coal into a cleaner fuel worldwide, although coal-burning electric plants remain at present major emitters of carbon dioxide, the primary greenhouse gas responsible for climate change. Cleaner technologies like coal gasification hold immense promise to cut down emissions of carbon dioxide and other pollutants that contribute to acid rain, smog and respiratory illness. Newer technologies focus on carbon-capture methods, whether in pulverized coal plants (which grind coal into a dust before burning it to make electricity) or in 'integrated gasification combined cycle', or IGCC plants (which convert coal into a gas that is burned to produce energy).

High oil and gas prices are also making the clean coal-to-liquids (CTL) technology attractive to coal-rich states. Gasoline, diesel, jet fuel and other petroleum products can be produced synthetically from coal through the CTL technology. The cost of production of such synthetic fuels ('synfuels') is less than $35 a barrel, in addition to the start-up commercial costs.[36] Invented before World War II by the Germans, the CTL technology was refined by an isolated South Africa in the 1980s during the apartheid-era international sanctions.

The clean-coal technologies raise the possibility of Asia satisfying its growing energy needs without accelerating climate change. The newer technologies, of course, are more expensive than conventional coal-burning methods. They are also challenging to commercialize. A combined-cycle, or IGCC, plant moves carbon dioxide deep underground, instead of releasing it into the atmosphere, with some sceptics raising concerns that such sequestration could trigger earthquakes. Despite the commercial attractiveness of CTL technologies, producing fuels from coal generates far more carbon dioxide than producing gasoline and diesel fuel from crude oil or using ordinary natural gas. CTL processes can sequester carbon dioxide but only a limited amount of that can be sold for industrial use and to soft-drink makers. As companies embrace the clean-coal technologies, the newer techniques will mature and their economics will cease to be an inhibiting factor for commercialization. Improved techniques may also make carbon sequestration commercially viable. Two state-owned Indian companies, the National Thermal Power Corporation (NTPC) and Bharat Heavy Electricals Limited (BHEL), for instance, have joined hands in setting up a 127-megawatt, IGCC prototype plant in Rajasthan state.

Turning coal into transportation fuel would, of course, offer the world a bright future. China already has several CTL pilot plants under construction in Inner Mongolia and other coal-abundant areas, and is considering investing billions of dollars in commercial-scale CTL production.[37] India, which has large reserves of the traditional 'black gold', also needs to make major investments in CTL projects in order to tap into a home-grown energy source and cut its growing reliance on imported oil.

For large-scale commercialization, a new capital-intensive technology like CTL demands sustained federal investments and assured, long-term buyers of 'synfuels'. Given the fact that the federal government in India maintains massive cross-subsidies in the oil and gas sectors, it can help kick-start the CTL industry in the country with assured investments and fuel-purchase contracts on behalf of the Indian military. By shifting to a single multipurpose synthetic fuel to run all its battlefield equipment, the Indian military can actually insulate itself from the effects of any potential disruption of the Persian Gulf oil-supply line to India. During World War II, Germany had powered its military with CTL fuels.

In India, the introduction of new coal technologies, however, has been made difficult by a sorry state of affairs in its coal sector. The nationalization of the Indian coal industry in the 1970s has led to the bizarre situation where India, with proven coal reserves that are among the highest in the world, has turned from a coal exporter to a coal importer. Although India's coal consumption is growing by 10 per cent every five years, low productivity and the high cost of coal production have made imported coal cheaper. Communist-led trade unions have stymied coal-sector liberalization, with the state-run Coal India Limited (CIL) controlling most of the country's mines.

If India is serious about energy security, it has no choice but to deregulate its coal industry and focus on newer technologies, including coal gasification and recovering coal-bed methane. During the process of coalification, whereby plant material is progressively converted to coal, large quantities of methane-rich gas get stored within the coal. India can emulate Beijing, which is developing its own CTL processes while having invited foreign firms like Sasol of South Africa and the Anglo–Dutch group, Shell, to conduct feasibility studies in China on employing their technologies to convert coal to synthetic gas and diesel fuel. Sasol is also exploring the commercial production of diesel fuel in India using a technology known as Fischer–Tropsch, for the German chemists who invented it in the 1920s. Using this technology, Sasol produces most of South Africa's diesel fuel from coal.

Attraction of Hydropower

Another obvious but underutilized source of energy in Asia is hydropower, which holds tremendous potential, for example, in the Himalayan and Central Asian regions. China, thanks to its annexation of vast Tibet, possesses a tenth of the world's potential hydropower resources, with such reserves estimated to total 700 gigawatt there. A sustainable energy future cannot be built in Asia or elsewhere in the world without embracing renewable energy sources (hydroelectric, geothermal heat pumps, wind, etc.) as a way to help cut fossil-fuel emissions.

The main attraction of hydropower is that, with no fuel cost, the electricity-generating costs decline over the lifespan of the venture. In contrast, the escalating costs of oil, gas, uranium and coal drive up the costs of electricity generated from such common sources of energy. Old Indian hydropower plants from the 1960s, such as at Bhakra (Punjab), Matatila (Uttar Pradesh), Rihand (Madhya Pradesh), Gandhi Sagar (Madhya Pradesh and Rajasthan) and Koyna (Maharashtra), now produce electricity at a ridiculously low price of 10 to 18 paise per kilowatt hour, while thermal stations of similar vintage, such as at Paras (Maharashtra), Nellore (Andhra Pradesh) and Bhusawal (Maharashtra), generate power at a much higher rate of 125 to 200 paise per kilowatt hour.[38]

The multipurpose nature of large hydropower projects makes them economically and socially very advantageous because they turn parched lands into farmlands through irrigation, bring drinking water to cities, and generate electricity. India's Himalayan region and the northeast, as well as the untapped resources in China's mountainous regions, provide ample opportunities for setting up major new hydropower projects.

Organized protests by non-governmental organizations over the displacement of local people by large hydropower projects, however, have acted as a damper to the promotion of hydroelectricity in democratic India. NGO protests have also driven up the costs of new hydropower projects in India. Such protests and inadequate public investments in this sector have contributed to the decline in hydropower's share of India's total electricity production from about 50 per cent in 1962–63 to 27 per cent in 2005. In China, the share of hydropower in total electricity production is 24 per cent.

Through careful planning, the number of local residents displaced can be minimized. However, China's Three Gorges Dam project — an emblem of that country's engineering might and its most ambitious construction since the Great Wall — has involved the relocation of 1.18 million residents since 1993 from 1200 villages and two towns. Located in central China's Hubei province, the

$24-billion, gargantuan project has replaced Brazil's Itaipu Dam as the world's largest hydropower and flood-control installation. The 2.3-kilometre-long Three Gorges Dam, which involves harnessing Asia's longest river, the Yangtze, has been built to power 26 generators to produce a staggering 18,200 megawatt of electricity. Designed to alleviate flooding on the Yangtze, it, however, has created some environmental problems downstream. Another massive hydropower project in China involves a series of dams on the upper portion of the Yellow River to help produce 15,800 megawatt of electricity through 25 generating stations.

Nuclear-Energy Hype

Commercial nuclear power generation is being emphasized by China, Japan, India and South Korea as a 'clean' source of energy and a means of reducing dependence on fossil fuels. Each of these states needs a mix of energy sources, and nuclear power definitely has a role to play in meeting national demands for electricity. A diverse energy portfolio, without doubt, serves as a strategic and commercial hedge against unforeseen risks. Yet it is important not to exaggerate the role nuclear power can play in Asia. Although nuclear power may no longer be a hobgoblin to some environmentalists, the growth of nuclear energy in Asia is unlikely to make any real dent in global carbon emissions or be a cost-effective answer to the growing electricity demands faced by demographic titans China and India. Australia, with nearly two-fifths of the known global uranium reserves, has so far not added nuclear power to its energy portfolio.

Independent studies worldwide have shown that contrary to the claims of the nuclear power industry and its powerful lobbying groups, electricity generated through currently available nuclear technologies is not cost-competitive with thermal power. That is one reason why nuclear establishments across the world are hesitant to share with the public transparent data on the costs of generating electricity, including associated expenditure on operational safety, radioactive-waste management and the retirement of old plants. With uranium prices skyrocketing, construction of new nuclear-power plants is hardly an attractive hedge against uncertain fossil-fuel costs. And with increased regulatory requirements, costs of decommissioning old reactors have escalated sharply. All in all, capital-intensive nuclear power may merit a place in a diverse energy portfolio but it cannot lead the world out of the fossil-fuel age.

China is planning one of the world's biggest expansions of nuclear power, with the number of commercial reactors in operation expected to increase sharply by 2020. Even then, the share of nuclear energy will be less than 5 per cent of China's total installed electricity-generating capacity.[39] The same is true about the nuclear-power expansion plans in India, where nuclear energy's share remains less than 3 per cent. Yet, the U.S.–India nuclear deal, which came to fruition in 2008, has spurred bloated hopes, with some peddling it as a sort of panacea to India's energy needs. The most limiting factor remains economics.

In fact, generating electricity from imported reactors dependent on imported enriched-uranium fuel makes little economic or strategic sense. Such imports will be a path to energy insecurity and exorbitant costs. Even if India were to invest a whopping $27 billion to increase its installed generating capacity by 15,000 megawatt through imported reactors, nuclear power will still make up only a tiny share of its total electricity production, given that nuclear plants take exceptionally long to complete and the share of other energy sources is likely to rise faster.

India can hardly seek to replicate in the energy sector the very mistake it has made on armaments. Now the world's largest arms importer, India spends some $6 billion every year on weapons imports, many of dubious value, while it neglects to build its own armament-production base. Should a poor India be compounding that blunder by spending billions more to import overly expensive reactors when it can more profitably invest that money to commercially develop its own energy sources?

In general, no state can correct its oil reliance on the Persian Gulf region by fashioning a new dependency on a tiny nuclear-supply cartel made up of a few state-guided firms. While oil is freely purchasable on world markets, the global nuclear reactor and fuel business constitutes the most politically regulated commerce in the world. In any event, nuclear energy cannot reduce India's or China's oil dependence or help cut either state's oil imports. Petroleum is no longer used to propel electric generators in most countries. Even the United States employs only a small percentage of its oil supply now as fuel for electrical production. Yet, an erroneous impression persists that a major expansion of commercial nuclear power in China and India can help reduce pressures on global oil prices.

A question India needs to face is whether it would like to get yoked to the nuclear-supply cartel while it still struggles to find energy leeway to loosen its bondage to oil-exporting states. That there is little sanctity of contract in the global nuclear reactor and fuel business is something India found out the hard way when the United States walked out midway through a 30-year nuclear cooperation pact it had signed with New Delhi in 1963. Although the 1963 pact had the force of an international treaty, the United States amended its domestic law to unilaterally rewrite its obligations and halt all fuel and spare-parts supplies to India.

In spite of such a bald-faced material breach and the expiry long ago of the 1963 pact, India has continued to exacerbate its spent-fuel problem at the General Electric-built Tarapur plant (near Bombay) by granting America a right it didn't have even if it had honoured that agreement — a veto on any Indian reprocessing of the accumulating discharged fuel. India has struggled on its own to resolve the safety and environmental concerns arising from the mounting spent fuel at Tarapur. Yet, by 2005, India came full circle, signing a nuclear deal with Washington and later concluding a new bilateral civil nuclear cooperation agreement with the United States, before the issues left over by the 1963 pact had been resolved with Washington.

India has transferred its nuclear technology to no other country, yet the United States was reluctant to grant it any of the favours it accorded China in a 1985 nuclear deal — a lax, elastic and unverifiable framework of cooperation that was signed at a time when Beijing had not joined the Nuclear Non-Proliferation Treaty and was engaged, as U.S. officials attested, in covertly assisting Pakistan's nuclear programme. A nuclear-weapons state under the NPT is a country that has conducted a nuclear test before 1967 and acceded to the treaty. In 1985, China was merely a *de facto* nuclear-weapons state, as India is today. It joined the NPT only in 1992. In 1985, it had refused to lend even outside support to the international non-proliferation regime.

When the U.S.–China accord was finally brought into force in 1998, President Bill Clinton, in his certification, said its implementation had been delayed for almost 13 years 'because of continuing questions about contacts between Chinese entities and elements associated with the Pakistani nuclear-weapons programme'.[40] While that accord specifically excluded the application of International Atomic Energy Agency inspections to U.S. exports to China, with Article 8(2) stipulating that safeguards 'are not required', America has imposed perpetual IAEA inspections on India that are to extend to 29 indigenous civil Indian facilities, including power reactors, heavy-water plants, fuel installations and premier research institutions. India has additionally agreed to dismember two other indigenous facilities — the Cirus plutonium-production reactor and Apsara, Asia's first research reactor — located at the Bhabha Atomic Research Centre at Trombay, just outside Bombay. Furthermore, India has agreed to what an opaque China will never do — a watertight civil–military segregation of its nuclear programme.

The world share of nuclear-generated electricity has remained constant at roughly 16 per cent for a decade,[41] despite persistent talk for years about a global nuclear-energy renaissance. In the United States, the promise of nuclear power dimmed following a reactor core meltdown at Pennsylvania's Three Mile Island nuclear power plant. The 1979 accident, strangely enough, occurred barely two weeks after the opening of a blockbuster film featuring Jane Fonda and Jack Lemmon, *The China Syndrome*, a fictional evocation of a reactor meltdown imperilling a city's survival.

Unlike the Three Mile Island plant, where the concrete containment structure prevented radiation from leaking into the environment, the subsequent accident in 1986 at Chernobyl, now in Ukraine, created widespread radioactive contamination. Chernobyl and Three Mile Island brought to a halt the building of nuclear power plants and fuel-production facilities in many nations — a situation yet to be reversed in most of the states that turned their back on new nuclear-power plants.

Despite being free of carbon and greenhouse gases during generation, nuclear power remains highly capital-intensive and faces the continuing challenge to become commercially competitive with thermal power, even when the costs of anti-pollution technology for the latter are included. Nuclear-generated electricity is costlier than coal-generated electricity even when coal has to be hauled more than 1000 kilometres from mines. Various studies comparing the costs of producing electricity from new nuclear, coal and natural gas plants have revealed that the baseline cost of new nuclear power remains higher worldwide.[42]

Such is the capital intensity of a nuclear power plant that two-thirds or more of its costs are incurred up front, before it is even commissioned. And while the international price of coal, measured in a two-decade timeframe, has dropped, the price of uranium tripled just between 2004 and 2006. Moreover, the price of nuclear-generated electricity in no nation includes the full potential costs of safe disposal of radioactive wastes. The back-end of a nuclear-fuel cycle is anything but clean, posing technological challenges and inestimable environmental costs. Finally, the costs are high to 'entomb' a nuclear power plant that has completed its useful life.

Still, indigenous nuclear reactors make sense to several nations, some of which have built large nuclear power industries. To them, nuclear power is part of their push for fuel diversity to help spread out potential long-term risks. However, no country has tried to build energy security by importing reactors of a type it has no intent to manufacture nationally and whose fuel requirements will keep it perpetually dependent on foreign suppliers.

Yet, this is the bizarre path India has embarked upon, seeking to import the proliferation-resistant light-water reactor (LWR), fuelled by low-enriched uranium. Actually, LWRs do not even fit with India's three-phase nuclear power development programme, which aims at overcoming the country's natural-uranium shortage through a shift from uranium-fuelled power reactors to fast-breeder technology. Fast-breeder reactors will employ uranium-plutonium mixed carbide fuel, with the plutonium inputs recycled from the spent fuel of uranium-fuelled plants. Given that India's has 31 per cent of the world's thorium reserves, the fast-breeder reactors, in turn, are to be replaced by thorium-breeder reactors.

New imported power reactors, despite their bad economics, can make energy-security sense only if they are part of a country's planned transition to autonomous capability. A good example is China, which is aggressively working to become self-sufficient in reactors and fuel despite entering the nuclear power field about two decades after India. As it is, India's indigenous reactors are unable to supply electricity to consumers at rates offered by the country's thermal power industry. That price differential will become appreciably higher when electricity begins to be produced from imported reactors.

For America, potential economic rewards were a key to its nuclear deal with India. Washington was counting on billions of dollars worth of Indian contracts to help revive its moribund nuclear power industry, which has received no new plant order since the 1970s. In fact, more than 100 planned reactors have been cancelled in the United States, including all ordered after 1973. Moreover, U.S. development of advanced reactors largely ended during the Clinton years, with Congress halting research on the advanced liquid metal reactor (ALMR) and the gas turbine modular helium reactor (GT-MHR). In 1998, Congress also cut off funding for improved versions of LWRs.

Little surprise the Bush administration sought congressional ratification of the deal with India in the midst of the worst U.S. financial crisis since the Great Depression, but only after it had extracted a commitment from India to import a minimum of 10,000 megawatts of nuclear-generating capacity from the U.S. As Condoleezza Rice put it, 'We plan to expand our civilian nuclear partnership to research and development, drawing on India's technological expertise to promote a global renaissance in safe and clean nuclear power'.[43]

The higher construction costs that nuclear power plants entail as compared to thermal plants have remained the main obstacle to the expansion of the U.S. nuclear power industry. According to a Congressional Research Service study, even with new plant designs, nuclear energy's 'total generating costs would still exceed currently projected costs for new coal- and gas-fired plants'.[44] Moreover, given its vast coal-burning infrastructure and refusal to adhere to the 1997 Kyoto Protocol's mandatory targets, the United States not only persists with its egregiously high discharge of fossil-fuel effluents, but also 'renders its nuclear industry uncompetitive', although many of the developed states abiding by the protocol obligations have 'declined to install more nuclear capacity as a means of meeting emissions targets'.[45]

Until newer, cleaner and more reliable alternatives to fossil fuels are commercially developed, fossils fuels will remain dominant the world over. At present, the environmental advantages of renewable non-conventional sources of energy are offset by prohibitive capital costs of electrical production (as in the case of solar photovoltaic power), or by limits placed by seasonal or climatic elements (wind power), or by large space requirements (solar power), or by other factors such as the source's technological limitation in producing sufficient and constant quantities of power to supply the national grid. Technological advances could make renewable non-conventional energy reliable and commercially viable in the form of big base-load plants. Alternatives such as hybrid vehicles that consume much less gasoline, or the use of hydrogen to power automobiles, look promising, and could help stem the rising global oil demand and move the world towards cleaner, more efficient energy.

Energy and Military Planning

A striking feature of a booming Asia is how energy demands are beginning to noticeably influence strategic thinking and military planning. With China seeking greater influence from the Pacific to the Himalayas, and from Central Asia to Africa, its rising dependence on oil imports has served to rationalize both its growing emphasis on the seas and its desire to carve out greater strategic space for itself. China's strategy for a forward naval presence in places like Burma, Sri Lanka's Chinese-aided Hambantota port and Pakistan's Chinese-built Gwadar port represents a direct challenge to India's interests in the Bay of Bengal, the Arabian Sea and the Indian Ocean — all critical areas for world trade and oil shipments.

Similarly, concerns over sea-lane safety and rising vulnerability to disruption of energy supplies are prompting India and Japan to explore avenues for joint cooperation in maritime security. Japan — despite being the largest producer of nuclear-generated electricity in Asia, and the third largest in the world — remains very vulnerable on the energy front. India's published maritime doctrine emphasizes the centrality to national security of the Indian Ocean — the only ocean named after a single country.[46] Tokyo and New Delhi have agreed on a string of joint-security measures, including exercises between the Japanese Maritime Self-Defence Force and the Indian Navy, military-to-military exchanges and high-level defence dialogue.

India's growing concerns over energy security arise from its fast-rising dependence on oil, liquefied gas and petroleum imports by sea from the Persian Gulf region. The critical importance of this region to India is manifest from the fact that it is the source of almost 75 per cent of India's oil imports. With some 3.7 million overseas Indian workers and merchants who remit home $8 billion annually resident in the Gulf region, India sees its interests extending far beyond the mouth of the Strait of Hormuz to cover most Arab states. Indeed, New Delhi treats the Gulf region as part of its extended neighbourhood.

In comparison to India, it is significant that China, the European Union and the United States source only 58 per cent, 30 per cent and 20 per cent, respectively, of their oil imports from the Persian Gulf states. The growing liquefied-gas imports by India also come mainly from the Gulf states, including Qatar (India's first LNG supplier) and Oman. In contrast, China and Japan buy much of their gas from Australia, Malaysia and Indonesia, while Europe relies on Russia and North Africa for its gas supply. The United States is largely self-reliant in gas.

Yet, the popular perception is that the heavy U.S. involvement in the Persian Gulf region — an involvement that includes propping up sheikhdoms and other autocratic regimes, and opposing the *mullah* government in Tehran — is linked to America's oil-import needs and the interests of its oil multinationals. The reality is that the American reliance on the Persian Gulf oil is low, and that most of the hydrocarbons in the Gulf region are owned by local state-owned firms.

India's heavy reliance on the Persian Gulf region makes it particularly vulnerable. Any disruption of energy supplies from the Gulf will hit India the most of all the major states in the world. A steep rise in energy prices, moreover, will exacerbate India's trade imbalance and budget deficit. Strategically, the heavy Indian dependence on the Persian Gulf for oil and gas has underscored the importance for India of protecting sea lanes vital to its economic and security interests. The Indian Navy, whose modernization had been neglected for more than 15 years, is now receiving special attention from policymakers in New Delhi, with naval spending rising sharply in recent years.

India is a peninsular country with a long coastline of 7516 kilometres and a vast EEZ measuring more than 2.02 million square kilometres. The movement by sea of 95 per cent of its external trade and 85 per cent of its oil makes India's maritime interests particularly susceptible. While military threats from across land borders can be anticipated, threats from the seas are less predictable because of the flexibility, mobility and stealth of naval forces. Threats from the sea can actually materialize in days or even hours, but building a strong navy is a task that takes many decades to accomplish. According to late Indian Prime Minister Jawaharlal Nehru, 'History has shown that whatever power controls the Indian Ocean has, in the first instance, India's sea-borne trade at her mercy and, in the second, India's very independence itself'.

Today, India's energy-security interests are encouraging its navy to play a greater role in the Indian Ocean region, a crucial international passageway for oil deliveries and for close to half of the world's overseas trade. In Indian perception, the maritime arc stretching from the Persian Gulf through the Strait of Malacca to the South China Sea and the Sea of Japan constitutes the 'new silk route'. The Indian Navy must protect not only vital sea lanes, but also the country's large energy infrastructure of onshore and offshore oil and gas wells, LNG terminals, refineries, pipeline grids and oil-exploration work within its EEZ.

In addition to enhancing its naval capabilities, India is attempting to build a safety cushion for itself through a web of strategic partnerships with key littoral states in the Indian Ocean region as well as with outside players like the United States, Japan, Israel and France. The partnerships, principally aimed at safeguarding the various 'gates' to the Indian Ocean, incorporate trade accords, military exercises, energy cooperation and strategic dialogue. India's primary focus is on states adjacent to chokepoints such as the Strait of Hormuz (Iran), the Strait of Malacca (Singapore, Indonesia and Malaysia), the Bab el-Mandab (Djibouti and Eritrea) and the Cape of Good Hope and the Mozambique Channel (South Africa and Mozambique). India's defence ties with Iran, the Maldives, Sri Lanka, Burma, Singapore and Thailand reflect the new emphasis on strengthening the Indian position in the Indian Ocean.

In recognition of the growing link between energy and security, India has been consciously seeking to play a naval role in its extended neighbourhood in recent years. That was illustrated by India's U.S.-encouraged action in 2003 in providing naval escort to commercial ships passing through the vulnerable, piracy-wracked Strait of Malacca. The action followed rising concerns that international terrorists might target vessels using this strait.

That six-month Indian undertaking, codenamed Operation Sagittarius, was primarily designed to safeguard high-value U.S. cargo from Japan passing through the Strait of Malacca on its way to Afghanistan. It was much later, after the Lloyd's Market Association's Joint War Committee listed the passageway as a 'war risk zone' in 2005, that Indonesia, Malaysia, Thailand and Singapore agreed — under intense U.S. pressure — to start joint naval patrols in the Malacca Strait. The LMA represents insurers working in the Lloyd's of London market. Seeking to allay international concerns over security in the world's busiest shipping lane, the four Southeast Asian states have contributed two aircraft each for their 'Eyes in the Sky' plan.

But it was the Indian Navy that showed Southeast Asian states the way to patrol the Malacca Strait. The Indian action prompted not only the 'Eyes in the Sky' plan, but also an Indonesian–Singaporean–Malaysian memorandum of understanding with the International Maritime Organization, the World Bank and a consortium of shipping firms to monitor every ship passing through the waterway. Due to the Indian patrolling, India's naval presence implicitly gained acceptance and legitimacy in Southeast Asia. One-third of the world's commerce and half of its oil imports pass through the waterways of Southeast Asia alone, with oil-tanker traffic through the Strait of Malacca projected to nearly double to 20 million barrels a day by 2020.

Another example was India's tsunami-aid naval diplomacy, which reinforced its role as the dominant power in the strategically critical Indian Ocean region.[47]

When the tsunami — a natural disaster of epic proportions — struck southern Asia on December 26, 2004, it was the Indian Navy that first came to the rescue and aid of people in the devastated areas of Sri Lanka, the Maldives and Indonesia's Aceh province.[48] This was the largest humanitarian relief operation the Indian Navy has ever conducted outside India's territorial waters.

Despite its own coastal areas in southernmost Tamil Nadu state and parts of adjacent Kerala state being battered by the tsunami, India came to the aid of Sri Lanka and the Maldives within hours of the devastation. When the first Indian aircraft with emergency personnel and supplies landed in Colombo the very day the tsunami struck, it signalled the start of what became the world's largest relief operation. The tsunami-relief operation jibed well with India's need to expand its naval role in the Indian Ocean region.

India's efforts to build strategic ties with Iran — a sore point in its warming relationship with the United States — have also been influenced by its energy and security interests, particularly the need to safeguard sea lanes and gain an access route to landlocked Central Asia. Iran, with which India shared a common land border until August 1947, is also critical to New Delhi's long-term strategy to neutralize Pakistan and to build closer engagement with Afghanistan. India has extended support to Iran in modernizing its Chabahar port, in building a rail line from Chabahar that links up with Iran's national railways, and in constructing a road northwards from that port. But New Delhi's efforts to deepen its strategic connections with Tehran have suffered a setback due to its pro-West stance on the Iranian nuclear issue. With the seemingly interminable conflict in Iraq, once the largest oil supplier to India, Indian interests risk further damage through a prolonged international confrontation over Iran. India recognizes that demonizing Iran can only provoke it to act like a demon. In a neighbourhood bristling with failed or failing states, the last thing India would want is a fresh hotspot of global conflict at its doorstep.

Japan — the only close U.S. ally maintaining friendly relations with Iran — has faced American pressure, like India, not to develop Iranian oilfields or sign long-term import contracts with Tehran, even though stable, long-lasting oil supply is the central objective of Tokyo's energy strategy. For instance, Washington mounted pressure on Tokyo to stop developing Iran's huge Azadegan oilfield, situated along the long and treacherous border with Iraq. The Tokyo-based Inpex, an energy giant that is partly owned by the Japanese government, won the right in 2004 to develop the field, which has confirmed reserves of 26 billion barrels of oil.

Like India, Japan has a lot more at stake in Iran than does the United States. Japan consumes 22 per cent of Iranian oil exports and is by far Iran's largest trading partner. Japanese investments in Azadegan are intended to develop the largest and most modern onshore petroleum fields in Iran since the 1979 Islamic revolution. While Washington is concerned that the Azadegan development will make Japan more dependent on Iran for oil, Tokyo views the project as securing committed energy resources for the world's second-largest economy. Any cutback by Japan and India of their financial and energy interests in Iran would be a boon to China, the second biggest buyer of Iranian oil after Tokyo.

China has pursued its interests with far less inhibition in Iran, its second largest oil supplier that delivers 14 per cent of Beijing's total oil imports. As part of its strategy to reduce reliance on oil imports by sea, Beijing wishes to build a 386-kilometre pipeline from Iran to link up with the Atasu–Alashankou pipeline from Kazakhstan to Xinjiang. China's advantage is that as a permanent member of the UN Security Council, it wields far more international clout than Tokyo or New Delhi. It can veto any UN sanctions proposal — a fact not lost on Tehran.

Beijing's ability to provide political cover is a fundamental element of its thriving commercial ties with a host of problem states, from Venezuela and Sudan to Iran and Burma.

How China's political advantage translates into commercial advantage over India can be seen from the way its oil company, Sinopec, signed a $70-billion deal in October 2004 to buy 10 million metric tons of LNG from Iran annually over a 25-year period. In exchange, Sinopec (also known as China Petrochemical Corp.) secured a 51 per cent stake in the giant Yadavaran oilfield in Iran's south, leaving a minority 20 per cent stake for India's state-owed companies led by ONGC Videsh Ltd. The 20 per cent stake in Yadavaran, along with a 100 per cent interest in Iran's small Jufeyr oilfield, came India's way as part of the major Indian deal to import Iranian LNG. Just between 2004 and 2009, China's state-run oil behemoths committed to invest a staggering $120 billion in Iran. That figure included a $5 billion contract to develop the massive South Pars gas field that Tehran awarded in mid-2009 after accusing the original developer, French oil producer Total SA, of delaying the project.

Strategically, India can expect to face growing competition from China in its own backyard, including the wider Indian Ocean region. China appears to be positioning itself along the vital sea lanes from the Persian Gulf to the South China Sea. It has helped Iran upgrade its Bandar-e-Abbas port. It is building a deepwater naval base and port for Pakistan at Gwadar, situated at the entrance to the Strait of Hormuz — the only exit for the Persian Gulf oil. China has begun close military cooperation with Bangladesh. And it has strategically penetrated Burma, a well-positioned country abundant in natural resources — ranging from precious gems and teak to nickel and natural gas. The Irrawaddy Corridor between China's Yunnan province and the Burmese ports on the Bay of Bengal has become a key economic and strategic passageway involving road, river, rail and harbour links.

As part of what an internal Pentagon study has called a calculated Chinese policy to fashion a 'string of pearls', Beijing desires to hold sway over vital sea lanes between the Indian and Pacific Oceans through a chain of bases, naval facilities and military ties. Sponsored by the Pentagon's director for net assessment and prepared by defence contractor Booz Allen Hamilton, the report titled, 'Energy Futures in Asia', states: 'China is building strategic relationships along the sea lanes from the Middle East to the South China Sea in ways that suggest defensive and offensive positioning [not only] to protect China's energy interests, but also to serve broad security objectives.'

The study sees China's strategy to underpin its interests along oil shipping sea lanes as 'creating a climate of uncertainty' and threatening 'the safety of all ships on the high seas'.[49] Added to that is the value Beijing attaches to secrecy, deception and surprise in its strategic planning and practice, as pointed out by another Pentagon publication — the 2006 annual report to U.S. Congress on China's military power.

One such 'pearl' in China's sea-lane strategy, Gwadar, will not only arm Pakistan with critical strategic depth against a 1971-style Indian attempt to bottle up its navy, but it will also open the way to the arrival of Chinese submarines in India's proximity, completing India's strategic encirclement by Beijing. Gwadar, one of the world's largest deep-sea ports that will double Pakistan's sea-trading capacity, already houses a Chinese electronic listening post. Islamabad has presented Gwadar, with its planned petroleum-handling facilities, as a potential export port for energy resources transported by pipeline from Turkmenistan. Beijing is reinforcing the strategic significance of Gwadar by linking it up with the Karakoram Highway to western China through the Chinese-aided Gwadar–Dalbandin railway extending up to Rawalpindi. In addition, the Chinese-supported Makran coastal highway links Gwadar with Karachi. Gwadar is a critical link in the chain of Chinese facilities that stretch from the Gulf of Siam to the Bay of Bengal and then to the Arabian Sea.

Chinese security agencies already operate electronic-intelligence and maritime reconnaissance facilities on the Coco Islands — transferred by India in the 1950s to Burma, which then leased them to Beijing in 1994. The main electronic-intelligence gathering station located on the Great Coco Island was completed quickly in 1994 itself, with its radars, antenna towers and other electronic equipment forming a comprehensive signals intelligence (SIGINT) collection facility. These agencies have also positioned their personnel at several Burmese coastal points, including the Chinese-built harbours at Kyaukypu and Thilawa, and other vantage locations close both to India's eastern strategic assets and to the Strait of Malacca, through which 80 per cent of China's imported oil passes. A railroad from Kunming via Dali in China links up with the traditional Mandalay–Rangoon railway as part of the Irrawaddy Corridor. A 40-kilometre southeastern railway spur will connect Rangoon with the new large port at Thilawa, built to receive Chinese goods both by barge down the Irrawaddy river and by ship from factories on China's eastern coast.[50] Beijing has also provided substantial military assistance to the junta in Burma, including a $1 billion arms and training package in the 1990s.[51]

Other moves by China include the building of container ports in Bangladesh at Chittagong (a desired military 'pearl' in Chinese eyes) and in Sri Lanka at Hambantota; an offer to fund a $20-billion canal that would cross Thailand's Kra Isthmus, thereby allowing ships to bypass the Strait of Malacca and permitting Beijing to set up port facilities there; and the construction of a railway from China through Cambodia to the sea. In addition to its creeping jurisdiction claims, Beijing is seeking to enhance its capability to project air and sea power into the South China Sea to help safeguard its energy and strategic interests. It has upgraded a military airstrip on Woody Island and stepped up its presence in the South China Sea through oil-drilling platforms and ocean-survey ships.

China's growing oil-import needs serve as justification for its new 'active defence' land-warfare doctrine, assertive maritime role and growing naval power. To help protect China's growing energy assets in Central Asia, the People's Liberation Army has set up at least two offensively configured, armour-heavy mechanized corps modelled after the Soviet Operational Manoeuvre Groups of the 1980s. Using Xinjiang as their springboard, these corps are designed to 'become China's new strategic weapon' in keeping with the new doctrine to fight deep inside enemy territory and secure oilfields.[52]

China is putting into service up to six nuclear-powered ballistic-missile submarines (SSBNs), part of the so-called 'Project 094'. That would considerably narrow the Sino–Russian gap in nuclear forces. Russia today has only two nuclear subs on patrol. In the years ahead, it is very likely that Chinese nuclear subs would appear in the Indian Ocean. The issue, in fact, is not 'if' but 'when'. As underlined by its plans to build a blue-water navy, Beijing clearly perceives the sea as a sphere of opportunity for extending its strategic, political and trade influence.

Japan and India can hardly ignore the military implications of China's energy-driven moves, including its use of commercial port facilities, diplomatic ties with other states and its own defence capabilities to police strategic chokepoints across a vast region. By assiduously cultivating regimes of strategically located states, Beijing has secured important naval or eavesdropping access, ostensibly for building maritime safety. New Delhi, for its part, has sought to encourage Japan to play a role in the Indian Ocean region, as is manifest from the March 2005 Indo–Japanese agreement to jointly explore for natural gas in the strategically sensitive Andaman Sea.

For New Delhi, the emergence of Chinese facilities on each flank, in Pakistan and Burma, represents a clear challenge to its command of the sea in its own backyard. Once the Chinese-built naval base-cum-port at Gwadar is complete, the Chinese Navy, with its access in Burma, will be able to operate on both Indian flanks. In addition, Beijing's broad-based military-cooperation agreement with Dhaka — Bangladesh's first such accord with any country — has four apparent objectives: to bring that country into the Chinese strategic orbit; gain naval and commercial access to Chittagong; develop Burma–Bangladesh road links; and secure a doorway to India's vulnerable northeast. The irony is that a power that tried hard, first to stop the birth of Bangladesh, and then to deny it United Nations membership, has now succeeded in presenting itself to that very country as a strategic friend and counterpoise to India.

It is inevitable that Tokyo and New Delhi will respond to the Chinese moves by building the required military capabilities to assert their maritime rights, safeguard security and maintain power equilibrium. In fact, India's determination to retain its dominant position in the Indian Ocean indicates that 'the ongoing reordering of the asymmetric relationship between the West and Asia will be centred as much in the Indian Ocean as in East Asia'.[53] Having been militarily outflanked by China, India has responded with its own naval-modernization programme that has included the purchase of a Russian aircraft carrier, the 40,000-ton *Admiral Gorshov*, and the Franco–Spanish Scorpene diesel submarines. Another piece on India's chessboard of naval power is the Israeli Phalcon system, an airborne early-warning and control system aboard three Russian-built Ilyushin-76 aircraft. The United States, whose technology is built into the Phalcon, barred Israel from selling the system to China but approved its sale to India.

If the Chinese Navy is to be pre-empted from challenging India's dominant position in the Indian Ocean, the Indian Navy will have to play a bigger role in the Strait of Malacca, a critical chokepoint for Chinese trade and energy lines. Indian naval policing of the Malacca Strait will not only vex China but also help keep direct Sino–Indian naval competition away from India's own backyard.

Russia is another important player in Asian energy-related geopolitics. With the Russian bear growling and brandishing its energy card, Moscow will seek to enhance its strategic space in Asia and underpin its military prowess through energy geopolitics. The emergence of Russia as an energy superpower has not only stemmed its geopolitical decline but also spurred a new assertiveness in Moscow's foreign policy that had been missing since the Soviet withdrawal from Afghanistan in the late 1980s. High energy prices will only help Moscow boost its leverage in Asia and elsewhere.

At the same time, Russia's growing reliance on energy exports to prop up its economy offers an opportunity to certain Asian states to diversify their oil and gas supplies away from the politically unpredictable Persian Gulf region. The commercial development of energy assets in the Russian Far East, in any case, demands the technical expertise and financial assistance of foreign partners, especially in Asia. That, in turn, mandates that the big energy consumers next-door to Russia — China, Japan and South Korea — coordinate their energy-import strategies to the extent of promoting market-favourable exploitation of Russian energy deposits.

To Northeast Asia at least, Russia can be a more secure energy supplier than the Persian Gulf. Yet the major oil importers of Asia need to thwart any attempts by supplier states — whether by Russia, Iran or any other big exporter — to use their considerable energy resources for political leverage or blackmail.

In the coming years, the voracious appetite for energy supplies in Asia is going to make the energy geopolitics murkier. The need to secure stable energy supplies will drive the larger players in Asia to increasingly integrate their energy policy with foreign policy, as they consciously promote diplomatic strategies geared towards seizing energy-related opportunities overseas.

Energy competition is already beginning to aggravate interstate rivalries in Asia. Mercantilist efforts to assert control over oil and natural gas supplies and transport routes certainly risk fuelling tensions and discord. Given the lack of regional institutions in Asia to avert or manage conflict, the sharpening energy geopolitics makes Asian economic and energy cooperation more pressing. A challenge for states in Asia is to manage their energy needs through more efficient transport and consumption and more cooperative import policies.

Notes and References

1. Wooed by all the major powers, Nursultan Nazarbayev has tried to play a balancing game while hedging his bets through diversification of energy exports. For example, in a March 1, 2006, policy speech, the Kazakh president listed 'increasing integration with Russia' as Kazakhstan's No. 1 foreign-policy priority. His other two main priorities, he said, were 'improving cooperation' with China and building a 'long-term, stable partnership' with America.

2. Wu Lei and Shen Qinu, 'Will China Go to War over Oil?', *Far Eastern Economic Review*, Vol. 169, No. 3 (April 2006), pp. 38–40.

3. Amnesty International, *People's Republic of China: Sustaining Conflict and Human Rights Abuses* (London: Amnesty International, June 12, 2006).

4. See Ronald O'Rourke, *China Naval Modernization: Implications for U.S. Navy Capabilities — Background and Issues for Congress*, CRS Report (Washington, D.C.: Congressional Research Service, November 18, 2005) and *Chinese Military Power*, Report of an Independent Task Force (Washington, D.C.:

Maurice R. Greenberg Center for Geoeconomic Studies, Council on Foreign Relations, 2003).

5. Stanley A. Weiss, 'Protecting the World's Arteries', *International Herald Tribune*, November 23, 2005.

6. See Worldwatch Institute, *State of the World 2006* (Washington, D.C.: Worldwatch Institute, 2006).

7. White House, *The National Security Strategy of the United States of America* (Washington, D.C.: White House, March 2006).

8. Pramit Mitra, 'India's International Oil Ties Risk U.S. Displeasure', *International Herald Tribune*, April 7, 2005.

9. For details of India's energy-consumption patterns, see the following links:
India's Ministry of Power
http://powermin.nic.in/
India's Ministry of Petroleum and Natural Gas
http://petroleum.nic.in/
Oil and Natural Gas Corporation Limited
http://www.ongcindia.com/
The Energy and Resources Institute
http://www.teriin.org/
Tata Energy and Resources Institute — North America
http://www.terina.org/
Energy Information Administration, U.S. Government — Country Information on India
http://www.eia.doe.gov/emeu/international/india.html

10. Robyn Lim, 'Asia Will Have a New Japan', *Asian Wall Street Journal*, September 13, 2005.

11. Michael Vatikiotis, 'China on the March', *International Herald Tribune*, September 30, 2005.

12. Friedrich Wu, 'The Globalization of Corporate China', *NBR Analysis*, Vol. 16, No. 3 (December 2005).

13. Steven R. Weisman, 'Rice and Australian Counterpart Differ on China', *New York Times*, March 17, 2006.

14. Chia-Peck Wong and Helen Yuan, 'China Hastens Quest for Metals', Bloomberg News, *International Herald Tribune*, September 22, 2005.

15. 'Australia: More Ore for China's Mills', *Business Week*, September 19, 2005.

16. UNCTAD Trust Fund Project, *The Iron Ore Market 2004–2006*, (UNCTAD, May 2005).

17. Mineral Information Institute, 'Iron Ore — Hematite, Magnetite and Taconite'. http://www.mii.org/Minerals/photoiron.html

18. http://www.thundersword.com/businesschina.htm#IRON%20ORE%20RESERVES

19. David Lague, 'China Corners High-Tech Element', *International Herald Tribune*, January 22, 2006.

20. Howard W. French, 'A Growing Power Lets a Growing Crisis Fester', *New York Times*, May 17, 2006.

21. White House, *National Security Strategy of the United States of America*.

22. Jamestown Foundation, 'China Brief: Beijing's Arms and Oil Interests in Africa', Vol. 5, Issue 21 (Washington, D.C.: Jamestown Foundation, October 13, 2005).

23. Ralph A. Cossa, 'You Are Judged by the Company You Keep', *International Herald Tribune*, September 6, 2005.

24. Robert S. Ross, 'Toward a Stable and Constructive China Policy', *NBR Analysis*, Vol. 16, No. 4 (December 2005).

25. Christopher Pala, 'China Pays Dearly for Kazakhstan Oil', *New York Times*, March 21, 2006. Also see Jason Singer and Guy Chazan, 'China Firm Refines Central-Asia Oil Deal', *Asian Wall Street Journal*, September 6, 2005.

26. Pala, 'China Pays Dearly for Kazakhstan Oil'.

27. Simon Romero, 'A Dispute Underscores the New Power of Gas', *New York Times*, January 3, 2006.

28. Strategic Forecasting, Inc., 'China: Pumping an Iranian LNG Deal for Oil' (Austin, Texas: Stratfor, March 22, 2006).

29. Reuters report, September 22, 2005.

30. The India–Sri Lanka Free-Trade Agreement, signed in 1998 and effective since April 2000, has served as a model of economic cooperation in South Asia and a forerunner to a South Asian FTA (SAFTA).

31. For further details, see following links: http://www.eia.doe.gov/emeu/cabs/bangla.html http://pubs.usgs.gov/bul/b2208-a/b2208-a.pdf

32. Eliza Griswold, 'The Next Islamist Revolution?', *New York Times*, January 23, 2005.

33. Burma is already exporting natural gas worth more than $1 billion a year to neighbouring Thailand from two other

fields. Alan Sipress, 'Asia Keeps Burmese Industry Humming: Trade, Both Legal and Illegal, Blunts Effect of U.S. Economic Sanctions', *Washington Post*, January 7, 2005, p. A11.

34. 'Gas Pipeline: Myanmar Takes India for a Ride', *The Times of India*, March 27, 2006.

35. Before that accord with India, Tehran in 2004 also agreed in principle to sell China 10 million metric tons of LNG over a period of 25 years.

36. See Brian Sweitzer, 'The Other Black Gold', *International Herald Tribune*, October 3, 2005. According to Sweitizer, a soil scientist and governor of Montana, 'synfuels' have unique properties: 'They are high-performing substances that run in existing engines without any technical modifications, and they burn much more cleanly than conventional fuels. The synfuel process, which is nothing like conventional coal use, removes greenhouse gases as well as toxins like sulphur, mercury and arsenic. And the technology has other applications: A synfuel plant can generate electric power, make synthetic natural gas, and produce the hydrogen that many (including Bush) believe is the energy source of the future.'

37. See, for example, Richard McGregor, 'China Looks At $24 Billion Coal-to-Oil Plan as Beijing Bets on Oil Price Staying High', *Financial Times*, September 27, 2005.

38. Pradip Baijal, 'Hydel Power Our Best Hope', *The Times of India*, September 20, 2005.

39. Estimate cited in: http://www.eia.doe.gov/emeu/cabs/china.html

40. On January 12, 1998, President Bill Clinton submitted his certification to U.S. Congress, contending that 'the Agreement will have a significant, positive impact in promoting U.S. non-proliferation and national security interests with China and in building a stronger bilateral relationship with China based on respect for international norms'. In doing so, he also waived a sanction imposed on China in response to its brutal 1989 Tiananmen Square crackdown.

41. Mohamed ElBaradei, director-general of the International Atomic Energy Agency, speech of October 10, 2005.

42. According to a 2004 Massachusetts Institute of Technology

(MIT) study by John Deutch and Ernest Moniz that assessed the aggregated cost of constructing, licensing and running a newly commissioned light-water reactor, the baseline cost of new nuclear power in the United States stood at 6.7 cents per kilowatt hour — higher that of a pulverized coal-fired plant (4.2 cents/kW hr). The same study also didn't find nuclear power competing well with a combined-cycle natural gas-powered plant (CCGT). The price of gas, however, has continued to rise in recent years.

43. Condoleezza Rice, 'Our Opportunity with India', *Washington Post*, March 13, 2006, p. A15. In the op-ed, Dr Rice argued that besides being 'good for American jobs', the nuclear deal will help make India 'less reliant on unstable sources of oil and gas' — a specious claim.

44. Mark Holt and Carl E. Behrens, 'Nuclear Energy Policy', Congressional Research Service Issue Brief No. IB88090 (Washington, D.C.: Congressional Research Service, March 22, 2001).

45. Pietro S. Nivola, 'The Political Economy of Nuclear Energy in the United States', Policy Brief No. 138 (Washington, D.C.: Brookings Institution, September 2004).

46. Integrated Headquarters, Ministry of Defence, *Indian Maritime Doctrine* (New Delhi: Integrated Headquarters, 2005).

47. See Satinder Bindra, *Tsunami: 7 Hours That Shook the World* (New Delhi: HarperCollins Publishers India, 2005).

48. Of the estimated 232,000 killed or presumed dead in the tsunami disaster that struck a dozen countries on December 26, 2004, more than two-thirds (some 169,000) were in Aceh alone.

49. Pentagon report cited in Bill Gertz, 'China Builds Up Strategic Sea Lanes', *Washington Times*, January 18, 2005, p. 1.

50. John W. Garver, 'Development of China's Overland Transportation Links with Central, Southwest and South Asia', *The China Quarterly*, No. 185 (March 2006).

51. Martin Smith, *Burma: Insurgency and the Politics of Ethnicity* (London: Zed Books, 1999), p. 426.

52. Martin Andrew, 'PLA Doctrine on Securing Energy Resources in Central Asia', China Brief, Vol. 6, Issue 11 (Washington, D.C.: Jamestown Foundation, May 24, 2006).

53. Donald L. Berlin, 'India in the Indian Ocean', *Naval War College Review*, Vol. 59, No. 2 (Spring 2006).

4

Equations in the Strategic Triangle

NOTHING WILL DETERMINE ASIA'S FUTURE PROSPERITY and security more than the equations between and among its three top powers — China, India and Japan. Constituting the Asian strategic triangle, these three countries are the largest economies and carry the most geopolitical weight in Asia. Each of them, in different ways, also poses a key challenge, regionally and globally. The bilateral China–Japan, India–China and Japan–India equations, as well as the relationship of each of the three players with the United States, will decisively shape the Asia of tomorrow.

'The storm centre of the world has shifted…to China', U.S. Secretary of State John Hay said way back in 1899 while unveiling America's 'Open Door' policy that sought commercial access in China identical to what other major powers enjoyed there. 'Whoever understands that mighty Empire…has a key to world politics for the next 500 years.' The same could be said today about the emerging Chinese colossus, an impenetrable empire with unconcealed ambitions.

Japan's quiet, undeclared transition from pacifism to a 'normal' state holds another key to the future of Asian and global geopolitics. Japan has come a long way from the time it concentrated mainly on economic modernization and relied on the United States to sort out the intricacies of international politics for it. In return for securing U.S. military and nuclear protection, Japan has for long allowed America to forward-base U.S. forces on its territory. The U.S.–Japan Security Treaty, in permitting Tokyo to single-mindedly focus on building economic strength, became, so to speak, 'Japan's highest source of authority, the functional successor to the pre-war emperor, "sacred and inviolate"'.[1] Today, even as it has reinvigorated its military ties with America, Tokyo is beginning to circumspectly shape an independent foreign policy and rethink its security.

The third major Asian player, India, has now come of age. It is displaying greater realism in its economic and foreign policies and moving gradually from doctrinaire nonalignment to geopolitical pragmatism. It has come to recognize that it can wield international power only through the accretion of its own economic and military strength. India will increasingly be aligned with the West economically. But politically it has multiple options, and there is no reason for it to put all its strategic eggs in one basket. It can advance its interests by forging issue-based partnerships with different players to create more strategic space for itself. That means it can progress from being nonaligned to being multialigned while preserving nonalignment's kernel — strategic and policy-making autonomy.

The China–Japan feud at a time when the Chinese economic juggernaut is gaining on Japan, the not-so-veiled Sino–Indian rivalry and the growing concerns in Asia (and rest of the world) over China's rising power make the future course of Asian security uncertain. In fact, the intensification of old rivalries and the assertion of national identities could presage a more volatile Asia, unless progress is made on a security framework to link the major states together through shared leadership and interests.

The Past Colours the Present

History casts a shadow on the major interstate political relationships in Asia, even as commercial ties continue to thrive and grow. Nowhere is the issue of history more troubling than in the China–Japan context, with a dire need to find a modus vivendi that could help the two to break free from the clutches of history once and for all. The burden of history, comparatively, is less onerous between China and India, which have expressed an interest in fashioning a 'strategic and cooperative partnership for peace and prosperity'. Yet, China and India are not finding it easy to overcome the past.

For Japan, which has been in search of leadership status, adjusting to China's ascent has been painful. It was in the decade since Japan's financial bubble burst in 1990 that China rose dramatically in Asia and the world. Japan's loss became China's gain. Having got used to making rapid economic strides and outmatching the performance of one European economy after another, Japan suddenly encountered a rising neighbour that was catching up with its own economic miracle.

India, meanwhile, also started rising economically, although more quietly. India is one country Tokyo had long neglected to cultivate despite abundant goodwill for Japan there. But after its nuclear-weapons tests in 1998, India's military potential could no longer be ignored. India's proven competence in information technology and other knowledge industries further raised its international profile. Japan is finally taking India's economic and military potential seriously.

Today, Japan is seeking to reclaim its international role, with assets that could be the envy of any society — a 100 per cent literacy rate, a stable political system, mastery of Western management techniques, surpluses and savings that have made it the world's second largest creditor nation, products with top international brand names, impressive soft-power resources and a military establishment more sophisticated than that of China except in the nuclear sphere. Japan's economic recovery was never in doubt except to the inveterate sceptics. Now it ranks 'first in the world in the number of patents, third in expenditure on research and development as a share of GDP, second in book and music sales, and highest for life expectancy'.[2]

Yet the fall in Japan's fortunes had been dramatic after 1990. From getting the United States so worked up in the 1980s about Japanese technological prowess as to bring Japan bashing into vogue, Tokyo slipped to the point that, through much of the 1990s, it began getting lectures from America on ways to stem its economic decline. After having played host to European and American businessmen who came in droves in the 1980s to study its model of success, Japan began hearing from the West on why it needed to radically reform that same success model. Japan's woes were compounded by its falling stock market and by deflation — a decline in property values and other prices that choked off borrowing and put pressure on its weak banking system. Now it faces the prospect of being eclipsed economically by China.

But throughout much of its history Japan has demonstrated its capacity to bounce back from a political slump or a seemingly hopeless situation. Take the situation in 1860, when anarchy stared Japan in the face following serious internal conflict and the assassination of the top official of the Tokugawa Shogunate. The eventual outcome of that chaotic situation was the Great Meiji success story that, over a nearly five-decade period, triggered a powerful renaissance that made Japan so powerful that it defeated Russia and China in separate wars. During the reign of the Meiji Emperor that ended with his death in 1912, Japan rose to world-power status.

Another example was the dramatic way Japan emerged as an economic superpower from the ashes of

World War II, after the United States had disarmed that country and imposed a pacifist constitution on it. In 1945, many Japanese cities lay in ruins, including two that had been incinerated by nuclear bombs; its industry was shattered; its people were scrambling for food; and its political will had been broken. Yet, by the late 1970s, it had risen spectacularly as a major competitor to the U.S. economy.

Now, even as its economy begins to rebound after years of stagnation — borne out by the rising corporate profits, the large inflows of foreign investment and the rise in the average stock price at the Tokyo Stock Exchange — Japan faces painful choices as a result of the global slowdown. Those choices go far beyond the need to rebuild debt-ridden public finances as a key component of its future economic strategy. Its aging and shrinking population, for example, underlines a more fundamental challenge. Before too long, China also will face the costs of its one-child policy. In fact, by 2040, it may lose its status to India as the world's most populous nation, unless, in the meantime, it reverses its official policy.

Japan, a country poor in natural resources that has all the same succeeded in turning manufacturing into the main engine of its nearly $5-trillion economy, seems set to lose its status to China as the world's second-largest economic powerhouse. It thus needs to focus on the development of new leading-edge technologies and the acquisition of special industrial skills. It can be rightly proud of its high-technology base. In a nation that makes a fetish of hygiene, Japan can boast of having the world's most high-tech toilets, including toilets with heated seats, bidet-like sprays, drying-action air blasts, built-in deodorizers and soothing river sounds. They are also available with music, built-in emitters of fragrance and a massage with warm-water pulsation. Japan's future, however, will be shaped not by comprehensive toilet comfort but by comprehensive national power.

In history, the Chinese and Indian civilizations have had a great effect on other societies in Asia, with the Indian influence visible to this day in Southeast Asia and the Chinese influence in East and Southeast Asia. In the coming age, while the battle for influence in Asia will be waged principally by the triumvirate of China, India and Japan, there will be other players too. As South Korea is demonstrating through its 'soft power', which extends to the material and spiritual realms as well as to the pop culture, Asia already has other important peddlers of influence.[3] The South Korean soft power is being developed in the crucible of a country whose deep-rooted insecurities have been tempered by a new-found confidence and yearning for international recognition. The competition for influence in Asia, however, is likely to be most intense among China, India and Japan. The Japan–China and India–China relationships have evolved in interesting but dissimilar ways.

Japan, as a loyal ally of the United States, did not restore diplomatic relations with China until after U.S. President Richard Nixon's 1971 'opening' to Beijing. It was Japanese Prime Minister Kakuei Tanaka's trip to Beijing that ended the 'abnormal state of affairs' between the two countries and helped 'establish diplomatic relations as from September 29, 1972', according to the joint communiqué issued at the end of that visit. In the communiqué ending nearly 80 years of Sino–Japanese enmity and friction, Japan accepted a one-China policy, while Beijing waived its demand for war indemnities from Tokyo. China and Japan then went on to sign the Treaty of Peace and Friendship in 1978. Another important accord, the Japan–China Joint Declaration on Building a Partnership of Friendship and Cooperation for Peace and Development, was initialled in 1998 during the first visit to Japan by a Chinese head of state. (See Appendices C, D and G for official texts of these accords.)

Over the past three decades and more, Japan has been a major source of capital, technology and equipment for China's economic-modernization drive. In recent years, however, China's major imports of capital equipment from Japan have aided the Japanese economy's recovery from recession.

India, in contrast, enthusiastically embraced China as soon as the communists led by Mao Zedong rode to power. Prime Minister Jawaharlal Nehru wrote to Chinese Premier Zhou Enlai on December 30, 1949, conveying India's decision to establish full diplomatic relations with China. Even as the new communist state annexed the large historical buffer of Tibet — an action that eliminated India's outer line of defence — Nehru's government continued to court China, seeing it as a benign neighbour that had like India emerged from the ravages of colonialism. New Delhi even opposed a discussion in the United Nations General Assembly in November 1950 on Tibet's appeal for international help. In fact, soon after coming to power, Mao confided in Soviet strongman Joseph Stalin that Chinese forces were 'currently preparing for an attack on Tibet' and inquired if the Soviet Air Force could transport supplies to them.[4]

Nehru later admitted he didn't anticipate the swiftness and callousness of the Chinese takeover of Tibet because he had been 'led to believe by the Chinese Foreign Office that the Chinese would settle the future of Tibet in a peaceful manner by direct negotiation with the representatives of Tibet'. Nehru, who brushed aside advice from level-headed colleagues and ran foreign policy like private policy, ended up bequeathing major security and foreign-policy problems to the future Indian generations of leaders. A classic example of Nehru's gullibility and lack of caution is the following note he recorded in July 1949 to close an internal debate on Tibet when a communist victory appeared imminent in China:

Whatever may be the ultimate fate of Tibet in relation to China, I think there is practically no chance of any military danger to India arising from any change in Tibet. Geographically, this is very difficult and practically it would be a foolish adventure. If India is to be influenced or an attempt made to bring pressure on her, Tibet is not the route for it. I do not think there is any necessity for our Defence Ministry, or any part of it, to consider possible military repercussions on the India–Tibetan frontier. The event is remote and may not arise at all.[5]

What Nehru credulously saw as a 'foolish adventure' was mounted within months by the Chinese communists, who gobbled up Tibet and gained control of its strategic crossroads, only to begin exerting direct military pressure on India. What Nehru averred was geographically impracticable became a geopolitical reality that has impacted on Indian security like no other development, and helped create a common land corridor to nurture the Sino–Pakistan axis. Tibet's annexation gave China, for the first time in its long history, a contiguous border with India, Burma, Bhutan and Nepal.

Nehru was such an unabashed panda-hugger that he even rejected the notion of India taking China's place in the United Nations Security Council. The officially blessed selected works of Nehru quote the then Indian prime minister as stating the following on record:

Informally, suggestions have been made by the U.S. that China should be taken into the UN but not in the Security Council and that India should take her place in the Council. We cannot, of course, accept this as it means falling out with China and it would be very unfair for a great country like China not to be in the Council.[6]

Little surprise that on the occasion of the 60th founding anniversary of the People's Republic of China in 2009, Nehru was identified in a poll conducted by the Communist Party's mouthpiece, *Global Times*, as being among the '60 foreigners who helped shape China's 60 years'.

In 1954, Nehru signed a largely one-sided pact with China, ostensibly establishing Sino–Indian friendship under the rubric of 'Panchsheel', or the 'five principles', of peaceful coexistence. The accord led to an uproar in the Indian Parliament, where it was dubbed the 'melancholy chapter of Tibet' by some amid cries of 'Shame! Shame!' Nehru stoutly defended the agreement, claiming it assured peace between the two Asian powers.[7] The Panchsheel principles greatly influenced India's foreign-policy doctrine and its adoption of nonalignment. Yet, historians are likely to record that the Panchsheel Agreement, as it became popularly known, was based on Indian naïveté and miscalculations, leading India into a war with a scheming communist China.

The agreement — 'born in sin', in the words of one analyst[8] — incorporated a formal Indian recognition of Chinese control over Tibet, with India forfeiting all the extra-territorial rights and privileges it had enjoyed in Tibet until the Chinese invasion. The accord recorded India's agreement both to fully withdraw within six months its 'military escorts now stationed at Yatung and Gyantse' in the 'Tibet Region of China' as well as 'to hand over to the Government of China at a reasonable price the postal, telegraph and public telephone services together with their equipment operated by the Government of India in Tibet Region of China'.[9] Up to the 1950 invasion, China maintained a mission in Lhasa, just as India did, underscoring Tibet's autonomous status.

Nehru in 1954 traded, in essence, an explicit concession for a self-perceived implicit gain — sacrificing

Tibet so that, in his words, 'our northern frontier should be considered a firm and definite one'. The formal acceptance of the Chinese claim over Tibet was a product of Nehru's zeal to befriend China.[10] Such was the ardour that Nehru signed away Tibet's long-held independence without reference to the wishes of the Tibetan people — that too in a pact with the occupying power. He did not even insist on China granting Tibet limited autonomy, despite Beijing's public charade that a 17-point agreement it imposed on Tibet in 1951 provided for autonomy. In the negotiations, India wanted the Panchsheel Agreement to use the term, the 'Autonomous Region of Tibet', but it caved in and settled for a reference to the 'Tibet Region of China'.

Nehru misconstrued the mention of specific border-trade mountain passes and posts in the 1954 accord as Chinese acknowledgement of where the Tibetan frontier with India lay. To make matters worse, he refused to pay heed to Beijing's statements that it had signed a border-trade accord and not a border accord with India. In fact, no sooner had the Panchsheel Agreement been signed than China laid claim to Indian frontier areas like Barahoti and then furtively intruded south of Niti and Shipki mountain passes — all specified border points in that accord. Before long, China began building a highway through India's Ladakh region to link rebellious Tibet with another vast, occupied region, Xinjiang, home to Turkic-speaking Muslim ethnic groups. (Before communist China enforced its writ on Xinjiang, a short-lived independent East Turkestan Republic had functioned up to 1949 in much of Xinjiang.)

Having reposed his implicit faith in China, Nehru cried foul when the same state deceived him. On October 20, 1962, just over eight years after the Panchsheel Agreement, China launched a two-front Himalayan war masterminded by strongman Mao Zedong that helped decisively humble India. While the Nehru government had been proclaiming, 'Hindi-Chini Bhai Bhai' (Indians and Chinese are brothers), the Chinese leaders had been reading the same slogan as, 'Hindi-Chini Bye Bye'. Then Indian President Sarvepalli Radhakrishnan called the invasion the outcome of India's 'credulity and negligence'.

In the style recommended by the ancient treatise, *The Art of War*, written by Sun Tzu — a general believed to have lived in the sixth century B.C. and said to be a contemporary of great Chinese philosopher Confucius — Mao chose a perfect time for taking on India: the launch of the attack, spread over two separate rounds, coincided with a major international crisis that brought the United States and the Soviet Union within a whisker of nuclear war over the stealthy deployment of Soviet medium-range ballistic missiles in Cuba.

The timing of the Chinese attack had been made even more favourable by two other developments — an American promise in July 1962 to hold Chiang Kai-shek from initiating hostilities across the Taiwan Straits that enabled China to single-mindedly mobilize forces against India, and Soviet leader Nikita Khrushchev's subtle yet discernible tilt towards Beijing on the Sino–Indian border issue in an apparent effort to buy Chinese support in the looming Soviet confrontation with the United States. A little over a month after launching the invasion of India, China announced a unilateral ceasefire that, significantly, coincided with America's formal termination of Cuba's quarantine.

As Jung Chang and Jon Halliday have revealed, Mao timed the attack very well because he had advance information from Khrushchev about the secret Soviet missile deployments in Cuba. That information, along with a request for Chinese help, had come, ironically, in response to Mao's 'feeler to the Russian ambassador [in Beijing] about how Moscow would react if China attacked India'.[11] According to the authors, as part of 'a hefty horse trade', Khrushchev agreed to 'stand by Beijing' in a war with India and to delay the promised sale of MiG-21s to New Delhi. The Mao–Khrushchev horse trade, however, didn't last long. The duplicitous Mao, by lashing out against the Russian agreement to pull out missiles from Cuba, compelled Khrushchev to backtrack on his initial support to Beijing. Indeed, by accusing Khrushchev of 'selling out', Mao vented his irritation that the United States and the Soviet Union did not come to nuclear blows — a mutual destruction that would have left China as the strongest power.

Mao had painstakingly masterminded the attack on India, with clear objectives in mind.[12] The 32-day war, which left some 3270 Indian soldiers dead and the Indian state in ignominy, was Mao's attempt to demolish India as an alternative democratic model and geopolitical rival to communist China. Mao heaped humiliation on India when it was militarily weak and least expected to be attacked by a neighbour whom it had been assiduously courting. In one stroke, Mao also wrecked the international stature of Nehru, the key architect of the global Nonaligned Movement. Defeat transformed Nehru from a statesman and towering figure on the world stage into a beaten, worn-out politician, hastening his death. He passed away on May 27, 1964.

The swiftness and brute power with which Mao managed to trounce India not only boosted China's international image, but also helped him to politically consolidate his position at home at a time when famines and other economic problems following his disastrous 'Great Leap Forward' had created grassroots turmoil. Success, after all, has a thousand fathers, while defeat leaves behind an orphan.

That aggression — the second bloodiest war India has faced since its independence — completely changed the fortunes of the two Asian giants. India, respected until then as a model pluralistic state in the developing world, has never fully recovered from that invasion. In contrast,

China, a backward state wracked by economic calamities in 1962, went on to successfully assert itself as a major power through a display of indomitable spirit and political single-mindedness.

Nothing can better explain China's 'perfidy' in attacking India from the occupied heights of the Tibetan massif than the words of India's most-famous panda lover. The day the Chinese invaded, a shattered Nehru confessed to the nation in the following words:

> Perhaps there are not many instances in history where one country has gone out of her way to be friendly and cooperative with the government and people of another country and to plead their cause in the councils of the world, and then that country returns evil for good.

Mao's premier, Zhou Enlai, had publicly admitted that the war was intended 'to teach India a lesson'. It definitely taught India a lesson. Principally, what the war helped draw attention to was that until India fully absorbs the fundamentals of international relations, it will continue to get 'evil for good'.

It was not until after Mao's own death on September 9, 1976, that India and China restored diplomatic relations. After all, the Indian Parliament had unanimously passed a bipartisan resolution on November 14, 1962, accusing China of betraying India's 'goodwill and friendship' and pledging the 'resolve of the Indian people to drive out the aggressor from the sacred soil of India, however long and hard the struggle may be. (See Appendix B for full text of the resolution.)

Although Sino–Indian commercial ties were re-established in 1978, it was not until the 1990s that bilateral trade really took off. It has grown so rapidly since then that China has emerged as India's largest trading partner. The border disputes between China and India, however, continue to fester, without a clearly defined line of control in the Himalayas still to separate the two giants. This is despite the two sides having signed three vaunted border-related accords — the 1993 agreement to maintain 'peace and tranquillity along the Line of Actual Control', the 1996 'confidence-building measures in the military field', and the 2005 deal identifying six 'guiding principles' for a settlement of the frontier disputes. (See Appendices D, E, F, H, I and J for texts of these accords.)

Today, despite the underlying problems and tensions, China and India, and Japan and China, are seeking to forge relationships based on equilibrium, not overt competition or confrontation. Both New Delhi and Tokyo believe their interests demand the building of peaceful, stable relations with Beijing on an equal footing. China, too, is desirous of putting its relationships with India and Japan on a more even keel to help underpin its power potential.

The Japan–China and India–China equations, however, are far from being steady and smooth. These relations, if not maintained and nurtured carefully, are such as to have a potentially corrosive effect on Asia's strategic stability in the coming years. It has now become imperative both to head off a cold war between Beijing and Tokyo and to put the accent on the positive in the Chinese–Indian relationship. For India, the potential emergence of a superpower on its northern borders that invaded it in the past, built up Pakistan as a military counterweight with transfers of nuclear-weapons and missile technologies and continues to hold captured Indian territories (including almost one-fifth of the original state of Jammu and Kashmir), is hardly a comforting thought. To Tokyo, it is disconcerting that a country whose economic modernization it aided by pumping in more than 3 trillion yen in aid between 1980 and 2003 alone should now whip up nationalistic passions at home against Japan.[13]

The political dimensions of these two pivotal bilateral relationships have come under pressure even as trade and economic cooperation between these states have continued to expand. In fact, Japan–China and China–India commerce is galloping to record levels. This only draws attention to the fact that growing trade cannot connote political progress by itself. China and Japan indeed have such close economic relations that in 'their breadth and intensity, the ties have begun to surpass those between the United States and Japan, whose economic relationship has often been called the most important in the world'.[14]

In 2004, when the Sino–Japanese trade crossed $178 billion, China overtook the United States as Japan's largest trading partner. Yet, by the spring of 2005, China had tacitly encouraged three anti-Japanese actions — a citizens-led petition drive against Japan's desire to be a permanent member of the United Nations Security Council, a popular boycott of Japanese goods and anti-Japanese mob protests. Beijing then used those actions as leverage to demand concessions from Tokyo. In India, a naïve belief persists among some that the growing Indian–Chinese trade — still small by China–Japan and U.S.–China levels — suggests an improvement in political relations. Such romanticists even hope that rising bilateral trade could help ameliorate India's security concerns vis-à-vis Beijing.

Trade and economic bonds can certainly help soften or mute political disputes. But without a resolution of the underlying political problems and suspicions, growing commerce can only bottle up the fundamental political pressures up to a point, beyond which they are likely to burst out in the open. It is an open question whether the Japan–China and India-China relationships are close to reaching that danger point, given what has been happening of late among the three. It is significant that as China's trade with the United States has grown, its political competition with Washington has also sharpened.

New Delhi should continue to expand its trade, economic and other cooperation with China, but without harbouring the illusion that it will change Chinese strategic objectives vis-à-vis India or lay the foundation for peaceful coexistence. With Sino–Indian trade growing at a phenomenal rate, a new boom in crossborder investment has become visible with Indian and Chinese companies hunting for business in each other's markets.[15] According to two analysts, 'history shows that close and interdependent economic ties do not guarantee moderation and mutual restraint in the face of deepening suspicion, acrimony and distrust'.[16]

If anything, the emergent Asia is showing that economic strength cannot by itself be the new international currency of power. Japan is learning the hard way that despite an economy thus far larger than China's, it does not enjoy the same international profile or influence as Beijing. A country's international standing depends on a host of factors, including its strategic vision and goals, leadership, military prowess, power-projection capabilities, economic strength, high-technology base, commercial competitiveness and soft power.

China epitomizes such attributes, even if some of them are still in the making. Its nuclear-weapons and missile armouries, coupled with its permanent seat at the UN Security Council, greatly aid its power-projection force capabilities. Those capabilities, in turn, arm Beijing with political and commercial leverage of a kind that is the envy of Tokyo and New Delhi. China also exemplifies how history can be wantonly used by a nation to further its foreign-policy interests.

An emblematic case was Beijing's 2004 spat with South Korea over the ancient kingdom of Koguryo, founded in the Tongge River basin of northern Korea.[17] At the heart of the politically inspired row was whether the kingdom that bestrode the period before and after Christ was Korean (as the Koreans and outside historians believe) or Chinese, as China's newly revised history claimed.

Triggered by the Chinese Foreign Ministry's posting of the revised historical claim on its official Website, the spat over the kingdom came out as an attempt by Beijing to reconstruct the past to prepare for the future. If the collapse of the rapidly corroding Stalinist state of North Korea helps establish Korean reunification, it will dramatically alter the geopolitics of Northeast Asia. By seeking to revise history, ostensibly at the instance of its state-funded researchers, China appeared to be hedging its options on how it will deal with a unified Korea, raising in the process the spectre of potential tensions over frontiers.

Like its proclivity to hedge, China's use of legend to pursue irredentist claims is renowned. An example was its 1992 promulgation claiming four-fifths of the South China Sea. With 60 per cent of its present territory comprising homelands of ethnic minorities, China has come a long way in history when the Great Wall represented the Han empire's outer security perimeter. Territorially, Han power is at its high point today. Yet, driven by legend, China continues to chase greater territorial and maritime claims. For the first time since the Ming dynasty, China is also pursuing security interests far from its shores.

Unsettled Frontiers

China continues to lay claim to more Indian territories, even as it holds on to Indian Himalayan areas it encroached on or captured in the 1950s and early 1960s. Sharing one of the world's longest and most rugged frontiers, China and India are the only two countries today without a fully defined frontline.

In the longest continuous border-negotiating process between any two nations in post-World War II history, China has held regular rounds of dialogue since 1981 with India to settle the festering Himalayan frontier disputes.

Yet, after almost three decades of continuous negotiations, the two neighbours have not achieved even the bare minimum — a mutually defined line of control separating them — even as they deceptively call their disputed frontline the 'Line of Actual Control', or LAC.

In the period since the negotiations began, China has emerged as a global economic and political force and thereby strengthened its negotiating leverage vis-à-vis India. Such leverage has also been boosted through its transfers of weapons of mass destruction (WMD) and missile technologies to Pakistan and its strategic penetration of Burma. Not surprisingly, as the border negotiations have proceeded, Beijing has shown a weakening inclination to settle the border or even to clarify the so-called LAC. The more the negotiations have dragged on, the less China has appeared interested in resolving the border disputes other than on its own terms.

Beijing's approach suggests that an unresolved, partially indistinct frontier fits well with its interests vis-à-vis India. Firstly, the status quo helps to keep India under Chinese strategic pressure. Secondly, it pins down along the Himalayas hundreds of thousands of Indian troops who otherwise would be available against China's 'all-weather ally', Pakistan. That is the third party whose interests China feels it cannot disregard. By compelling New Delhi to maintain sizable forward-troop deployments along the Indo–Tibetan frontier, Beijing in effect ensures that there is a closer military parity on India's western flank with Pakistan. In other words, just as the Pakistan-aided Islamist insurgency in Indian Kashmir has bottled up a significant number of Indian forces there, the People's Republic of China has helped lock in many Indian troops along the Himalayas, keeping them away from the Pakistan frontier. Thirdly, an unresolved border arms Beijing with the option to turn on military heat along the already-tense frontier if India dared to play the Tibet card or enter into an overt, anti-China military alliance with the United States.

What is more, China is sitting pretty on the upper heights, having got what it wanted, either by furtive encroachment or by conquest. It certainly sees no reason to strategically assist a potential peer competitor by lifting pressure on the borders through an amicable settlement. Consequently, despite long-lasting negotiations with India, it still seeks to apply the brakes on the negotiating process with jingles such as: 'Time and patience hold the key'; 'what is left over from history demands a step-by-step approach'; and 'the need is for meaningful and mutually acceptable adjustments'.

Yet, by persisting with the border dialogue with New Delhi and singing the virtues of 'give and take', Beijing all the same seeks to influence Indian policy and conduct through engagement, even as it is constantly looking to 'take' more, such as its astounding claim to the Indian Buddhist district of Tawang as a cultural extension to annexed Tibet. Without the strategically located Tawang, India's position in its upper northeastern belt would become more vulnerable. Engagement and contrived flexibility on the border issue also help China to advertise its peaceful rise.

Given the hard-nosed Chinese approach, a succession of Indian prime ministers, starting with Indira Gandhi in the early 1980s, gave priority to the clarification of the line of control while remaining open to any Chinese proposal for a complete border settlement. The parallel process to institute Sino–Indian confidence-building measures (CBMs) since the 1980s was pivoted on the elimination of LAC ambiguities so as to help stabilize the military situation on the ground and ensure enduring peace and tranquillity. But with Beijing dragging its feet on fully defining the frontline, the confidence-building process has advanced far ahead of the LAC-clarification process.

The way the two sides have got carried away by the confidence-building exercise is illustrated by their 1996 accord to farcically prohibit certain military activities at specific distances from a line of control whose ambiguities they still have to purge. The CBMs enshrined in that agreement require the two countries, among other things, not to fly combat aircraft 'within 10 kilometres of the line of actual control' (Article V.2) and not to 'conduct blast operations within two kilometres of the line' (Article VI), when the reality is that there is no agreed frontline on maps, let alone on the ground.

With almost their entire 4057-kilometre border in dispute and their frontline neither defined nor delineated, India and China have a major task to complete. The Indo–Pakistan frontier, in sharp contrast, is an international border, excepting in Jammu and Kashmir, where there is a Line of Control that has been both clearly defined and delineated. Only in the 110-kilometre northernmost tip of the Indo–Pakistan frontier at Saltoro Ridge, encompassing the disputed Siachen Glacier, is the frontline ill-defined. It took almost two decades of bloody skirmishes on Siachen's icy pinnacles, where temperatures can fall below −55° Celsius and more soldiers die in avalanches than by gunfire, for the two sides to thrash out and enforce a ceasefire there since November 23, 2003.

Barring some strips of land, China has settled its land-border disputes with all its neighbours other than India and Bhutan, even as it remains embroiled in serious maritime territorial disputes with several states and tetchily presses its irredentist claim over Taiwan. First, China's frontier disputes with India involve larger tracts of territories than any other land-border problem China has faced. This is especially true if one takes the Chinese claim over India's Arunachal Pradesh state at its face value and not as a rhetorical bargaining chip. Arunachal Pradesh ('Land of the Rising Sun') is nearly three times as large as Taiwan.

Second, China has a track record of clinching land-border settlements with declining states, with the exception of its deal with Vietnam. Beijing prefers to do border deals with weakened states where domestic conditions are deteriorating so that it can impose the majority of its claims, as it did with a rudderless Russia before Vladimir Putin became president and with an internally troubled Kazakhstan, Kyrgyzstan and Tajikistan.

It took China two full decades of border talks with India before it agreed to even exchange maps relating to just one border sector. The Chinese side literally had to be shamed into exchanging maps with India in 2001 showing each other's military positions in the least-controversial middle sector. That step was to be followed up with a promised exchange of maps of the western sector in 2002, and finally of the eastern sector in early 2003. The completion of the exchange of maps showing each other's presently held military positions was intended, without prejudice to rival territorial claims, to define where *actual control* lay. Through such clarification of the frontline, the two sides intended to proceed towards mutual delineation on maps and perhaps even demarcation on the ground, pending a final settlement. However, the Chinese side reneged on the promised exchange of the maps of the particularly thorny western and eastern sectors, upsetting the 'Joint Working Group' (JWG) negotiations on the clarification of the entire line of control.

Having broken its word, Beijing then injected confusion on purpose by suggesting that the two sides abandon years of laborious efforts to define the frontline and instead focus on finding an overall border settlement. That more clearly appeared to be a dilatory tactic intended to disguise its breach of promise. If Beijing is not willing to take even an elementary step — clarifying the frontline with India — why would it be willing to commit itself to something far bigger: resolving the festering border problem through a package settlement?

The frontline clarification, after all, is to be without prejudice to rival territorial claims. A final border settlement, in contrast, would be a complex process involving not only a full resolution of the territorial claims but also the drawing of a clear-cut frontier through a lengthy three-part process to first define, then delineate on maps, and then finally demarcate on the ground that border. Put simply, a disinclination on Beijing's part to define the existing line of control connotes an aversion to clinch an overall border settlement.

The idea of a package settlement is not new. China has been peddling a package-settlement idea now and again, although till date it has not put forward a single concrete proposal for consideration. In fact, it first dangled that carrot before India in 1960 as a kind of red herring to deflect attention from its aggressive designs. If not before the 1962 war, the outlines of an overall deal have been clear at least since 1981, when border talks began in earnest. Any package deal has to involve a simple trade-off — India giving up its claim to the territory it lost to China, in return for Beijing's abandonement of its astounding claim to India's northeastern state of Arunachal Pradesh (which the Chinese military invaded in the 1962 war, only to withdraw almost wholly after the ceasefire).

In other words, if China agreed to forfeit its Arunachal Pradesh bargaining chip, India would formally cede its claim to the Chinese-occupied area of Ladakh in Kashmir that is almost the size of Switzerland — an area that is of critical strategic importance to Beijing because it provides a land corridor between Tibet and Xinjiang, and a passageway to ally Pakistan. Since seizing that 38,000-square-kilometre area, known as Aksai Chin, China has been fortifying its hold. It has built an all-weather highway through Aksai Chin that links remote western Tibet with Xinjiang, where the Han Chinese (long regarded by the Turkic-speaking Uighurs as invaders) now form the majority. One of the highest and coldest roads in the world, this highway from Lhasa to Kashgar runs mostly at over

4000 metres. It is a vital logistical route for the Chinese military through two restive regions — one region where it faces non-violent, low-key resistance and the other where Beijing seeks to tar the Turkic separatists with the Al Qaeda brush.

The Indian public and lawmakers have always supported reconciliation with China despite Beijing's 1962 stab in the back. There is nothing in the November 14, 1962, Indian Parliament resolution that could thwart an attempt by a government in New Delhi to reach a reasonable border deal with China. The resolution, passed during the height of the Chinese aggression, records the 'resolve of the Indian people to drive out the aggressor from the sacred soil of India, however long and hard the struggle may be'. But it neither calls for the recovery of every inch of lost Indian territory, as some Indian analysts have fancifully claimed, nor does it bar an Indian peace settlement with Beijing.

The relevant question, however, is whether the Chinese idea of a package settlement has been real or just a gambit to buy time in order to keep India under strategic pressure. The border talks have brought out unmistakably that Beijing is not willing to settle on the basis of the status quo. That China has been far from sincere in ballyhooing such a settlement model is also apparent from its reluctance till date to put forward or even bilaterally discuss a concrete package deal. By making an outlandish claim over India's Tawang region, China has further dispelled the notion that a settlement would involve a simple, uncomplicated swap, with New Delhi giving up what it doesn't control in the west in return for Beijing allowing it to keep what it already controls in the east. China has even refused to have any discussion with India on the future status of the trans-Karakoram tract comprising mainly the Shaksgam Valley — a sizable area in Pakistani-occupied Kashmir that Islamabad ceded to China under the 1963 Sino–Pakistani Frontier

Agreement. India does not recognize this territorial ceding to China.

The borders of India, China and Pakistan converge at Kashmir. Indeed, the core territorial disputes between India and China, and India and Pakistan, centre on Kashmir, which ranks as the world's largest and most militarized zone of contention, with China holding 20 per cent of it, Pakistan 35 per cent and India the remainder 45 per cent. Pakistan has never explained why it gifted away to China the trans-Karakoram tract when it claims the whole original state of Jammu and Kashmir. Conveniently, Pakistan shows the Chinese-occupied Aksai Chin as part of the People's Republic of China, while Beijing's official maps depict the Pakistani-held portions of Kashmir (the so-called 'Azad Kashmir' and Northern Areas) as part of Pakistan and its own acquired Kashmir areas as PRC territory. But the same Chinese maps portray Indian-administered Kashmir as disputed. The Chinese army, with its vantage positions atop the towering peaks and glaciers of the trans-Karakoram tract and Aksai Chin, peers down at Indian military formations in Kashmir.

Against this background, the still-hazy Sino–Indian line of control remains a powerful lever in Beijing's hands against India, as do its claim on Arunachal Pradesh and its strengthened hold on a fifth of the original state of Jammu and Kashmir. For similar reasons of leverage, China has accepted the 1914 McMahon Line with Burma but not with India, finding it more profitable to rail against the colonial-era line in its interactions with India since the 1950s. The line, defining the border between the then-independent Tibet and the northeastern stretch of the British Indian Empire, runs along the crest of the Himalayas until it reaches the great bend in the Brahmaputra River, which flows from Tibet into the Assam Valley.

The McMahon Line was crafted at a meeting on the sidelines of a conference at Simla, India. Britain and Tibet, represented by Sir Henry McMahon and Lonchen Shatra, respectively, reached agreement on defining the line at that meeting, to which the Chinese delegate at the Simla conference was not invited because all parties at that time, including China, recognized Tibet's sovereign authority to negotiate its boundary with India.[18] Had communist China not annexed autonomous Tibet, the McMahon Line — a boundary upheld by Tibet — would officially have been the Indo–Tibetan frontier in the east, running from Bhutan to Burma. Having seized Tibet in violation of international law, the non-recognition of the McMahon Line became essential to China to lay claim to areas south of that line, like Arunachal Pradesh.

That backdrop is essential to comprehend the contemporary setting, including China's wilful determination to go slow on clarifying its frontline with India. Yet, with China continuing to drag its feet on that issue, then Indian Prime Minister Atal Bihari Vajpayee sprang a major surprise during his mid-2003 China visit when he decided to turn Indian policy on its head and shift the focus from LAC clarification to the elusive search for a border settlement. His concession to the hosts in agreeing to initiate a new framework of discussions between designated 'senior representatives' not only stalled the process of clarifying the frontline, but it has also taken India back to square one — to discussing the 'principles' and 'basic framework' of a potential settlement. He also propitiated China on another front: he formally recognized Tibet as 'part of the territory of the People's Republic of China', formally completing the process of India's sacrifice of its northern buffer.

In Beijing, Vajpayee appeared less like the leader of a nuclear-armed India determined to engage China on equal terms and more like a tribute payer to the fabled Middle Kingdom. His visit also contributed to an unflattering international linkage being drawn between troubled Tibet — a major international issue that refuses to fade away because of the continuing resistance to Chinese rule — and peaceful Sikkim, a non-issue, with the natives (and the rest of the world) having accepted the tiny Himalayan state's 1975 merger with India.

In return for his kowtow on Tibet — handing Beijing the Indian formulation on Tibet it wanted — Vajpayee claimed credit for beginning 'the process by which Sikkim will cease to be an issue in India–China relations'. China had long ploughed a lonely international furrow on Sikkim, refusing to accept the change in status of that territory from an Indian protectorate to part of the Indian union. Before Vajpayee, however, no Indian prime minister had viewed Sikkim as an issue on which India needed to engage China and seek concessions.

Beijing, before agreeing to incrementally halt its cartographic depiction of Sikkim as an independent kingdom, succeeded in getting the Vajpayee government to unequivocally recognize as part of the People's Republic of China the area it officially calls the Tibetan Autonomous Region (TAR) — the central plateau where much less than half of all ethnic Tibetans live. Vajpayee's formal recognition of TAR as 'part of the territory of the People's Republic of China' continued a pattern of self-damaging Indian betrayal of Tibet that began under Nehru, who not only gave up the extra-territorial rights India had inherited in Tibet from the British but also acknowledged the 'Tibet region of China' in the 1954 Panchsheel Agreement. Moreover, by narrowing Tibet to just TAR, Vajpayee implicitly conceded the forcible incorporation of Tibet's large outer territories into the Chinese provinces of Qinghai, Sichuan, Gansu and Yunnan. Qinghai, for example, is the Chinese name for Greater Tibet's Amdo region, where the present Dalai Lama was born.

The sphinx-like Vajpayee's motivations were short-sighted and tied to domestic electoral politics. With national elections due the following year in India, Vajpayee wished to face the voters as the leader who had initiated rapprochement and peace with the country's main adversaries — China and Pakistan. It was not an accident that about two months prior to his China visit, Vajpayee had, out of the blue, reversed his government's policy on Pakistan by extending a hand of friendship to that country without securing a halt to Pakistani- sponsored terrorist acts against India.[19] Chasing dreams of winning a Nobel Peace Prize, Vajpayee suffered the humiliation of being swept out of power by the voters in the 2004 general elections.

Vajpayee's 2003 diversionary decision to explore anew the principles and framework of a border settlement not only rewarded Beijing for an act of bad faith, but also put off China's compliance with the joint commitment to exchange maps of the western and eastern sectors. Worse, what was touted as a new framework of dialogue at the political level to help add impetus to the process has turned out to be yet another mere change of label — from 'senior-level' negotiations since 1981, to a Joint Working Group after 1988, and to now discussions between 'senior representatives'.

Despite the labelling ingenuity in dressing up the border discussions, China has since 1981 steadfastly maintained its participation in the talks at the level of a vice foreign minister, while the Indians have, with every change to the label, upgraded their representation in the negotiations from secretary (East) in the Ministry of External Affairs, to foreign secretary, and then to national security adviser — all positions held by bureaucrats. This despite the fact that the national security adviser is senior in protocol to China's 'special representative', Dai Bingguo, the first of the eight vice foreign ministers. Through creativity in labels, New Delhi and Beijing have sought to demonstrate 'progress'. But progress has been difficult to come by.

A well-known strength of Chinese diplomacy is to discuss and lay out 'principles', and then reinterpret them at Beijing's convenience to suit its interests, as the experience of the past half a century or more attests. Take the case of 'Panchsheel', or the 'five principles' of peaceful co-existence, which China began quietly violating no sooner than it had incorporated them in the much-trumpeted 1954 accord that helped lull India into complacency. Within nine years of signing the 'Panchsheel' Agreement, China invaded India.

The consequence of the new twist in 2003 has been that China and India have gone from the practical task of clarifying the frontline to a conceptual enunciation of vacuous principles and discussions on a new framework to resolve their border disputes. The two countries' special representatives are now enmeshed in giving meaning to and implementing the abstract principles that were agreed upon in April 2005 during the New Delhi visit of Chinese Premier Wen Jiabao.

Called the 'Agreement on the Political Parameters and Guiding Principles for the Settlement of the Boundary Question', the 2005 accord defines the following six principles: (1) 'a fair, reasonable and mutually acceptable solution to the boundary question through consultations on an equal footing'; (2) 'meaningful and mutually acceptable adjustments to their respective positions' so as to 'to arrive at a package settlement to the boundary question'; (3) 'due consideration to each other's strategic and reasonable interests, and the principle of mutual and equal security'; (4) 'take into account, *inter alia*, historical evidence, national sentiments, practical difficulties and reasonable concerns and sensitivities of both sides, and the actual state of border areas'; (5) the 'boundary should be along well-defined and easily identifiable natural geographical features to be mutually agreed upon'; and (6) 'safeguard due interests of their settled populations in the border areas'.[20] It did not, however, take Beijing long to repudiate the last principle.

The Chinese regime's touted interest in a package settlement remains nothing more than a rhetorical bait, lacking substance and specificity. In any event, after almost three decades of negotiations, any two sides will run out of new ideas to discuss. The way the talks are carrying on, China and India can only consolidate the record they hold for the longest, most-barren border negotiations. India needs to face up to the reality that China has little stake in an early border resolution. Indeed, the never-ending process appears to jibe well with Beijing's India policy of engagement with containment.

In keeping with the fact that the disputes relate to the Indo–Tibetan frontier, India ought to introduce a caveat in its negotiations with China: any border delineation and resolution between New Delhi and Beijing would be subject to a final settlement between the Dalai Lama's government and the People's Republic of China. This would parallel China's caveat in Article 6 of the 1963 Sino–Pakistan Frontier Agreement that the transfer of a Pakistani slice of Kashmir to it was subject to 'the settlement of the Kashmir dispute between Pakistan and India'.[21] Consistent with the historical fact that Tibet was free when it was illegally occupied and also to help build leverage against China, India could begin border negotiations with the Dalai Lama's government to mutually settle the Indo–Tibetan border in full beyond the McMahon Line.

Good fences make good neighbours. But the world's two most populous nations, sharing one of the longest interstate land borders, lack the first requisite to good-neighbourly relations — a well-defined frontline. Yet their entire border-related confidence-building process is predicated on the existence of such a mutually defined line of control. It is unclear how long India and China can continue to go round and round the mulberry bush without achieving success in either removing the ambiguities that bedevil their line of control or reaching a settlement on their simmering border disputes.

The territorial and maritime disputes between China and Japan are more limited in scale, although not in intensity. Their conflicting claims to potentially rich natural-gas and oil deposits in the East China Sea took a belligerent turn after two Chinese destroyers entered the area in January 2005, provoking Tokyo to up the ante. The decades-old dispute actually had escalated earlier in 2003 after China reached agreement with four Chinese and Western firms to explore for gas in the East China Sea, and then commenced test drilling for gas in May 2004 in a large field that straddles the median line between the two countries. In reprisal, Japan allowed a private Japanese company, Teikoku Oil, in mid-2005 to carry out exploratory operations in the same field but on the Japanese side of the median line.[22]

Japan, responding to China's hard-line stance that its Exclusive Economic Zone stretches to the very edge of the continental shelf, has insisted that the median line in the East China Sea serve as the Sino–Japanese maritime boundary. After intrusions by Chinese maritime research vessels into the Japanese EEZ, a Chinese nuclear attack submarine entered Japanese territorial waters in November 2004, further inflaming Japanese nationalistic passions barely three months after violent protests had erupted against the Japanese national soccer team at the Asia Cup in China. However, nothing has rattled the Japanese public more in recent times than the officially scripted anti-Japan mob protests in China in April 2005. Tens of thousands of Chinese participated in such protests in major cities, attacking Japanese diplomatic and commercial offices, before authorities stepped in to end the demonstrations that threatened to go out of control.

The tussle in the East China Sea also involves rival territorial claims to islands to the south by three different parties. Japan controls the Senkaku Islands, which China claims and calls the Diaoyu Islands. In fact, to assert its claims, Beijing incorporated those islands into its territory under its law on the territorial sea. But Taiwan has also defined its territory through national legislation in a way to include the very same islands — a group of five small volcanic islands and three 'rocks' located about 145 kilometres northwest of the Japanese Ishigaki Islands and 170 kilometres northeast of Taiwan's Keelung.

While Japanese administrative control of the islands dates back to 1895, China and Taiwan pressed their unofficial claims to the atolls separately for the first time in 1971 after a U.S. geological survey indicated potential oil fields in the East China Sea. However, a formal Chinese claim to the islands, part of Japan's Okinawa Prefecture, came much after the United States returned Okinawa to Japan. Indeed, after World War II, the islands were administered by the United States and were included in the Okinawa area returned to Japan in 1972. Shortly thereafter, China first pressed an exploratory claim. But it was not until the 1980s that Beijing went from a tentative to a definite claim. According to one reporter, 'When Japanese diplomats visiting Beijing in the mid-1980s asked for a clarification, Deng Xiaoping called the issue a "dispute", and recommended it be resolved in the future. Tokyo objected to what it saw as a device to grab territory by declaring it disputed'.[23]

Actually, the disputes over the Senkaku/Diaoyu Islands intensified publicly after the Japanese Youth Association, which built a lighthouse on the main 4.3-square-kilometre island of Uotsuri-jima in 1988, erected another lighthouse on a second atoll in 1996, triggering anti-Japanese protests in Hong Kong and Taiwan. Some of the protesters then managed to evade Japanese security patrols and reach the main island to plant the flags of China and Taiwan, but not before one of them drowned. The uninhabited islands — too tiny to be depicted on most maps — are important because the maritime area round them holds potentially major oil, gas and mineral deposits. The U.S. military continues to use the islands as practice grounds for bombing runs, even as Tokyo in 2005 put them under the direct administration of its coast guard.

The Sino–Japanese maritime-boundary issues raised by the disputes over the Senkaku/Diaoyu Islands are complex and difficult to resolve on the basis of international law, including the UN Convention on the Law of the Sea. The islands are located on the Asian continental shelf, which stretches hundreds of kilometres in the East China Sea. The disputes pit China's right under the Law of the Sea to the continental shelf area (and to the oil and mineral wealth therein) against Japan's legal right to an EEZ extending 370 kilometres to the west of the Ryukyu Islands chain in the Okinawa Prefecture.

With Japan's EEZ overlapping with the Asian continental shelf, Tokyo has sought to limit its claim to a median line. Although this line is halfway between the Ryukyu Islands and the Asian mainland, Japan's EEZ still overlaps China's right to the continental shelf and the latter's claim to the disputed islands and to the gas and oil deposits in the surrounding maritime zones.[24] The intricacy of the boundary issues is further intensified by the fact that the islands themselves are entitled to both an EEZ and a continental shelf under the Law of the Sea.

More broadly, the Sino–Japanese territorial and maritime disputes have turned into hot-button issues. By contrast, the Sino–Indian disputes, although involving much larger tracts of territory, had been better managed, with both sides eschewing inflammatory rhetoric in public until Chinese cross-border military incursions escalated, putting the spotlight on border tensions in 2009.

Japan is also involved in a territorial row with South Korea over a set of disputed islets, which are surrounded by rich fishing waters and located halfway between the two countries, with Seoul calling them Dokdo and Tokyo naming them Takeshima. Such are the passions aroused by the dispute over the South Korean-controlled islets that sit atop unexploited energy resources that the then President Roh Moo Hyun of South Korea thundered: 'The Dokdo issue has become a matter that can no longer be managed in a quiet manner.' He went on to say in a nationally televised speech on April 25, 2006: 'We will react strongly and sternly against any physical provocation. This is a problem that can never be given up or negotiated, no matter at what cost or sacrifice.'

Japan and South Korea, America's closest allies in East Asia, also dispute each other's claim to the seabed near the volcanic outcroppings in the Sea of Japan (the 'East Sea' to South Korea and China). Tokyo and Seoul, in fact, have sought to put their own monikers on places such as undersea basins and ridges in a wrangle that strikes a raw nerve among many Koreans, who consider Japan's claim a leftover from the 1910–45 Japanese colonial rule over the Korean peninsula. Roh, for instance, called Japan's claim to the islets and surrounding waters 'an act that denies Korea's complete liberation'.

Japan's recent attempts to map waters in the disputed zone have met with strong South Korean protests and gunboat threats. As one Japanese analyst has put it, 'Between Japan and South Korea, shared democratic values are not yet proving to be a source of affinity'.[25] The outcome of the dispute with Seoul matters to Tokyo because it could have a bearing on its own island feuds with China, Taiwan and Russia.

Of course, more significant are the Sino–Japanese disputes in the East China Sea, where rival nationalistic sentiments and strategic ambitions have spurred mutual rancour. The East China Sea disputes have regularly flared in public in recent years and helped harden domestic feelings in Japan and China. An assertive China has sent research and naval vessels into Japan's side of the midpoint line between the Ryukyu Islands and the Asian mainland. It also attempted to declare a disputed area off limits to shipping to facilitate its gas-exploration activity. China's approach has also been tough on the disputes in the South China Sea, with Beijing refusing to jointly discuss with Vietnam, the Philippines, Malaysia and

Brunei ways to settle rival claims.

In the East China Sea, a February 2001 pre-notification agreement between China and Japan has not been successful in halting all incursions because it was vaguely worded, with its framework too broad. Such is its fuzzy language that it requires Beijing and Tokyo to give advance notification before entering waters in an area in which the other side 'takes interest'. To make things more difficult, neither side is willing to submit the bilateral disputes to the International Court of Justice for adjudication.

Fiery Irredentism

The disputes between China and India, and China and Japan involve more than rival territorial or maritime claims. In essence, they centre on the politics of national identity, historical grievances that have not yet been put to rest and the pursuit of national power. Resurgent nationalism and competing economic, security and energy interests have further fuelled their rivalries and disputes, making progress on a resolution of the bilateral problems more difficult. Yet, at the same time, Sino–Japanese and Sino–Indian economic bonds continue to deepen, with bilateral trade increasing every year.

The baggage of history remains a serious impediment to greater political cooperation. The new, defiant Japanese approach towards China on the issue of history was exemplified by Prime Minister Junichiro Koizumi's visits to the Yasukuni Shrine, which memorializes Japan's war dead, including the 14 who were labelled war criminals by the Allied powers following World War II. The defiance has been spurred by a rightist backlash in Japan over China's nationalism-mongering and blatant political use of the history card. Ever since they seized power in 1949, the Chinese communists have employed purported history to lend legitimacy to their actions in gobbling up Tibet, seizing or laying claim to Indian territories, asserting China's claims in the East and South China Seas, and seeking Taiwan's 'return'.

Although Taiwan has become the Holy Grail of Chinese foreign policy, the shrill cry for 'reunification' is shakily anchored in history. China certainly has a more than 3000-year history, but significant Chinese settlements in Taiwan did not begin until the first half of the seventeenth century, when southern Taiwan was under Dutch control and the north under Spanish domination. Even as imperial Chinese rule was facilitated by the new settlers, who swamped and dispossessed the native Malayo-Polynesian people over a period of 100 years, Taiwan was not declared a province of China until 1886, or barely nine years before the Manchus — defeated in the Sino–Japanese war — ceded Taiwan to Japan in perpetuity.

After Japan's own defeat in World War II, the United States did not 'return' Taiwan to China, as Beijing claims, but authorized Chiang Kai-shek's army to exercise provisional control over the island as a 'trustee on behalf of the Allied Powers'. For more than a century now, Taiwan has been outside the direct, lawful control of mainland China. In fact, India has a stronger historical claim to Pakistan than China has to Taiwan, which geographically is closer to the Philippines than to mainland China. But no right-thinking Indian makes that claim.

Nevertheless, Taiwan remains at the centre of what a tetchy China perceives as its unfulfilled historical quest. If cultural or racial ties were to confer historical entitlements, India could claim the entire region from Nepal to Mauritius. But that would be as much a travesty of history as China's single-minded aim to recolonize Taiwan, defying both the island's separate, distinct history and the wish of the majority of its citizens to stay autonomous.

As Philip Bowring has put it, 'Few object to the notion that in an ideal world all Chinese people should be under one political umbrella. Like world government, it is a remote prospect, but not one worth arguing with'.[26] But when an authoritarian China puts a democratic Taiwan under a permanent threat of force — with the intent to absorb it with or without open war — it becomes more than an abstract proposition. From its erstwhile history books referring to Taiwan first as an area 'outside the pale of Chinese civilization' and then as a 'base for pirates',[27] China has, in more recent times, laid claim to Taiwan as its 'integral part', even promulgating a menacing Anti-Secession Law in March 2005.

In keeping with the teachings in the ancient treatise, *The Art of War*, famed for insights such as, 'winning without fighting is the best strategy of all', China's preferred option on Taiwan is to absorb it without war. In order to achieve a major political objective without direct military action, the adversary's weaknesses need to be identified and exploited — a thesis also to be found in the writings of contemporary Chinese strategists.[28] To help absorb Taiwan without open aggression, Beijing is using the openness of the Taiwanese political system to influence the politics and public discourse on the island. The intent is to suborn Taiwan to the extent that it becomes like 'a frog being lulled to sleep in a pot of gradually heating water'.[29] Beijing also believes that the greater the military gap between the mainland and the island, the more likely Taiwan will accept 'mother' China, even if in the framework of a Hong Kong-style confederation arrangement. Through its rapid military build-up, China wishes to create a reality that so compresses Taiwan's options that the island is left with little choice but to politically integrate with the mainland.

That the issue of cross-strait relations has become a divisive subject in Taiwan aids the publicly enunciated strategy of the People's Liberation Army to wage 'three wars' against the island — psychological, legal and information. To underpin the three-war strategy, China holds out a credible threat to employ force, mirrored in its growing missile and other weapon deployments against Taiwan. Even so, China is also preparing for the 'fourth war', if the right opportunity were to arise — a swift and forcible absorption of Taiwan.

China's fierce irredentism is founded partially in the easy way it was able to gobble up a large buffer state over which it had even a less plausible historical or ethnic claim — Tibet. With Tibet's occupation, a 'natural and cultural buffer zone between India and China disappeared'.[30] A triumphant annexation, like a successful revolution, engenders its own force of legitimacy. As China has tightened its hold over Tibet, challenges to its claim over what is called 'the roof of the world' have become academic. Yet, with China's continued use of purported history to advance other extravagant claims, the past can hardly be forgotten.

This is especially so because China has employed success as a licence to extend its gains territorially. For example, China's claims on Indian territories, including those already seized through furtive encroachment or conquest, flow from its claims on Tibet's alleged historical ties with those areas. Instead of straightforwardly contesting China's right to move troops hundreds of kilometres south to create a military frontier with India for the first time in history, New Delhi from the beginning played into Chinese hands by retreating to a border-definition exercise with Tibet's occupiers. With its ambitions whetted, China has not only been loath to define a line of control with India, but it has also laid claim to India's Tawang region as a cultural patio to annexed Tibet.

Although Chinese mythology presents Tibet as one of the tributary states of the fairy-tale Middle Kingdom, Tibet has been an independent political entity since the earliest times and culturally distinct from China. China and Tibet were enemies from the second century B.C. to the thirteenth century. In fact, during the seventh to ninth centuries, the Tibetan kingdom extended across Central Asia, including to large areas of modern-day China.

The only time Tibet was part of China was under the Yuan dynasty, from 1279 to 1368. The Yuan dynasty, however, was not Han but Mongol. It was the Mongols under Genghis Khan who conquered China and compelled Tibet, without invading it, to accept their authority, thereby bringing the Han and Tibetan societies under their dynasty. It was the historical equivalent of Burma having been part of the British India Empire until 1937. During their imperial rule, the Mongols imbibed Tibetan religious and cultural values, just as the Romans had drawn inspiration from ancient Greece. In a misappropriation of the Genghis Khan legacy, however, China's official history treats the Yuan dynasty as Chinese.

During China's Ming Dynasty (1368–1644), Tibet was independently ruled by the Pagmodru, Rinpung and Tsangpa Tibetan dynasties. In the latter half of the seventeenth century, China itself was conquered by foreigners again, this time by the Manchus. Tibet, meanwhile, had been ruled independently from 1642 to 1682 under the fifth Dalai Lama, who gradually demilitarized the country. To avoid maintaining a military, the Dalai Lama negotiated a protective alliance with the Manchu emperor.

It is a fact of history that the Manchu (Qing) dynasty aggressively conquered and colonized surrounding non-Han regions. Revisionist history in China under the continuing communist rule, however, has indoctrinated citizens to think of the Mongol and Manchu empires — the Yuan and Qing dynasties — as Han, with the result that educated Chinese have come to feel a sense of righteous ownership about every territory involved with those empires.

Objective history cannot justify Chinese revanchism or territorial expansion, just as it cannot validate Japan's occupation of Korea in 1910 or its rule over the rich strategically located Manchuria or its invasion of Han China in 1937. What Beijing refers to as its 'integral' regions are, at the most, imperial spoils of earlier foreign dynastic rule in China.[31] Yet Maoist China helped create new geopolitical realities, as exemplified by its absorption of Tibet and Xinjiang. In the case of Tibet, it went quickly from claming shadowy suzerainty to declaring the high plateau an integral part of the People's Republic.

The geopolitical ramifications of China's annexation of the resource-rich Tibet can be gauged from just one piece of information: Tibet, as it existed independently up to 1950, comprises approximately one-fourth of China's land area today. Tibet's fall gave China, for the first time in its long history, a contiguous border with Burma, India, Bhutan, Nepal and Kashmir (of which, as described earlier in this chapter, it subsequently gained a one-fifth slice). Additionally, the annexation has given China access to the vast mineral wealth of Tibet, which has 126 different mineral resources, including significant reserves of uranium, chromite, boron, lithium, borax, copper and iron.

While the Mao Zedong-led 'Cultural Revolution' attempted to systematically obliterate Tibet's art, culture and history, today the survival of Tibet as a distinct ethnic and cultural entity is seriously threatened by its rapid Sinicization, reflected in the mass influx of Han settlers and the economic marginalization of the native people.[32] Both in Tibet and Xinjiang, government projects have been designed not to develop local manufacturing industry but to help transport mineral and energy resources to the east. The large income disparities in China are the greatest in Tibet, where 'almost all the rich are Han settlers' and the 'poor and powerless' are Tibetans.[33]

The mid-2006 opening of the $6.2-billion China–Tibet rail link from Gormu to Lhasa, which will accelerate the already-devastating exploitation of the Tibetan plateau's natural resources, militarily strengthens China's hold over

Tibet and also its offensive military capability against India while making more vulnerable the fragile ecology of Tibet — the starting point of almost all the great Asian rivers. For example, a train station has been built within the Gulu Wetlands, a pristine breeding ground for Tibet's famed black-neck cranes and yellow ducks. The railroad's construction through wildlife habitat also endangers musk deer and chiru antelopes (whose meat is a great Chinese delicacy and whose shahtoosh wool is internationally renowned).

The railroad links Tibet with the eastern Chinese coastal belt, and helps tighten China's hold over 'the roof of the world'. The new 1118-kilometre stretch, which begins in Tibet's Amdo region (now the province of Qinghai) and traverses 600 kilometres of permafrost to the Tibetan capital, ranks as the highest elevated railway in the world, requiring train carriages to be sealed like aircraft to protect passengers from high-altitude sickness and necessitating turbochargers to make engines run with enough oxygen. Completed in five years ahead of schedule, the railroad is a staggering engineering feat, confirming the arrival of China as a technological force. It was originally conceived by Mao in the 1960s to help cement his forcible absorption of Tibet. When the first train ever to travel from Beijing to Tibet arrived in Lhasa on July 3, 2006, it marked the realization of his dream.

For much of its run to Lhasa from Gormu, the railway functions at altitudes higher than many small planes can fly, as it passes through 30 mountain tunnels or bridges, including a 1686-metre-long tunnel through the Kunlun mountain range.[34] A southward railway spur from Lhasa to Xigatse — seat of the Panchen Lama's Tashilhumpu monastery — further strengthens China's military-transport and reinforcement capabilities against India. At short notice, the People's Liberation Army can intensify military pressure on India by rapidly mobilizing up to 12 divisions. A string of new Chinese military airfields along the frontier with India have also come up, even as China builds up its missile strength on the Tibetan plateau.

Just as the southbound strategic roads that China built in the 1950s in Tibet were later used for aggression against India, the new Tibetan railroad greatly strengthens Beijing's capability to rapidly deploy its forces and overwhelm Indian defences. And just as the new highways into Tibet helped dramatically increase Han migration, the railroad to Lhasa and Xigatse will result in an even bigger Han influx, threatening the very survival of Tibet's distinct religious, cultural and linguistic identity. In fact, just days before he cut the ribbon on the first train to Lhasa, President Hu Jintao named as the new party chief in Tibet the commander of the Xinjiang Production and Construction Corps, responsible for promoting Han immigration into Xinjiang. Hu himself served as the party chief in Tibet and presided over a brutal martial-law crackdown there after a series of pro-independence protests in 1989.

Furthermore, the railroad helps augment China's missile-transport capability. Not only does the railway aid the easy transport of intermediate-range missiles, but also it allows China to rail-base and conceal the location of its intercontinental ballistic missiles, in Russian-style. In fact, China's latest ICBMs, the DF-41 and DF-31A, are rail-mobile weapons.

All in all, by beefing up Chinese logistic support in Tibet, the railroad arms China with multiple strategic benefits vis-à-vis India: enhanced power-projection force capability; the option to step up direct military pressure; superior transport links with states that are part of the Indian security system (Nepal and Bhutan); a greater potential to meddle in India's restive northeast; and the ability to dump goods in the Indian market via Nepal and the Chumbi Valley's Nathu-la Pass. Eventually, China would like to extend the Tibetan railway to Kathmandu even as it presently expands its road links with Nepal. It has also held out the prospect of connecting Lhasa by rail to the Chumbi Valley and to Nyingchi, or 'Throne of the Sun,' just north of Arunachal Pradesh at the tri-junction with Burma.

Ever since the elimination of Tibet as the outer buffer, India has regarded Nepal and Bhutan as its inner strategic buffers. India's security would be gravely imperilled if it were to lose the two inner buffers. Chinese efforts to make strategic inroads into those buffers thus challenge Indian security. During 2005–06, Beijing signed contracts worth several million dollars to supply Nepal 25,000 rifles, 18,000 grenades, five armoured personnel carriers, two aircraft and other unknown arms.[35] The Chinese arms supply began after India, the United States and the United Kingdom suspended military aid to Nepal in response to the now-ousted monarch there seizing direct power on February 1, 2005.

Having vastly upgraded its support infrastructure in Tibet and having begun expanding its transportation capabilities right up to its southernmost borders, China has developed greater influence over Nepal and Bhutan, which strongman Mao Zedong had once described as two of the fingers of the Tibetan palm — the others being the Indian states of Arunachal Pradesh (shown as Chinese territory in maps published by the People's Republic), Sikkim and Kashmir (one-fifth of which China occupies).

In recent years, China has sought to aggressively extend its influence in politically troubled Nepal, with which India shares a long, open border. To reduce Nepal's and Bhutan's economic dependence on India, China would like to employ its growing transportation capabilities to help link them to Tibet's economy. Its interest is greater in Nepal, where incipient state atrophy and lawlessness have increased Beijing's manoeuvring room and strengthened the very domestic forces that wish to bring about a communist revolution by chipping away at core state institutions. While united in seeking to overthrow what they perceive as a decadent feudal social order, the communists in Nepal come in two hues — the Maoists and the assorted communist groups that form the Unified Marxist–Leninist alliance. Many of these elements are attracted to the idea of viable Nepalese economic links with China-annexed Tibet as a means to undercut India's leverage over Nepal.

Unfettered Sino–Indian trade through the strategic Chumbi Valley could help China to gain influence in India's vulnerable northeast. For long, Beijing had called for trade with India through the Chumbi Valley, located at the tri-junction of Sikkim, Bhutan and Tibet. To that end, it offered bit-by-bit concessions on Sikkim, without declaring that it fully recognizes Sikkim's status as an integral part of India. Despite presenting an official map showing Sikkim in the same colour as the rest of India and signing a joint statement that carried a reference to Sikkim being in India, Beijing has been loath to surrender its Sikkim card the way India relinquished its Tibet card.

China's admission that Sikkim is presently under Indian control — a self-evident reality — does not mean that it now formally recognizes Sikkim to be part of India. Indeed, Beijing's acknowledgement of Indian control over Sikkim seems limited to the purpose of facilitating trade through the vertiginous Nathu-la Pass, the scene of bloody artillery duels in September 1967 when Indian troops beat back attacking Chinese forces. Yet China succeeded in getting what its premier had sought during his 2005 India visit — trade through Chumbi 'at an early date'. Unlike the inconsequential trade through the opening of the passes at Shipki-la (Himachal Pradesh) and Lipulekh (Uttaranchal) between 1992 and 1993, the reopening of Chumbi's Nathu-la Pass could pave the way to the gradual revival of the ancient Lhasa–Kalimpong and Lhasa–Calcutta trade routes that were Tibet's economic lifeline.

The road through the Nathu-la-Pass is the only direct route to India from Lhasa, where Tibetans are already a minority. The repening of the pass for trade works to Beijing's commercial advantage: while China can supply goods to the densely populated parts of eastern India, the potential for Indian exports via Nathu-la is limited in comparison. Beijing's interests, however, are more than commercial. One of its strategic objectives is to gain a foothold in the northeastern Indian region. It is also seeking to carve out separate doorways to that region through its military cooperation with Bangladesh and Burma. China's accumulating power is becoming the single biggest instigator of qualitative change in the geopolitical landscape of southern Asia.

Balance-of-Power Politics

Fundamentally, China's hard-nosed pragmatism and assertive projection of power far beyond its shores have contrasted sharply with Japan's pacifist constitution and India's smug, didactic worldview for long. It was inevitable that this kind of dissimilarity would spur strategic change at some point in Tokyo and New Delhi. China, through its policies and actions, is now beginning to influence the public thinking and discourse in Japan and India. It is also prompting the United States to pursue a strategy whose publicly declared intent is to 'encourage China to make the right strategic choices for its people, while we hedge against other possibilities'.[36]

As pacifist sentiment in Japan has declined, popular demands have grown there for revision of its U.S.-imposed Constitution's Article 9, which renounces war and armed forces. Removal of the constitutional shackles, in turn, will impel a larger change in Japanese strategic thinking and doctrine. In India, there is growing recognition of the country's need to pursue a practical, non-ideological foreign policy that surmounts the country's didactically quixotic past to pursue mutually beneficial strategic partnerships with other key players in Asia and the wider world.

Despite the emergent realism in India, the country — with its traditional goody-goody approach — has shied away from a doctrine pivoted on strategic balancing. While important states have pursued strategies of 'balance of power', 'balance of threat' or 'balance of interest', Indian foreign policy has never borne a distinct strategic imprint, except for a short period under Indira Gandhi. India is still loath to use the Tibet or Taiwan card for building countervailing leverage against China. The Dalai Lama's 2004 statement forsaking Tibet's independence as his life's mission was a cry of despair. Short of expelling him and denying refuge to more Tibetans fleeing their homeland, India has over the decades bent over backwards to please China. New Delhi's customary see-no-evil, do-no-evil policy on China only played into the hands of Beijing, encouraging it to expand its strategic leverage against India.

China, quite the opposite of India, has been a practitioner of classical balance-of-power politics. It has consistently pursued ties with India valuing the multiple strategic cards it holds against New Delhi, including a Himalayan line of control it steadfastly refuses to define; its commitment to maintain Pakistan as a military counterweight to tie India down south of the Himalayas; its setting up of novel strategic passageways to India via Burma, Nepal and Sri Lanka; its budding military ties with Bangladesh; the continual improvements in its firepower, communications and mobility on the Tibetan plateau; and its cartographic aggression in depicting an entire Indian state — Arunachal Pradesh — as Chinese territory, paying no heed to the wishes of the local people who count themselves among the most patriotic Indians.

Hemming in India from all four sides — Tibet, Pakistan, Sri Lanka and Burma — is the favoured way by which Beijing has sought to impose limits on the capabilities of its rival. As Eric Margolis puts it, the Chinese strategy 'confronts India with the spectre of simultaneously facing serious strategic threats on its western, northern and eastern borders',[37] even as China challenges India's dominance in the Indian Ocean. With its new wealth, China has been inventively building strengthened trade and transportation links to further its strategic designs. Such links around India's periphery are already bringing that country under strategic pressure on multiple flanks.

China is fashioning two north–south strategic corridors on either side of India — the Trans-Karakoram Corridor stretching right up to Gwadar, at the entrance to the Strait of Hormuz, and the Irrawaddy Corridor involving road, river and rail links from Yunnan right up to the Burmese ports. In addition, it is shoring up an east–west strategic corridor in Tibet across India's northern frontiers. With China beginning to challenge the pre-eminent Indian role in the Indian Ocean region by securing naval or eavesdropping access at points along the vital sea lanes of communication, a Chinese threat to India from the south may also emerge before long. China's intent clearly is to position its navy along routes vital to India's security and economy.

A lynchpin of Beijing's new emphasis on the seas surrounding India is Gwadar, a Chinese-built, deep-water Pakistani naval base-cum-port protected by cliffs from three sides that makes an Indian aerial attack extremely tricky. Gwadar, already home to a Chinese electronic-listening post, is a critical link in the emerging chain of Chinese forward-operating facilities in India's periphery. With its petroleum and military facilities, Gwadar is also intended to serve as a key base in China's strategy to secure greater Gulf energy resources.

By Beijing's own admission while launching the project in 2001, Gwadar's strategic significance is equivalent to the Chinese-built Karakoram Highway that has linked western China with Rawalpindi since opening in 1969, serving as the passageway for covert Chinese nuclear and missile transfers to Pakistan and helping to reinforce the Sino–Pakistan nexus. Beijing is buttressing Gwadar's strategic significance by linking it up with the Karakoram Highway through the Chinese-assisted Gwadar– Dalbandin railway. The transportation link to connect Gwadar to China through the Karakoram Highway is bound to have a strategic-multiplier effect.

In fact, with access to Gwadar and Burmese facilities, the Chinese navy will be able to operate on both Indian flanks. Seizing on the strategic importance of the Irrawaddy Corridor that stretches up to the Bay of Bengal, Beijing has already positioned its security personnel at several Burmese coastal points, including the Chinese-built Kyaukypu and Thilawa harbours. Chinese security agencies operate electronic-intellience and maritime-reconnaissance facilities on the two Coco Islands — transferred by India in the 1950s to Burma, which then leased them to Beijing in 1994.

Just as China covertly built a plutonium-producing reactor near Khushab in Pakistan when the process of rapprochement with India was in full swing (and just after it had assumed international non-proliferation obligations by acceding to the Nuclear Non-Proliferation Treaty in 1992), it began the Gwadar project at a time when the chill in Sino–Indian ties over the 1998 Indian nuclear-weapons tests had given way to peace overtures and high-level visits. Similarly, China started opening a new strategic flank against India via Burma after the much-trumpeted 1988 China visit of then Prime Minister Rajiv Gandhi had lulled New Delhi into complacency. Even while getting ready to invade India in 1962, as pointed out by Captain Amarinder Singh in his book on military history, 'the Chinese had been putting up a smokescreen of peace and deliberately creating confusion' on the Indian side.[38] After all, in the words of Sun Tzu, 'all warfare is based on deception' — a maxim Beijing follows tenaciously by employing diplomacy to camouflage its true intentions or to justify its actions.

Gwadar opens the way to the arrival of Chinese submarines in India's backyard, completing its strategic encirclement. Yet, in public, Beijing continues to deliver its now-familiar spiel — that China and India, as two ancient civilizations, need to live in peace so as to concentrate on economic progress; that China wants peaceful borders with all its neighbours; and that the two neighbours should not regard each other as a threat.[39] Such patter is no different from China's calculated presentation of itself to the wider world as a benevolent, non-interfering, peace-loving power, 'whose bland and benign visage is meant to lull the world until such time as China has finished rebuilding and is ready to engage the world on its own terms'.[40] India has known first-hand since the Nehru years that China's words rarely match its deeds. Indeed, Beijing treats India as a potential peer rival to be put down, with calibrated Chinese strategic pressure and intimidation designed to keep it in check. China's friendship diplomacy has always sought to underpin a win-win posture with India — engagement with containment.

As a consequence, Beijing's saccharine talk has given way to coarse talk each time India has asserted its rights, such as when it conducted the 1974 and 1998 nuclear tests. Few Indians can forget the Chinese ultimatums to India in the 1965 and 1971 wars with Pakistan, or the 1999 Chinese military manoeuvres across the line of control in Ladakh while the Kargil war was raging between the Indian military and Pakistani invaders on Ladakh's opposite front. As Jung Chang and Jon Halliday have revealed, Mao Zedong, even after the 1962 invasion, was itching in 1965 to use 'Pakistan's war with India...to score another victory over India' by opening a Himalayan front against it. 'He moved troops up to the border, and issued two ultimatums, demanding that India dismantle alleged outposts on some territory Beijing claimed within three days'. But Mao found himself out on a limb and 'deeply frustrated' when, despite his urging to fight on, Pakistan suddenly accepted a ceasefire before the expiry of China's deadline.[41]

When Indian forces were battling to evict Pakistani army encroachers from their holdouts inside Indian territory in Kargil in 1999, the People's Liberation Army carried out provocative actions at that very time so as to build military pressure on India. These actions included the construction of a track linking Point Spanggur to Lake Pangong Tso in Ladakh; an exercise to build a road in Ladakh's disputed Trig Heights and gain control of that strategically important area; a brief incursion south of the line of control in the Demchok region of eastern Ladakh; and the deliberate initiation of a military standoff with Indian forces in Arunachal Pradesh's West Kameng district by setting up temporary posts at a place called Chantze.[42]

By testing India's military alertness and response capability and thereby keeping Indian troops bottled up along the Himalayas, China was seeking to aid the Pakistani military during the Kargil war — an aim also underlined by the promptness with which it made the PLA conventional-weapons chief available for advice in Islamabad on how the encroaching Pakistani forces could better direct their firepower against the Indans. To help bail out Pakistan, Beijing wanted India to keep Kargil as a limited, localized war by refraining from doing what any military would do when confronted with aggression in one sector — relieve pressure by opening another front where the foe is weak or ill-prepared.

Beijing's actions thus were intended to ensure that India was not relocating any forces from the Tibet frontier to the Pakistan border. Due to its own leadership's pusillanimity, India ended up fighting the entire Kargil war on its territory on terms dictated by the aggressor state, with the U.S.-midwifed outcome leaving a wounded, not a vanquished, enemy. Before long, the wounded foe responded by stepping up terror attacks against India, with crossborder terrorism in the post-Kargil period rapidly morphing from hit-and-run attacks to daring suicide assaults on Indian military camps and national emblems of power, such as the Red Fort and Parliament.

In recent years nothing has better exposed Beijing's true attitude than Jiang Zemin's spiteful dig at India in a private conversation with French President Jacques Chirac in late 1999. Referring to the Chinese cross-frontier military forays earlier that year to test Indian defence preparedness along the line of control, the then Chinese president mockingly told Chirac: 'Each time we tested them by sending patrols across, the Indian soldiers reacted by putting their hands up.' Jiang raised his own hands up to drive home the point to a horrified Chirac.[43] Blaming the 1962 war on Indian 'aggression', Jiang went on to warn: 'If India were to attack China again, we will crush it.' He squeezed his hands together to stress the word 'crush' in what was a live demonstration to his French host of the creeping Chinese arrogance.

The People's Republic of China remains scornful both of India's aspiration to be a permanent member of the United Nations Security Council as well as of its status as the world's biggest representative democracy. In the way Mao derided the Indian model and Jiang ridiculed India, Chinese Vice Foreign Minister Wang Yi, in a 2003 meeting with American academics, dismissed as meaningless all talk of China learning from India's democratic experience, calling India 'a tribal democracy' with an uncertain future.[44] It is no wonder that China tried to exclude India from the East Asian Summit (EAS) and the proposed East Asian Community (EAC).

Yet, over the years, India has steadily eroded its leverage and room for manoeuvre vis-à-vis its main long-term rival. Unwilling to shape up to the challenge posed by Beijing's accumulating power and strategic plans, India has become averse to treating China even as a competitor, preferring to shelter behind the calcinatory rhetoric of cooperation. But cooperation on equal terms demands at least the political will to face the competition. Without being at a disadvantage, India can cooperate with China on what? On promoting a multipolar world, when China seeks to fashion a unipolar Asia? On regulating competition or energy assets, when China's egotistical autocrats revel in outbidding others, even if it jacks up prices to artificial levels? On building defence cooperation, when bilateral exchanges and exercises remain tokenistic and Beijing persists with inimical actions?

Just because India poses no threat to China doesn't mean the converse is also true. Yet romanticized visions of cooperation have remained popular in India, even as China has continued to pursue ruthless pragmatism. Despite New Delhi's pronounced accent on cooperation, Beijing is not going to shy away from ploughing more and more of its resources into activities and capabilities antithetical to Indian interests and security.

Through its ambitions and actions, however, China is unwittingly contributing to changes in strategic thinking and policy in Asian states, particularly in Japan and India. Also, inadvertently, Beijing is aiding the establishment of a closer equation in the third part of the strategic triangle — between Japan and India.

Godzilla and Eagle Warm Up to Tiger

Japan, as if to make up for decades of neglect, is enthusiastically recognizing India's potential as an investment destination and strategic partner. Reversing a long-standing pattern, Tokyo now provides more development loans to India than to China. After having provided China with nearly $30 billion in official development assistance (ODA) over a quarter century, Japan under Prime Minister Koizumi cut development aid to China in half, with the intent to phase it out entirely by fiscal 2008. The biggest beneficiary has been India, which now tops the list of recipients of such concessionary credit.[45]

Japan's interest in India noticeably increased after China's April 2005 anti-Japanese mob protests, which reminded Japanese businesses of the risks they face in China. The protests psychologically rattled Japanese portfolio investors in particular. To help hedge their risks in China, Japanese institutional investors began to plough funds in a major way into the Indian stock markets, where dozens of companies boast market capitalizations greater than $1 billion each and where more than $400 billion of equity is traded. Such has been the inflow of Japanese funds to India since then that high stock valuations have spurred concern over a foreign-funded bubble in Indian equities.

In media comments just before departing from India in April 2005, visiting Chinese Premier Wen Jiabao bluntly laid out what lower-level Chinese diplomats had hinted at for weeks earlier: China will not allow Japan to secure a UN Security Council permanent seat until it 'faces up to history squarely'. It didn't occur to Wen that before asking Japan for yet another apology for its atrocities during World War II, Beijing should face up to its own historical misdeeds. Nor did it occur to him that his verbal assault on Japan would set in motion events disadvantageous to China but favourable to his host India.

The bountiful liquidity resulting from the Japanese-led global institutional inflows has had a twofold effect in India. India's foreign-exchange reserves have continued to swell. And the frenzied buying has blunted the attraction of Indian equity valuations, despite sporadic but feeble attempts at market correction. According to Lipper, a fund research unit of Reuters Group Plc., money from Japan alone accounted for 40 per cent of the net inflow from all foreign institutional funds to Indian equities in 2005, with some 500 billion yen ($4.3 billion) flowing into Indian stock markets in that year. The gush of Japanese institutional funds entering the Indian stock markets since then could presage a similar pattern in Japanese direct investment. Shifts in foreign direct investment patterns become visible, however, only over an extended period.

At least in the short term, China's loss has been India's gain. In the coming years, India is likely to increasingly benefit from closer ties with Japan, as the latter seeks to stay economically competitive with China and re-emerge as a 'normal' military power. An India–Japan strategic partnership involving, among other things, maritime cooperation to protect the vital sea lanes of communications could help stem the emerging power disequilibrium in Asia. For Japan and India, energy security and trade flows are dependent on secure routes through the Indian Ocean region. Given the ongoing Japanese reassessment of China, India should aggressively woo Japanese businesses to move some of their investments to its secure location. India needs Japanese technology and investment to sustain a GDP growth rate beyond 7 per cent annually.

An India–Japan strategic alliance can help offset the deleterious effects for New Delhi of the long-standing Sino–Pakistan nexus. While Beijing managed to uncouple the New Delhi–Moscow strategic link by building close ties with Russia and gaining access to important Russian military technologies, India has failed to dismantle the China–Pakistan nexus despite reaching out to Beijing politically and boosting bilateral trade. Beijing has always valued its Pakistan card to keep India boxed in on the subcontinent and prevent its rise as a peer competitor. Such is Pakistan's strategic worth in Chinese calculations that Beijing has continued to provide major aid to the Pakistani nuclear-weapons and missile programmes even after joining the NPT, paying little heed to its international legal obligations. In more recent years, Beijing has stepped up its strategic squeeze of India through Burma, Bangladesh and even Sri Lanka and Nepal — traditional pockets of Indian influence.

The effects of China's anti-Japanese mob protests and gunboat diplomacy, while already instilling caution and reappraisal in Japan, are likely to linger in Japanese public opinion, especially as Beijing gives further vent to its nationalistic ambitions. There has been no dearth of incidents vitiating the bilateral atmosphere, including the 2004 suicide of a Japanese diplomat in Shanghai who was reportedly the target of a Chinese intelligence honey trap.[46] Two days before the 2005 Japanese national election, a Japanese P-3C Orion maritime reconnaissance aircraft spotted five Chinese warships near the Chunxiao gas field in the East China Sea. It is unclear how long the vibrant Japan–China commercial ties can survive without harm from the sharpening political rhetoric and new mistrust.

With the Japan–U.S. security ties reinvigorated, the new U.S.–India global strategic partnership appears to foreshadow a geopolitical realignment in Asia. Such realignment, founded on an emerging geopolitical confluence of interests, will have an important bearing on global power relations. In an Asia characterized by a growing imbalance of power, a U.S.–India partnership can help contribute to long-term stability, order and equilibrium.

The July 2005 U.S.–India nuclear deal was a product of, not a precursor to, an Indian strategic shift. Before America agreed to consider relaxing civilian nuclear export controls against India, New Delhi had already consented to team up with Washington on matters vital to U.S. interests — from participating in U.S.-led 'multinational operations' and assenting to 'conclude defence transactions' and share intelligence[47] to joining the U.S.-directed non-proliferation regime (the first step of which was the May 2005 enactment by India of the Weapons of Mass Destruction Act).

When the controversial nuclear deal was unveiled on July 18, 2005,[48] it constituted just four paragraphs in a long 'Joint Statement' which roped in India as America's collaborator on yet more fronts — from a 'Global Democracy Initiative' to an enduring, military-to-military 'Disaster Response Initiative' designed, in the White House's words, for 'operations in the Indian Ocean region and beyond'. It is thus not a surprise that America believes that, 'India now is poised to shoulder global obligations in cooperation with the United States in a way befitting a major power'.[49]

For India, its warm ties with Washington both mirror and spur a major shift in public opinion at home. Such ties also boost India's international profile. Yet, to avoid the pitfalls and to better capitalize on those ties, India needs to fully absorb U.S. strategic aims. Moderation, pragmatism and subtlety should guide India's U.S. policy, not sentiment, hyperbole or false expectation. No durable partnership can be built without both sides being sensitive to each other's legitimate security and economic concerns.

For Japan and China, too, their relations with Washington remain central to their foreign-policy and economic interests. Beijing would like to emphasize cooperation with the United States where national interests overlap, while minimizing and managing the disrupting nature of the divergent interests. So convinced is China that its overall foreign-policy and economic objectives depend on a cooperative, if not benign, relationship with America that it has been gone to the extent of signalling that its domestic priorities, including fighting political corruption, rural unrest and widening income disparities, leave it with neither the will nor the means to challenge U.S. global primacy. At present, America's financial dependence on Chinese purchases of its debt is balanced by China's economic dependence on trade with the United States.

With the rhetoric of shared values sharper than ever, the U.S.–Japan security and commercial relationships have further expanded. U.S. officials have called the alliance 'the indispensable foundation of Japan's security' and 'the lynchpin of American security policy in Asia'. U.S. policy in recent years has been influenced by an October 2000 bipartisan report prepared under the leadership of former Deputy Secretary of State Richard Armitage, which recommended turning Japan into a full-fledged military partner — America's 'Britain in the East'. The growing strategic cooperation between Tokyo and Washington is symbolized by Japan's contributions to the U.S. missile-defence programme and the agreement the two countries hammered out in 2006 on the biggest restructuring in decades of the U.S. military in Japan. Under Prime Minister Koizumi, Japan loosened its constitutional constraints to transform the U.S.–Japan alliance into one with global reach. After sending Japanese naval tankers to the Indian Ocean to support U.S. and British forces operating in Afghanistan, Tokyo despatched about 600 troops to southern Iraq on a non-combat humanitarian mission. And when Koizumi finally decided to bring home the ground troops from occupied Iraq, he made the decision in consultation with the United States. The growing U.S. cooperation with Tokyo and New Delhi also helps smooth the progress of Japanese–Indian ties.

Shaping the Future

As they manage their own trilateral relationships, China, India and Japan will find that their ties with the U.S. carry both opportunity and risk, given America's determination to reinforce its strategic primacy in Asia. A new range of issues will constantly challenge the equations of the Asian strategic-triangle states with

America. The potential conflict-creating elements of the U.S.–China relationship are obvious. But America's lukewarm support to Japan's and India's bids for a permanent seat on the UN Security Council — and local opposition in Japan to U.S. military bases and in sovereignty-conscious India to America's efforts to influence Indian policies — underline the complexity of the various power permutations and relationships in Asia.

Furthermore, China and India are too big to effectively contain each other, and too proud to allow themselves to be used by another power. They have flirted with the idea of joining hands with Russia in a Eurasian 'strategic triangle' — a concept first floated by then-Russian Prime Minister Yevgeny Primakov in New Delhi in December 1998. Russia has not taken kindly either to America's establishment of military bases in Central Asia, Romania and Bulgaria or to NATO's 2004 expansion into the Baltic states in breach of post-1991 assurances that NATO would not push the alliance perimeter up to the Russian frontier. The United States not only has set up military bases along Russia's borders from the Baltic states and Poland to the Caucasus and Central Asia, but it also supported various 'colour revolutions' around the Russian periphery and unilaterally withdrew from the 1972 Anti-Ballistic Missile (ABM) Treaty — actions that were seen in Moscow as part of the 'strategic suppression' of an already-weakened Russia. The consequent rise of nationalism has led to Russia's transformation from a military superpower to an energy superpower that openly employs its oil and gas wealth for political ends. It has assertively sought to counter U.S. moves to persuade ex-Soviet states in Central Asia to build oil and gas pipelines that are outside of Moscow's control. Through internal consolidation, Russia has also worked hard to take Chechnya out from the East–West chessboard of big-power politics. Like Moscow, Beijing has been concerned over U.S.-backed 'colour revolutions' and U.S. military expansion in Central Asia.

Ever since Foreign Ministers Igor Ivanov of Russia, Yashwant Sinha of India and Tang Jiaxuan of China held the first-ever high-level 'triangular' meeting on the sidelines of the UN General Assembly in New York in 2002, there has been increased international interest in the follow-up to the idea. Russia-India-China (RIC) trilateral meetings have since become an annual feature, reflecting an effort to pluralize the global order. The expansion of RIC into a separate BRIC (Brazil-Russia-India-China) grouping has created a potentially powerful bloc, given the projections that the BRIC nations could surpass the present leading economies by the middle of this century. Yet it is true that there is little in common among the BRIC states, prompting cynics to call BRIC an acronymic ingenuity with no substance.

If China, India and Russia were to coalesce into a Eurasian anti-NATO axis, the threat to U.S. global pre-eminence would be self-evident: it would bring together formidable military and nuclear resources in the global heartland — and about 2.6 billion people — in an effort to build multipolarity in international relations.[50] In fact, China and India, the two biggest buyers of Russian weapons, have in recent years accounted for about 60 per cent of Russian arms exports.[51] The reality, however, is that all the three potential triangle members, despite their misgivings about American policies, value their relationship with the United States more than their ties with each other. Also, Sino–Indian and Sino–Russian relations remain riven by mutual suspicions and distrust.[52] Consequently, the concept of an axis has yet to be fleshed out in concrete terms.

Japan and India would like to build greater strategic manoeuvring room vis-à-vis the United States. To do so, they need to manage their relations with China in a way that increases such room. A sharp deterioration in ties with Beijing will increase Tokyo's or New Delhi's strategic need for U.S. help. Moreover, history testifies that a smaller power's partnership with a globally dominant power has never been easy, given the inherent asymmetry. What is more, such a partnership has rarely helped the smaller power secure a reliable friend. Tokyo and New Delhi thus face the challenge of building closer strategic engagement with Washington without weakening their autonomy in decision making.

Broadly, the dynamics of international relations in Asia are changing fundamentally in a way that carries important global ramifications, with the rapid rise of China serving as a major catalyst.[53] In the years ahead, the main challenge in Asia will be to prevent the increasingly overt strategic competition among the major powers from descending into a strategic clash. The success in meeting that challenge will largely be determined by how relations evolve within the China–India–Japan strategic triangle, including in conjunction with America's promotion of its interests in the Asia–Pacific region. The U.S. role, centred on expanding security and economic interests primarily through robust partnerships and a forward military-deployment posture, will have a significant bearing on equations within this triangle.

Just as China's accumulating power presently is the single biggest contributor to geopolitical change in Asia, the future course pursued by that communist-ruled state will be the principal determinant of Asian stability and security, even as major power relations on the continent become more and more multidimensional. An open question is how long the Chinese Communist Party will succeed in retaining its monopoly on power through economic growth and heightened nationalism, without the state being compelled by events to carry out major political reforms. Like the rise of most powers in world history, China became a military power first before becoming an economic power. While it was still poor and economically backward, it armed itself with nuclear weapons and developed its first intercontinental-range ballistic missile. But now, as it showcases its arrival as an economic powerhouse, its economic might is coming in handy to bolster its military capabilities.

China has evolved in important ways but its authoritarian political structure remains intact, mirrored in the arbitrary detention of citizens, unfair trials and the execution each year of the largest number of people anywhere in the world. Yet the benign portrayal of the emerging China is best exemplified by the 2006 book of Qian Qichen, a highly influential former Chinese vice premier who contends that his country will threaten no one but only make the rest of the world wealthier as it gets wealthy.[54] China's neighbours certainly hope that the 'Middle Kingdom' will pursue a 'peaceful rise', but none can bet its future on such an ascent. As one analyst has put it, 'punditry about Beijing's true intentions is about as dicey as predicting the fertility of mating pandas'.[55] The combination of a vibrant centralized economy, growing military might and increasingly fervent nationalism has turned China into a central player in Asia and a major force in international institutions.

History, geopolitics and conflicting national goals will continue to cast a shadow on equations in Asia's strategic triangle. China pursues its Asian strategy in keeping with its larger goal to emerge as Asia's 'natural leader'. In fact, its strategic alliances and partnerships suggest that it is seeking to manoeuvre towards a dominance of power in Asia. For Japan, the challenge is to prevent the strategic balance in East Asia from changing adversely against its interests.

For India, there is now just one credible option — a single-minded pursuit of comprehensive national power. If instead of industrializing rapidly through infrastructure growth, reform of antediluvian labour laws and open competition in labour-intensive manufacturing, India remains content with an average GDP growth of 7 per cent or less versus China's 9.6 per cent, it will find it more difficult to build a level-playing field with Beijing. And if it continues to pare down its defence spending, it will enlarge the asymmetry. While China has maintained double-digit growth in annual military appropriations since before 1990, India has allowed its defence spending to plummet from 3.59 per cent of GDP in fiscal 1987–88 to barely 2 per cent in 2009–10. If India is to be recognized as a major international power, it has to start behaving and acting like one. So far, it has displayed the airs of being a great power without demonstrating the stomach or the spine to be one.

Resolving the disputes over history in Asia will not be easy, especially because they have become politically tied with issues of national identity and even jingoism. While a booming China, having embarked on a dizzying kind of an economic and strategic waltz, wishes to make the most of the history card, the national debates over history textbooks even in democracies like Japan and India indicate the difficulty in ensuring objective history.

History, after all, is written by victors and abounds in well-cultivated myths. For example, the myths about Mao Zedong, including his military exploits and triumphs over imperialism and capitalism, have helped sustain the Chinese communists in power, even as a transformed China now practises capitalism and presents itself as a large empire with even larger imperial ambitions. But while there is room for debate and correction of historical interpretations in democracies, there is none in dictatorships 'that use history as one more tool to maintain power'.[56] The target of Beijing's revisionism, which was the Soviet Union at one point and is now Japan, could become America when China gains political ascendancy in Asia. In the short term, however, Beijing desires a stable, non-confrontational relationship with the United States to help accumulate additional strength and spread its influence wider.

Despite the daunting challenge posed by issues of history,

Asia needs to find ways to ensure that unassuaged historical grievances do not cast a shadow on its building of a better future. If not, the Asian renaissance may be stillborn. Indeed, a more cooperative and integrated Asia cannot emerge without its major states backing away from nationalism and the political use of history. While drawing appropriate lessons from their history, Asian states need to move on, without being weighed down by ugly memories of the past. China illustrates the counterproductive use of history: not only has Beijing stirred nationalistic passions in Japan, but also it has made it more likely that the Chinese will come to confront what they would have liked to avert — a resurgent, assertive Japan.

While Asia wrestles with history, the disputes over how to correctly interpret the past seemingly invoke the Orwellian dictum that he who controls the past controls the future, and he who controls the present dictates the reading of the past. The controllers of the present want to manipulate the way the past is portrayed so that it more fittingly gives credence to their goals for the future.

Notes and References

1. Masaru Tamamoto, 'Is Japan Re-entering the World of International Power Politics? Japanese Discovery of Democracy', Japan Institute of International Affairs (JIIA) Commentary No. 1 (Tokyo: JIIA, April 26, 2006).
2. Joseph S. Nye Jr., 'Soft Power Matters in Asia', *Japan Times*, December 5, 2005.
3. Norimitsu Onishi, 'A Rising Korean Wave: If Seoul Sells It, China Craves It', *International Herald Tribune*, January 3, 2006.
4. Jung Chang and Jon Halliday, *Mao: The Unknown Story* (London: Jonathan Cape, 2005). Mao could confide in Stalin as the Soviet strongman had played an important role in Mao's own rise, according to the book.
5. Cited in Brahma Chellaney, 'Fatal Attraction', *The Hindustan Times*, August 22, 2001.
6. H.Y. Sharada Prasad, A.K. Damodaran and Sarvepalli Gopal

(eds.), *Selected Works of Jawaharlal Nehru,* Second Series, Vol. 29, 1 June–31 August 1955 (New Delhi: Oxford University Press, 2005). The volume, cited 'as an indispensable reference for research into modern India', on p. 231, also reveals the following significant statements contained in the minutes of Nehru's meeting at Moscow on June 22, 1955 with Soviet Premier Marshal Nikolai Aleksandrovich Bulganin:

> BULGANIN: While we are discussing the general international situation and reducing tension, we propose suggesting at a later stage India's inclusion as the sixth member of the Security Council.
>
> NEHRU: Perhaps Bulganin knows that some people in USA have suggested that India should replace China in the Security Council. This is to create trouble between us and China. We are, of course, wholly opposed to it. Further, we are opposed to pushing ourselves forward to occupy certain positions because that may itself create difficulties, and India might itself become a subject of controversy. If India is to be admitted to the Security Council it raises the question of the revision of the Charter of the UN. We feel that this should not be done till the question of China's admission and possibly of others is first solved. I feel that we should first concentrate on getting China admitted.

7. Defending the Panchsheel pact, Nehru said in Parliament: 'Several Honourable Members have referred to the "Melancholy Chapter of Tibet". I really do not understand.... What did any Honourable Member of this House expect us to do in regard to Tibet at any time?... The fact is, and it is a major fact of the middle of the 20th century, that China has become a great power, united and strong.'

8. Claude Arpi, *Born in Sin: The Panchsheel Agreement — The Sacrifice of Tibet* (New Delhi: Mittal, 2004).

9. Item Nos. 1 and 2 in the 'Notes Exchanged' concurrently with the 'Agreement between the Republic of India and the People's Republic of China on Trade and Intercourse between Tibet Region of China and India'. (See Appendix A for full text).

10. Once the People's Liberation Army (PLA) came to occupy Tibet,

'Nehru completely changed his policy tactics towards the PRC. There was virtually nothing, he and [K.M. Panikkar, his adviser] concluded, that India could do militarily to dislodge the PLA from Tibet. Therefore, rather than fruitlessly antagonize Beijing by maintaining the old British policy, New Delhi should befriend New China by all means and at almost any cost. This friendship policy was expected to reduce or neutralize the security threat from the PLA stationed in Tibet, as well as enhance Asian solidarity. The Panchsheel Agreement (1954), which sacrificed Tibet's historical status at the altar of Sino–Indian friendship (*Hindi–Chini bhai bhai*), should be seen in this perspective'. Dawa Norbu, 'Tibet in Sino–Indian Relations: The Centrality of Marginality', *Asian Survey*, Vol. XXXVII, No. 11 (November 1997), pp. 1083–84.

11. Chang and Halliday, *Mao: The Unknown Story*.

12. For a detailed account drawing on new Chinese material on how Mao planned the attack on India to achieve a swift, decisive victory, see Roderick MacFarquhar, *The Origins of the Cultural Revolution*, Vol. 3: *The Coming of the Cataclysm 1961–1966* (New York: Oxford University Press and Columbia University Press, 1997). Discrediting Neville Maxwell's thesis, *India's China War* (New York: Pantheon Books, 1970), MacFarquhar, in a section titled 'Mao's India War', details how the Chinese carefully planned the offensive and used Nehru's unguarded remarks ('our instructions are to free our territory') to brand India the aggressor (pp. 308–10).

13. Japan provided this official development assistance (ODA) to China largely as long-term, low-interest yen loans that helped finance major infrastructure projects, such as the construction of harbours and railways. 'Phasing out China's ODA', editorial, *Japan Times*, March 23, 2005.

14. Howard W. French and Norimitsu Onishi, 'Economic Ties Binding Japan to Rival China', *New York Times*, October 31, 2005.

15. Howard W. French, 'India and China Woo Cross-Border Business', *International Herald Tribune*, November 8, 2005, p. 13 and Niraj Dawar, 'Prepare Now for Sino–Indian Trade Boom', *Financial Times*, October 30, 2005.

16. Minxim Pei and Michael Swaine, 'Simmering Fire in Asia: Averting Sino–Japanese Strategic Conflict', Policy Brief No. 44 (Washington, D.C.: Carnegie Endowment for

International Peace, November 2005), p. 1.

17. See, for example, Edward Cody, 'China Gives No Ground in Spats Over History', *Washington Post*, September 22, 2004, p. A25.

18. The Simla conference, from October 1913 to July 1914, was a tripartite one, with Tibet an equal party. While Tibet demanded recognition of its sovereignty, China seemed willing to let Inner Tibet be autonomous if Outer Tibet recognized Chinese 'suzerainty'. The conference, however, broke down over additional Chinese demands on Tibet.

19. Just as Atal Bihari Vajpayee returned from Lahore in 1999 with a shared 'vision of peace' with Pakistan that he swore constituted 'a defining moment' in Indo–Pakistan relations, he came back from his 2003 China visit vowing that Beijing now 'fully reciprocates our desire for mutual goodwill'.

20. Official text of the Agreement between the Government of the Republic of India and the Government of the People's Republic of China on the Political Parameters and Guiding Principles for the Settlement of the India–China Boundary Question, signed on April 11, 2005 (New Delhi: Government of India). (For the text, see Appendix K.)

21. Article 6 of the 1963 Sino–Pakistan Frontier Agreement reads: 'The two parties have agreed that after the settlement of the Kashmir dispute between Pakistan and India, the sovereign authority concerned will reopen negotiations with the Government of the People's Republic of China on the boundary as described in Article Two of the present agreement, so as to sign a formal boundary treaty to replace the present agreement, provided that in the event of the sovereign authority being Pakistan, the provisions of the present agreement and of the aforesaid protocol shall be maintained in the formal boundary treaty to be signed between the People's Republic of China and Pakistan.'

22. Associated Press, 'Japan Approves Teikoku Oil's Request to Drill in East China Sea, Sets Off Showdown with Beijing', July 14, 2005.

23. Robert Marquand, 'Japan–China Tensions Rise over Tiny Islands', *Christian Science Monitor*, February 11, 2005.

24. Koji Taira, 'The China–Japan Clash over the Diaoyu/Senkaku Islands', *The Ryukyuanist* (Spring 2004).

25. Tamamoto, 'Is Japan Re-entering the World of International

Power Politics?'

26. Philip Bowring, 'Understanding Taiwan's History', *International Herald Tribune*, May 20, 2000.

27. John F. Copper, *Taiwan: Nation-State or Province?* (Boulder, Colorado: Westview, 1996), pp. 31–32.

28. An example is *Unrestricted Warfare*, authored by two PLA senior colonels, Qiao Liang of the PLA Air Force Political Department, and Wang Xiangsui of the Guangzhou Military District PLA Air Force Political Department. Published in February 1999, the book focuses on winning asymmetric warfare by a variety of means, including unconventional.

29. Chong-Pin Lin, 'Beijing Speaks Softly to Taiwan', *International Herald Tribune*, March 29, 2006.

30. Arpi, *Born in Sin: The Panchsheel Agreement*.

31. See, for example, Peter Perdue, *China Marches West: The Qing Conquest of Central Eurasia* (Cambridge, Massachusetts: Belknap Press, 2005) and Emma Jinhua Teng, *Taiwan's Imagined Geography: Chinese Colonial Travel Writing and Pictures, 1683–1895* (Cambridge, Massachusetts: Harvard University Press, 2004).

32. A recent study, using official Chinese statistics, shows how ethnic Tibetans are becoming increasingly marginalized in the local economy. Andre Martin Fischer, *State Growth and Social Exclusion in Tibet: Challenges of Recent Economic Growth* (Copenhagen: Nordic Institute of Asian Studies Press, 2005).

33. Howard W. French, 'Railroad Marvel Conquers China's Terrain: But Route to Tibet Ignores Its People', *International Herald Tribune*, September 10–11, 2005.

34. *Renmin Ribao*, September 27, 2002.

35. For details, see Amnesty International, *People's Republic of China: Sustaining Conflict and Human Rights Abuses* (London: Amnesty International, June 12, 2006).

36. Section VIII titled, 'Develop Agendas for Cooperative Action with the Other Main Centres of Global Power', in White House, *The National Security Strategy of the United States of America* (Washington, D.C.: White House, March 2006).

37. Eric Margolis, *War at the Top of the World: The Struggle for Afghanistan, Kashmir and Tibet* (London: Routledge, 2002).

38. Amarinder Singh, *Lest We Forget* (Patiala, Punjab: Regiment of Ludhiana Welfare Association, 1999).

39. For example, then Chinese Premier Zhu Rongji, during a

visit to New Delhi in January 2002, declared: 'China has never viewed India as a threat nor do we believe India will regard China as a threat.'

40. Howard W. French, 'Letter from China: U.S.–China Relationship Isn't the Most Vital One', *International Herald Tribune*, May 3, 2006.

41. Chang and Halliday, *Mao: The Unknown Story*.

42. General V.P. Malik, *Kargil: From Surprise to Victory* (New Delhi: HarperCollins India, 2006), pp. 297–98.

43. For full details of Jiang's dig at India, see Brahma Chellaney, 'Belligerence Unprovoked: Jiang Zemin Ridicules India', *The Hindustan Times*, January 31, 2000, p. 1.

44. Mohan Malik, 'India's Dragon Delusions', *Asia Times*, October 17, 2003, at:
http://www.atimes.com/atimes/South_Asia/EJ17Df03.html

45. A total of $1.3 billion in Japanese concessionary credit was earmarked for India for the fiscal year ending in March 2007, making New Delhi the top recipient of Japanese loans for the third consecutive year.

46. It was not until late 2005 that the Japanese government blamed 'regrettable actions', in violation of the Vienna Convention on Diplomatic Relations, by Chinese security agencies for the suicide. The diplomat, in charge of encrypted communications at the Japanese consulate in Shanghai, was allegedly being blackmailed over his affair with a hostess to provide classified intelligence to Chinese agents. 'Ministry Defends Not Telling Koizumi of Diplomat's Suicide', *Japan Times*, January 12, 2006, p. 1.

47. These elements form part of the June 28, 2005, defence-framework agreement between the United States and India.

48. The four-paragraph nuclear 'deal' in the July 18, 2005, Joint Statement signed by President George W. Bush and Prime Minister Manmohan Singh reads as follows:

Recognizing the significance of civilian nuclear energy for meeting growing global energy demands in a cleaner and more efficient manner, the two leaders discussed India's plans to develop its civilian nuclear energy programme. President Bush conveyed his appreciation to the Prime

Minister over India's strong commitment to preventing WMD proliferation and stated that as a responsible state with advanced nuclear technology, India should acquire the same benefits and advantages as other such states. The President told the Prime Minister that he will work to achieve full civil nuclear energy cooperation with India as it realizes its goals of promoting nuclear power and achieving energy security. The President would also seek agreement from Congress to adjust U.S. laws and policies, and the United States will work with friends and allies to adjust international regimes to enable full civil nuclear energy cooperation and trade with India, including but not limited to expeditious consideration of fuel supplies for safeguarded nuclear reactors at Tarapur. In the meantime, the United States will encourage its partners to also consider this request expeditiously. India has expressed its interest in ITER [International Thermonuclear Experimental Reactor] and a willingness to contribute. The United States will consult with its partners considering India's participation. The United States will consult with the other participants in the Generation IV International Forum with a view toward India's inclusion.

The Prime Minister conveyed that for its part, India would reciprocally agree that it would be ready to assume the same responsibilities and practices and acquire the same benefits and advantages as other leading countries with advanced nuclear technology, such as the United States. These responsibilities and practices consist of identifying and separating civilian and military nuclear facilities and programmes in a phased manner and filing a declaration regarding its civilian facilities with the International Atomic Energy Agency (IAEA); taking a decision to place voluntarily its civilian nuclear facilities under IAEA safeguards; signing and adhering to an Additional Protocol with respect to civilian nuclear facilities; continuing India's unilateral moratorium on nuclear testing; working with the United States for the conclusion of a multilateral Fissile Material Cut-off Treaty; refraining from transfer of enrichment and reprocessing technologies to states that do not have them and supporting international efforts to limit their spread; and ensuring that the necessary steps have been taken to secure nuclear materials and technology through comprehensive export control legislation and through harmonization and adherence to Missile Technology Control Regime (MTCR) and Nuclear Suppliers Group (NSG) guidelines.

The President welcomed the Prime Minister's assurance. The two leaders agreed to establish a working group to undertake on a phased basis in the months ahead the necessary actions mentioned above to fulfil these commitments. The President and Prime Minister also agreed that they would review this progress when the President visits India in 2006.

49. White House, *The National Security Strategy of the United States of America.*

50. Tyler Marshall, 'Russia, China and India: Do Closer Ties Bode U.S. Ill?', *Los Angeles Times*, September 28, 1999.

51. Victor M. Gobarev, 'India as a World Power: Changing Washington's Myopic Policy', *Policy Analysis*, No. 381 (September 11, 2000).

52. The Sino–Russian Treaty for Good Neighbourliness, Friendship and Cooperation signed in 2001 and the subsequent border agreement have done little to assuage Russian concerns over a China that is economically and militarily ascendant and poses a demographic challenge to thinly populated Eastern Serbia and the southern part of Russia's Far East — areas which came under the sway of the strong Manchu Empire before the treaties of 1858 and 1860 returned them to Russia.

53. See David Shambaugh (ed.), *Power Shift: China and Asia's New Dynamics* (Washington, D.C.: Brookings Institution, 2006).

54. Qian Qichen, *Ten Episodes in China's Diplomacy* (London: HarperCollins, 2006).

55. Tom Plate, 'Engaging with China Beats Other Options', *Japan Times*, April 2, 2006.

56. Fred Hiatt, 'China's Selective Memory', *Washington Post*, April 18, 2005, p. A17.

5

Averting Strategic Conflict in Asia

T HE MAJOR GEOPOLITICAL CHANGES UNDERWAY IN THE world are most conspicuous in relation to Asia. The rising importance of Asia at a time of the ongoing shifts in global economic and political power foreshadows a much different world — a world characterized by greater distribution of power as well as new opportunities and uncertainties. Fortifying its renaissance, Asia will be a central player in the emerging world. But the shifts in world geopolitics will also test Asia's ability to assume a leadership role in international relations.

A fundamental and qualitative reordering of power in Asia characterized by tectonic shifts is already challenging strategic stability and effecting equations among the continent's three major powers that hold the key to a cooperative security environment. As they manoeuvre for strategic advantage, China, India and Japan are transforming relations between and among themselves in a way that portends closer strategic engagement between New Delhi and Tokyo, and sharper competition between China on one side and Japan and India on the other.

Yet, given the fact that India and China point across the mighty Himalayas in very different geopolitical directions and that Japan and China are separated by sea, they need not pose a threat to each other, especially if they were to abstain from hostile actions against one another and strive to avoid confrontation. The interests of the three powers are getting intertwined to the extent that the pursuit of unilateral solutions by any one of them will disturb the peaceful diplomatic environment on which their continued economic growth and security depend.

Ensuring that the Japan–China and China–India competition does not slide into strategic conflict will nonetheless remain a key challenge in Asia. That, in turn, demands that a strong China, a strong Japan and a strong India find ways to reconcile their interests in Asia so that they can peacefully coexist and prosper. Never before in history have all three of these powers been strong at the same time. In fact, there is no previous history of the three powers having been involved in a bilateral or trilateral contest for pre-eminence across Asia.

The emergence of China as a global player is transforming the geopolitical landscape like no other development. Not since Japan rose to world-power status during the reign of the Meiji Emperor has another non-Western power emerged with such potential to alter the global order as China has today. However, as history testifies, the rise of a new world power usually creates volatility in the international system, especially when the concerned power is not a democracy. Such has been the transformation of China that, while preserving communist rule and Confucian culture, it has gone in one generation from all ideology and token materialism to all materialism and token ideology.

China's ascent, however, is dividing Asia, not bringing Asian states closer. Economic powerhouse Japan is determined to shore up its security and, despite its concerns over fraying ties with Beijing, wishes to ensure that China does not call the shots in East Asia. After its World War II ignominy, Japan turned a necessity into a virtue by defining an anti-war identity anchored in its U.S.-imposed Constitution and a strategy emphasizing economic modernization and global peace. Now, it is starting to shed decades of pacifism and reassert itself in world affairs. India's continued economic rise, coupled with its political realism and growing self-confidence, has made it a key factor in Asian geopolitics. It will be unwilling to cede its leadership role in southern Asia.

In the emerging Asia, the two major non-Western democracies, India and Japan, look like natural allies as China drives them closer together. An India–Japan strategic partnership, involving naval cooperation to protect vital sea lanes of communication, could help adjust balance-of-power equations in Asia and build long-term stability and equilibrium. After all, whether a multipolar Asia or a Sino-centric Asia emerges will be decided in the Indian Ocean region, not in East Asia, where the power balance is largely clear.

Battle for the Heartland of Asia

How the China–Japan, China–India and Japan–India equations evolve in the coming years will have a crucial bearing on Asian and global security. Concerned over dragon China's lengthening shadow over Asia, Godzilla Japan and tiger India are bracing for a strategic challenge in the Asian heartland, not to gain pre-eminence but to thwart pre-eminence.

After extraordinary economic growth since the late 1970s — a period which also saw its emergence as a global military power armed with intercontinental ballistic missiles (ICBMs) — China is seeking to be the pre-eminent power in a vast region stretching from the Mongolian steppe to the Indian Ocean and to the Philippines, while aspiring for greater political and economic influence in Africa and Latin America. It is also working to position itself along the vital sea lanes from the Persian Gulf to the South China Sea.

With the Chinese giant already well-entrenched across the Himalayas on the Tibetan massif, India now is gearing up to the likely arrival of Chinese submarines in its strategic backyard — the Indian Ocean, which is vital to world trade and oil shipments. Close to half of the world's overseas commerce, and much of the global oil export supplies, pass through the Indian Ocean region. Japan's defence posture is also undergoing a subtle but visible change in response to the relentless advance of the Chinese juggernaut. The Japan Defence Agency has been elevated to full ministry status as popular support has grown for creation of more security options.

China's rise as an international power — and as a potential superpower — has already become a principal catalyst in the shift of the world's centre of gravity to Asia. China's emergence as a global economic giant is evident from just one fact — its international trade volume was $2.5 trillion in 2008, or 57 per cent of its GDP, making it one of the most trade-dependent economies in the world. Given the huge investments it has made in setting up a lot of factories and producing more goods than its economy can possibly absorb, China will continue to relentlessly seek greater markets for exports and thereby keep its trade surplus at a high level.[1] Its fiscal policy indeed promotes major price distortions that favour goods-producing and exporting industries.

At the same time, China's foreign-currency reserves (another important measure of a country's economic progress) went from $11 billion in 1990 to more than $2.2 trillion in 2009. Yet, its entrenched authoritarianism, vibrant centralized economy, growing military might and unbridled ambition to be 'a world power second to none' underscore the larger challenge it poses as it aims to change the international status quo in its favour. Its accumulating military capabilities have already begun to decisively shift the balance of military power in Asia.

But just as China's moment in the sun began arriving, the land of the rising sun, Nippon or Japan, is feeling threatened by the lengthening shadow of a neighbouring giant whose economic modernization it helped spur by providing nearly $30 billion in cheap yen loans over a quarter century. As if to make this threat look real, China's sharpening rhetoric against Japan has unwittingly shaken Tokyo out of its complacency and diffidence, setting in motion the political resurgence of Japan and its return as a 'normal', or even a great, military power. It is only a matter of time before Japan comes out of its pacifist cocoon.

Such a move would include Japan transforming its Self-Defence Forces into a real military, revising Article 9 of its U.S.-authored Constitution, and asserting its rights on the Asian and global arenas. Japan's $53.3 billion annual military budget is nearly twice that of India, although it makes up less than 1 per cent of the Japanese GDP. Japan is smaller than California but, with 127.28 million citizens, is over four times more crowded than California. Yet it remains an economic giant, with a per capita GDP of $34,300. Per-capita income in China is still less than a tenth that in Japan, although China has a population 10 times larger.[2] Technologically, Japan has world-class capabilities in several fields. The Japan Aerospace Exploration Agency's successes, for example, have helped pave the way for Japan's entry into the international commercial rocket business.

Japan and Germany have been spectacular economic-success stories, rising from the ashes of their World War II defeat and occupation. Today, both Japan and Germany — whose histories, significantly, have run in parallel since the 1930s — are asserting their right to permanent seats at the UN Security Council after having loosened their constitutional constraints on sending military forces overseas. Both are desirous of emerging fully from the shadows of history. Yet their past, including notions of racial purity and superiority that drove their aggressions, remains a hindrance to their gaining wider acceptance to play a leadership role in their respective continents and the larger world.

Unlike Germany, however, Japan today faces a direct challenge from a neighbouring power that is assertively expanding its strategic space, even at Tokyo's expense. That power, China, also does not shy away from using the history card against Japan — for unabashedly political ends. It is true that by not coming to terms with its past as satisfactorily as Germany, Japan has made itself more vulnerable to the use of the history card against it. But it is equally true that few countries face up to history fully.

In fact, China is an egregious example of a country that covers up its communist-era historical misdeeds to whip up nationalism at home over more distant history. Even if Japanese politicians were to stop paying homage at the Yasukuni Shrine — a Shinto memorial to Japan's 2.5 million war dead, including top leaders such as Hideki Tojo, the wartime prime minister, who were convicted of 'crimes against peace' by the Allied powers' war crimes tribunal and exceuted — China is unlikely to cease employing its history card against Japan. In that situation, Beijing would still be able to exploit the textbooks issue and what it sees as insufficient Japanese penitence for past atrocities. However, if China's rulers had the capacity to take the long view and to think about the broader constellation of their national interests, they would not be inciting nationalism in Japan.

Although China and India are immediate neighbours today, sharing a long, disputed Himalayan frontier, they were separated throughout history by Tibet, a large buffer. The Chinese and Indian military frontiers met for the first time only in 1950 when China annexed Tibet. The Sino–Indian border dispute, which is still unresolved despite the 1962 war, is a consequence of China's forcible absorption of Tibet and its subsequent refusal to grant that region any autonomy. Sino–Japanese animosities have longer historical roots in contrast, with Japan inflicting a humiliating defeat on China in 1894–95, carving off Manchuria in 1931–32 as an independent state and invading the Chinese mainland in 1937.

At a time when the democratization of affluence is creating a new upwardly mobile class of Indians, the implications of the rising power of China are sinking in deeper in New Delhi. Indians can hardly forget that when China was poor and backward, it occupied Tibet, invaded India and began transferring weapons of mass destruction (WMD) technology to Pakistan. In the same way that India bore the brunt of the rise of international terrorism because of its geographical location next to the Afghanistan–Pakistan region, it now confronts the prospect of being frontally affected by the growing power of a next-door opaque empire practising classical balance-of-power politics. In fact, just as India has begun to shore up its decision-making autonomy and expand its role beyond its immediate region, it has to cope with an antagonistic China that strives to constrict Indian strategic space through direct and surrogate moves.

In that light, India can ill-afford to persist with its traditions of escapism. An India that remains soft and confused but miraculously enjoys international power due to its size or exemplary behaviour is a fantasy. India's main concern now should be to grow rich and strong speedily. The best way it can respond to the challenge from China is by emulating that country's single-minded focus on the development of comprehensive national power while steering clear of China's negative nationalistic elements and its mix of crony capitalism and widespread, state-dispensed patronage. There is absolutely no reason for it to develop China paranoia.

Interestingly, while China is reinterpreting the ideological basis of its revolution through the prism of nationalism, its friends in India's political and intellectual classes remain ideologically indebted to it. Such is the fidelity of many Indian communists to Beijing that they resist India undertaking the very measures that are making China powerful. As China dumps cheap manufactured goods in the Indian market, these powerful friends of Beijing oppose India acquiring similar capability through reform of its antediluvian labour laws and open competition in labour-intensive manufacturing — steps that will help accelerate an industrial renaissance in the country. Without a broad, labour-intensive manufacturing boom, India will continue to import more than it exports while being unable to alleviate unemployment and inequality. With its low wages and easy availability of labour, however, India is well placed to emerge as a manufacturing hub as the gold-rush mentality that drove multinationals to China gives way to greater corporate realism and a desire to hedge risks by diversifying production.

Income disparities are greater in Chinese than Indian society, according to the UNDP's yearly Human Development Reports; yet Maoism now has more followers in India than China. That only goes to show that citizens in China, by and large, have forsaken ideology and taken to capitalism like fish to water. At least on one score — political corruption — India is virtually level with China. The effects of corruption on any system are insidious. In China, rampant corruption represents both a lack of confidence in, and a threat to, the communist system. In the case of India, where a free, open system demands transparency and public accountability, unchecked corruption risks undermining the faith of citizens in democracy.

To sustain its pride as the world's largest democracy, India has to demonstrate that fair elections bring not just new governments but also good, clean, national interest-focused governance. Having disproved that its inherited social values are a barrier to rapid economic growth, India can now show that those values do not promote a lack of accountability or a tolerance of corruption. Without a check on corruption, India will find it difficult to realize its great-power ambitions.

More broadly, a nation's prosperity, security and international standing depend not only on its domestic policies but also on how it projects itself externally and to what extent it is able to advance its interests with other states. The strength of any nation's foreign and trade policies depends on the vitality of its institutional processes of decision making, on the unwavering pursuit of realistic goals through astute strategies and tactics, on the timely exploitation of opportunities thrown up by external conditions and on prudent, clear-minded diplomacy. The battle for the heartland of Asia will be shaped by how China, India and Japan measure up to such demands of statecraft.

Corralling the Nationalism Demon

Resurgent nationalism is the single biggest threat to Asian renaissance. Take the salient case of China. For a rapidly rising power that barely disguises its aim to dominate Asia, it is counterproductive to kindle fear among its neighbours through truculent actions or words. Given its accumulating economic and military power, China should be consciously seeking to do the opposite — to allay the concerns of countries in Asia and elsewhere by eschewing both strident nationalistic rhetoric and sabre rattling.

Yet, the domestic political imperatives of replacing the increasingly ineffectual communist ideology with fervent nationalism have prompted the Chinese leadership to act short-sightedly and set off alarm bells in other lands. From the threat to nuke Los Angeles, to allowing slogan-chanting, unruly protestors to take to the streets against Japan and to aggressively bidding for overseas energy assets, the neo-Leninists in Beijing have only helped present their country as a threat to others. Consequently, the leadership's calculated efforts to camouflage in soft terms Beijing's wielding of hard power have not carried credibility, including the claims about China's 'peaceful rise' and its 'win-win' engagement with the rest of the world. In fact, the seemingly benign theory of a 'peaceful rise' has been propounded to carry an evocative message: that China's emergence as a great power is inevitable and that the rest of the world needs to accommodate and adjust to that rise.[3]

As the fabled Middle Kingdom, China has claimed to be the mother of all civilizations, weaving legend with history to foster an ultra-nationalistic political culture centred on the regaining of supposedly lost glory. It even sees a historical entitlement to superpower status. In territorial size, China has come a long way in history since the time the Great Wall represented the Han empire's outer security perimeter. Nonetheless, self-cultivated myths have driven China to chase greater territorial and maritime claims.

China, admittedly, has displayed a new foreign-policy subtleness in recent years, which is a far cry from the coarse image its earlier communist rulers presented, especially when they set out, in then Premier Zhou Enlai's words, to 'teach India a lesson' in 1962, or when, to quote late strongman Deng Xiaoping, they similarly sought to 'teach a lesson to Vietnam' in 1979. The refinement is happening under the same party that directed those military adventures at a time when China was impecunious and internally troubled, lacking the power-projection force capability it has since developed. Yet the new subtleness is being undermined by the way the Chinese leadership is willing to openly mix history with its politics, as the scripted anti-Japanese mob protests in the spring of 2005 and the more recent Himalayan border provocations exemplified.

Another case in point occurred at a 2005 Bombay seminar when the Chinese consul-general — throwing diplomatic norms to the wind — audaciously talked down to the Indian defence minister at the meeting and then received public support from his ambassador in New Delhi. At the seminar, the Indian defence minister had fleetingly referred to two plain facts — 'the Chinese invasion of 1962' as a defining moment that set in motion India's new thrust on defence production and the still-festering border problem with China, which he said has resolved its land-frontier disputes 'with all its neighbours except India and Bhutan'.

Diplomatic propriety dictated that if the Bombay-based consul-general found the Indian defence minister's articulation of facts offensive, he should have written to his ambassador in New Delhi who, in turn, could have sought instructions from Beijing. Instead, the consul took his host nation's defence minister head-on, castigating him at the seminar for using the term 'invasion' and claiming 'China did not invade India'. As if to show the consul's conduct was no aberration, the Chinese ambassador in New Delhi later criticized the defence minister's reference to 1962, telling the Indian media, 'Whatever happened in the past is history and we want to put it back into history'.

What the incident revealed is the way China contradictorily deals in history vis-à-vis its neighbours to further its foreign-policy objectives. While it wants India to forget 1962, it misses no opportunity to hit Japan over the head with the history card. Its aim is not to extract more apologies from Tokyo for its World War II atrocities but to continually shame and tame Japan. In fact, visiting Chinese Premier Wen Jiabao had wantonly used Indian soil in April 2005 to demand that Japan 'face up to history squarely', setting the stage for his country's orchestrated anti-Japanese protests.

It didn't occur to the premier that before asking Japan for yet another apology for its atrocities during World War II, China should face up to its more recent history of naked aggression by apologizing to the Tibetans, Indians and Vietnamese. While railing against the risk of renewed Japanese militarism in Asia, the premier appeared oblivious to the fact that his country has fought wars on four separate flanks in the years since it came under communist rule. Nor did it occur to him that his verbal assault on Japan would set in motion events disadvantageous to China. That is the kind of political short-sightedness that could one day spell doom for the communist hold on power.

Another way China manipulates history is by reconstructing the past to prepare for the future. This was illustrated by the Chinese Foreign Ministry's posting on its Web site a revised historical claim that the ancient kingdom of Koguryo, founded in the Tongge River basin of northern Korea, was Chinese. The Koguryo kingdom bestrode the period before and after Christ and, at its height, included much of Manchuria. The posting of the claim in 2004 was seen as an attempt to hedge China's options with a potentially unified Korea. Then there is China's continued use of purported history to advance extravagant territorial claims. Its maps show an entire Indian state — Arunachal Pradesh — as well as other Indian areas as part of China.

China has yet to grasp that a muscular approach is counterproductive. Had it not set out to 'teach India a lesson',[4] that country probably would not have become the significant military and nuclear power that it is today. It took a long time for India to break out of the battered-victim syndrome fostered by the 1962 humiliation, the lessons of which still reverberate in New Delhi. What the invasion did achieve was to help lay the foundation of India's political rise. In that sense, the aggression did help 'teach India a lesson'.

This has a reflection today. Just a decade ago, Beijing was content with a Japan that was pacifist, China-friendly and its main source of low-interest loans. Now, it is locked in an emergent cold war with Tokyo, with its growing assertiveness and ambition reawakening Japanese national consciousness and spurring a politically resurgent Japan. Even the consul-general's impudence counterproductively returned the focus onto an invasion that Beijing seeks to put out of public discussion and about which it hides the truth from its own people. The impertinence only underlined the fact that China remains unapologetic for its major stab in the back that shattered India's pacifism and hastened the death of its first prime minister, Jawaharlal Nehru.

Japan certainly needs to come to terms with its disastrous era of militarism, colonialism and war crimes that culminated in its World War II defeat. But just as Japanese textbooks and the museum attached to the Yasukuni Shrine in central Tokyo glorify Japan's past, Chinese textbooks and the military museum in Beijing distort and even falsify history. The key difference is that Chinese foreign policy seeks to make real the central legend that drives official history — China's centrality in the world.

Eagle Eye at Play

The deteriorating geopolitical dynamics between Beijing and New Delhi, and between Beijing and Tokyo, have taken attention away from the quieter though more intense U.S.–China competition for influence in Asia. The United States will remain a key player in Asia through its security arrangements and other strategic ties with an array of regional states. Its policies and actions will also have an important bearing on the strategic calculus of the players in the China–India–Japan triangle. During the Clinton years, Washington went out of its way to befriend China, even if such courtship slighted Japan. As Condoleezza Rice put it before joining President George W. Bush's administration, 'Never again should an American president go to Beijing for nine days and refuse to stop in Tokyo or Seoul'.[5]

Under President Bush, the primacy of Japan in America's Asia policy was re-established, even as a new thrust was unveiled to build a durable, long-term strategic partnership with India. But the creeping Sino-centricity in America's Asia policy became obvious under President Barack Obama. To some in Washington, a partnership with a rising India is potentially capable of performing the same role in anchoring the global order as America's special relationship with Britain. In the words of one analyst, 'A century ago, America found its destiny by forging a partnership with the British lion; tomorrow, the same can — and should — happen with the Indian elephant'.[6] A strategic partnership with India jibes well with the 'realist' thesis Dr Rice published in January 2000 in *Foreign Affairs*: U.S. foreign policy should 'focus on power relationships and great-power politics' rather than on other countries' internal affairs.[7]

The emerging U.S.–India global strategic partnership presages a geopolitical realignment in Asia that will have an important bearing on international power relations. History testifies that a major geopolitical realignment can cause unease and even tensions in the near term. But a geopolitical realignment can also help build long-term stability, order and equilibrium. That is what a U.S.–India partnership can do. In Asia, it can help stem the trend towards power disequilibrium. Internationally, it can play a role in shaping the emerging new world order.

A true U.S.–India partnership can emerge only on the basis of a tangible strategic shift in policy towards one another, backed by strong public support in each country. The global-opinion polls by the Washington-based Pew Research Centre over the past decade have consistently shown that more respondents in India expressed a positive view of America than in most other nations surveyed. For example, in the 2009 survey, 76 per cent of Indians held favourable views of the United States. This rating was higher than in the countries closely aligned with the United

States, including Canada, Britain and Israel. In fact, in that poll, taken in 24 nations, as well as in the Palestinian territories, the only places where the U.S. positive rating was higher than in India were Kenya (partly attributable to Obama's Kenyan roots) and Nigeria. Among the publics in India's adversarial neighbours, China and Pakistan, America's favourable rating stood at 47 per cent and 16 per cent, respectively, with 64 per cent of Pakistanis and 24 per cent of Chinese identifying the U.S. as an enemy.[8] The poll found that the greatest support in the world for U.S.-led anti-terrorism efforts was in India, which finds itself on the frontlines of the fight against Islamic terrorism.

Even when the U.S. image took a beating globally during the Bush years, America's favourable rating in India remained impressive. The Indian public has always been pro-Western, given India's liberal, secular, pluralistic ethos. And despite Abu Ghraib, Guantánamo, Haditha and other potent symbols of abuse, President Bush was better rated in India than in any other country, including his own. Faced with a dire leadership deficit at home, Indians possibly saw in Bush a bracing contrast to their lily-livered leadership.

On the other hand, the warmth of Indians towards the United States and American people is not equally reciprocated in U.S. attitudes towards India or Indians. For instance, a BBC poll on U.S. attitudes, released in February 2006, showed that only 39 per cent of Americans viewed India positively.[9] One-sided favourable views, of course, cannot serve as a reliable foundation for a lasting partnership.

Another issue to be considered is whether there is sufficient policy shift in both Washington and New Delhi to facilitate a durable partnership. Or is the strategic shift more in one country than the other? India, clearly, is undergoing a tectonic tilt towards the United States. New Delhi's increasingly closer ties with Washington spring from and aid a major shift in public opinion at home. India has entered into far-reaching strategic ventures with the United States (or 'coalitions of the willing', in U.S. parlance), including the 'Global Democracy Initiative' and the military-to-military 'Disaster Response Initiative'. In addition, New Delhi has pledged to participate in U.S.-led 'multinational operations', to uphold the US-designed nuclear non-proliferation regime and to share intelligence with Washington.

While New Delhi is reorienting its foreign policy fundamentally, is there a corresponding strategic shift in U.S. policy towards India? In an increasingly uncertain world characterized by rapid change and an altering balance of power, America needs new allies and partners. The strategic importance of India is obvious to U.S. policymakers. As Bush himself put it in New Delhi during his India visit, 'The United States and India, separated by half the globe, are closer than ever before, and the partnership between our free nations has the power to transform the world. The partnership between the United States and India has deep and sturdy roots in the values we share'.[10] In recognition of that, Obama honoured India with his first state dinner.

India's growing geopolitical weight and abundant market opportunities have certainly nudged America to strive for a long-term partnership with New Delhi. American businesses are enthralled by India's large market, with the Indian middle class now numbering 300 million people — more than the entire U.S. population. India's economic rise and the growing prosperity of many of its citizens create more commercial opportunities for U.S. companies. Also, many among India's elites have seemingly convinced themselves that the way for India to carve out a larger international role for itself is to bandwagon with the United States, instead of the country following China's example and rapidly developing comprehensive national power. Being with America, according to this line of thinking, helps India gain the benefits and prestige that flow from association with the world's sole superpower.

Two factors, however, complicate America's relations with India. The first is that the United States, used to dictating to its allies, expects a new partner to toe its line. In a twenty-first-century world, Washington is unlikely to get a major new partner willing to be a Japan or Germany to the United States. In India, the independence streak remains deeply entrenched in thinking, with the nuclear-weapons programme serving as the emblem of the country's accent on sovereignty. Even Tokyo and Berlin are now beginning to discreetly reclaim their foreign-policy autonomy. In fact, when the United States in 2005 came out publicly against Germany's bid for a United Nations Security Council permanent seat, it sent out an unflattering message. By opposing the aspiration of a close ally that still provides it wide military and intelligence access of a kind it is unlikely to secure in India, the United States only helped advertise the limits of any partnership.

The second factor is that the United States endeavours to seize strategic and commercial opportunities in India without the readiness to make the necessary commitment that a long-term partnership entails, including being sensitive to each other's legitimate security concerns and interests. Not content with fattening the terrorism-exporting Pakistani military with generous aid, the Bush administration armed 'key ally' Pakistan with lethal weapons that can only be used against India. After announcing the transfers to Islamabad of P-3C Orion dual-role naval aircraft, C-130 military transport planes, TOW missiles, Aerostat surveillance radars, 155-mm self-propelled howitzers, Phalanx systems and Harpoon anti-ship missiles, the United States unveiled its largest-ever arms package for Pakistan in mid-2006 — a $5.1 billion deal that included satellite-guided bombs, advanced targeting systems and 36 F-16C/D Falcon fighters. It also has upgraded the existing Pakistani F-16 fleet. Continuing weapon transfers threaten to erode India's edge over Pakistan in naval and air power.

Obama, like Bush, has sought strategic partnerships with both India and Pakistan to 'fight terrorism' and 'advance democracy'. That approach slights India's democracy and the victims of Pakistan-orchestrated terror. Also, while playing the China card in India, Washington has tried to use the ingenious nuclear deal not only to draw New Delhi into the non-proliferation net but also to block India from emerging as a full-fledged nuclear-weapons state — an objective whose unwitting effect would be to thwart India's rise as a true strategic peer to China.

The India–U.S. nuclear deal may have been founded on good intentions, and its goal was certainly bold — to eliminate a decades-long source of acrimony between the two countries and open the way to building a durable strategic partnership. At the practical level, however, the deal, far from adding momentum to bilateral ties, helped inject controversy and complexity when the direction of the relationship had already been set — towards closer engagement. Because the deal is rife with unsettled issues and ambiguities, there is potential room for more controversy.

While it is clear that America and India are getting increasingly closer, it is less certain that their emerging global partnership will translate into New Delhi becoming Washington's junior partner against China and parts of the Muslim world. It is more likely that instead of trimming its sails before the American wind, India will seek to underpin its interests by retaining its strategic options and autonomy even as it forges closer links with Washington. Engagement with the United States is likely to proceed with a clear appreciation of where mutual interests diverge.

Take the issue of combating global terror. What is India's terror focus is exactly what America doesn't want to be the international focus — the role of Pakistan-based, state-supported groups in fomenting global *jihad*. In fact, America's constant endeavour is to deflect international attention from what India sees as the vortex of extremism, terrorism and nuclear proliferation — Pakistan. It would derail America's global agenda if the spotlight were to be on Pakistan, its gateway to military engagement in Afghanistan and covert reconnaissance missions into Iran. As a result, the United States not only attempts to play down India's concerns over Islamabad-directed terrorism, but also the U.S. national-security strategy report has gone to the extent of portraying Pakistan as a victim of terror. According to the report, India is not even among the 12 identified countries where 'terrorists have struck'. In fact, India — with the world's highest incidence of terrorist attacks, according to the U.S. Central Intelligence Agency's Office of Terrorism Analysis — finds no mention in the report's extensive chapter titled, 'Strengthen Alliances to Defeat Global Terrorism and Work to Prevent Attacks Against Us and Our Friends'.[11] This is just one illustration of why U.S. pronouncements on India need to progress from statements of good intent to concrete policy changes. America also needs to reconcile its avowed offer to help India become a world power with its actual policy that aims to build Indo–Pakistan nuclear and conventional 'balance' and thereby tie New Delhi down regionally.

In the coming years, India will increasingly be aligned with the West economically. But, strategically, it can avail of multiple options, even as it moves from Jawaharlal Nehru's nonalignment to a contemporary, globalized practicality. In keeping with its long-standing preference for policy independence, India still retains the option to forge different partnerships with varied players to pursue a variety of interests in diverse settings. That means that from being nonaligned, it is likely to become multialigned, while tilting more towards Washington, even as it preserves the core element of nonalignment — strategic autonomy. In other words, India is likely to continue to chart its own course and make its own major decisions. A multialigned India pursuing omnidirectional cooperation for mutual benefit with key players will be better positioned to advance its interests in the changed world.

The larger reality in Asia is that in the period since the September 11, 2001 terrorist attacks in the United States, China has expanded its strategic influence across the continent. An illustrative example of Beijing's spreading influence is Southeast Asia — a region where Japan still remains the main contributor of development aid and the United States the largest trade and security partner. Yet China's charm offensive has led to Southeast Asia increasingly accepting it as a key player in the region. Given Southeast Asia's desire to hedge against the rise of Chinese power, fears that ASEAN might come to acquiesce in hegemonic Chinese suzerainty, however, seem unjustified.[12]

What is clear is that the Bush administration's fusing of the war of necessity against terrorism that began on 9/11 with the war of choice in Iraq has had wider, unmanageable implications for U.S. policy and Asian geopolitics. The mess in Iraq, and the continuing difficulties in pacifying Afghanistan, have not only constricted U.S. policy options vis-à-vis China and scofflaw states like North Korea and Iran, but also helped increase Beijing's strategic leeway in Asia and elsewhere. America also has had to pay a price in terms of international political influence and soft power.

America's growing problems at home and abroad may have actually emboldened the Chinese leadership to search for more strategic advantages and even step up nationalistic rhetoric. Rising Chinese assertiveness — rooted in the belief that it is only a matter of time before China attains a commanding position on the world stage — has had the unintended effect of persuading Japan to jettison its doubts about U.S. security commitments and to reinvigorate its military relationship with Washington based on the long-standing U.S.–Japan Security Treaty. Tokyo, however, remains uncomfortable with its increased security dependency on the United States. It wishes to fashion more strategic manoeuvring room for itself and safeguard its economic stakes by halting the downward course in its ties with China — a task neither easy nor realizable without Beijing's active cooperation.

Fundamentally, the key U.S. interest in the Asia–Pacific region remains what it has been since 1898 when America took the Philippines as spoils of the naval war with Spain — the maintenance of a balance of power. During the first part of the Cold War, the United States chose to maintain the balance by forging alliances with Japan and South Korea and also by keeping forward bases in Asia. By the time the Cold War entered the second phase, America's 'ping-pong diplomacy' led to Richard Nixon's historic handshake with Mao Zedong in 1972 in an 'opening' designed to reinforce the balance by employing an assertive, nuclear-armed China to countervail Soviet power in the Asia–Pacific region.

Just like it played the China card against the Soviet Union, the United States propped up Pakistan militarily and politically over the years largely for its countervailing value vis-à-vis India. As Lloyd Rudolph and Susanne Hoeber Rudolph put it, 'For roughly 50 years, the United States destabilized the South Asia region by acting as an offshore balancer. Its actions allowed Pakistan to realise its goal of "parity" with its much bigger neighbour and to try to best that neighbour in several wars.... Why and how did offshore balancing come to the South Asia region? Its origin can be found in the geostrategic ideas of Olaf Caroe, the last foreign secretary for the British Raj in India (1939–45).... For a variety of reasons he facilitated, and then welcomed the partition of India. Caroe used the circumstance of India's Partition to help launch Pakistan on a 50-year career as the vehicle of America's practice of offshore balancing against Indian hegemony in South Asia'.[13]

Pakistan's uncompromising resolve to thwart India's regional pre-eminence has always jibed well with the U.S. balancing strategy. In the past, the United States turned a blind eye to Pakistani nuclear proliferation for the same reason that China aided Islamabad's nuclear and missile ambitions. Not only did the CIA shield Pakistani nuclear-smuggling ring mastermind Abdul Qadeer Khan from arrest and prosecution in Europe in 1975 and 1986 — as revealed by former Dutch Prime Minister Ruud Lubbers in August 2005[14] — but it also had a likely hand in the disappearance of Khan's legal files from the Amsterdam court that convicted him, according to the judge, Anita Leeser.[15] Khan, who became known as the 'father' of the Pakistani nuclear-bomb programme, publicly confessed in February 2004 to having covertly provided nuclear-weapons technology to three other states — Iran, Libya and North Korea. He then was immediately pardoned by his country's dictator, General Pervez Musharraf, who cited Khan's status as a national icon to justify his action. In fact, it was to hide the role of the principal actors in the proliferation ring — the Pakistan military and intelligence — that the entire blame was pinned on a group of 12 'greedy' scientists led by Khan. Washington not only went along with that charade, but it also sought to make the world believe that Khan set up and ran a nuclear Wal-Mart largely on his own. In fact, the twenty-first-century fable of an A.Q. Khan-run nuclear supermarket busted by the United States has now become part of American nuclear folklore.

Today, as China, India and Japan assert themselves on the Asian stage, America still views the maintenance of a balance of power as a central strategic goal in Asia. It would not want any single state to dominate the continent or any region there. The defiant 1998 Indian nuclear-weapons tests challenged U.S. interests as much as they did Chinese interests. It was thus not merely a moment of aberration when then U.S. President Bill Clinton provocatively reacted by urging China, on Chinese soil, to be the non-proliferation cop in South Asia, despite Beijing's proliferation role in both continually expanding its nuclear arsenal and directly aiding Pakistan's nuclear and missile ambitions. Yet, the U.S. hedging strategy's need to rope in India as a possible future balancer in Asia had led Washington by mid-2005 to sign a controversial nuclear deal that explicitly recognized that country's nuclear military programme.[16]

The United States is certainly concerned about China's aim to dominate Asia — an objective that runs counter to U.S. security and commercial interests. But America at present also shares important interests with China, including keeping the oil flowing from the Persian Gulf, maintaining peace on the Korean peninsula and seeking strategic stability in the Pacific and South Asia. Furthermore, U.S. and Chinese regional interests still converge on Pakistan vis-à-vis India. On issues of congruent interest, the United States is willing to work with China on Pakistan, for example, or discuss China with India. Similar balance-of-power politics is played out in other theatres as well.

As a matter of fact, the U.S.–China relationship, underpinned by closely intertwined economic ties and three decades of political cooperation on a broad range of regional and global issues, has a wider and deeper base than U.S.–India relations. From being allies of convenience in the second half of the Cold War, the United States and China have gradually emerged as partners tied by interdependence. America depends on Chinese surpluses and savings to finance its supersized budget deficits,[17] while Beijing depends on its huge exports to America both to sustain its impressive GDP growth rate and subsidize its military modernization. A quarter or more of all Chinese exports go to America alone.

By ploughing more than two-thirds of its foreign-currency reserves into U.S. dollar-denominated investments, Beijing has gained significant political leverage. The United States has tolerated a mammoth trade deficit with China largely because cheap Chinese-made goods help keep US inflation down. By outsourcing lower-cost manufacturing to China, the U.S. economy can concentrate on high-value productivity. The same consideration encourages U.S. companies to outsource back-office work to India. It is thus hardly a surprise that many U.S. firms have business process outsourcing and information technology subsidiaries in India or tie-ups with Indian companies.

In fact, in the manufacture of many products, multinational companies in the United States, Japan and elsewhere are merely using China as the final assembly station in their vast global-production chain so as to help lower their costs and boost their profits. This has resulted, among other things, in computer-assembling work moving from Japan and Taiwan to China and garment-stitching operations shifting from Hong Kong to China. For example, Panasonic has 70,000 employees and Samsung 50,000 employees working in China. According to Chinese customs data, about 60 per cent of China's exports are controlled by foreign companies.

Such practices have allowed China to get the wage benefits of globalization more than the commercial profits of globalization. The relocation of the final assembly floor of several major industries to China has helped create millions of jobs for China's low-wage migrant labourers, who earn on an average about 75 cents an hour. But the very reasons that make China attractive for basic manufacturing and final assembly — such as easy availability of cheap labour and land — have also acted as a dampener to the prospects of many Chinese companies to upgrade to higher-value activity, including design work. In any event, unlike America's freewheeling culture favourable to interdisciplinary fusion, China's regimented and deferential culture is hardly conducive to innovation.

In sharp contrast to the way Japan and South Korea created their own international brands, China can only boast of a couple of global brands like Lenovo and Haier. Yet China has remained a hot destination for foreign capital. Thanks partly to its cheap labour and undervalued yuan, China received some \$465 billion in foreign direct investment between 1995 and 2004 alone. China's case illustrates, as Joseph Nye has pointed out, why 'simple projections of economic-growth trends can be misleading. Countries tend to pick the low hanging fruit as they benefit from imported technologies in the early stages of economic takeoff, and growth rates generally slow as economies reach higher levels of development. In addition, the Chinese economy faces serious obstacles of transition from inefficient state-owned enterprises, a shaky financial system and inadequate infrastructure. Growing inequality, massive internal migration, an inadequate social safety net, corruption and weak institutions could foster political instability. Creating a rule of law and institutions for political participation has lagged behind the economy'.[18]

Given the vast disparity it faces in military and economic power with the United States, China's approach to handling America's global primacy is a model of canny tactics — a carefully calibrated balance of inconspicuous submission, modest resistance and circumspect competition. Despite Sino–American ties slowly fraying, Beijing will dare not behave towards the United States the way it spits fire at Japan or condescendingly treats India. The Chinese leadership clearly recognizes that close economic ties with Washington are critical to China's becoming a developed nation.

China's role at the UN Security Council illustrates how it engages in rhetorical condemnation of U.S. actions but is unwilling to press its opposition, such as by casting its veto. A classic example of calculated Chinese equivocation was the 2003 U.S. invasion of Iraq. It was France and Germany that spearheaded the opposition at the UN while Beijing played naked opportunism. Yet, at the same time, China appears keen to help moderate U.S. power. It thus desires a multipolar world, even as it seeks a unipolar Asia in which it replaces America as the main player and arbiter.

All told, the United States and China are far from developing into enemies, and the basis of their future ties is open to all options — from amity to hostility. Although China's rise has split Republicans and Democrats alike in the United States over how their country should respond,[19] containing China in the way America tried to isolate the Soviet Union is certainly not a credible U.S. policy option. Any U.S. balancing of China, if the need were to arise, will be very different, given America's reliance on Chinese capital and China's own role as an engine for U.S. economic growth.

As the U.S. Defence Department's last Quadrennial Defence Review (QDR) states, U.S. policy 'remains focused on encouraging China to play a constructive, peaceful role in the Asia–Pacific region and to serve as a partner in addressing common security challenges. U.S. policy seeks to encourage China to choose a path of peaceful economic growth and political liberalization'. The four-year review of U.S. military strategy identifies the three giants — China, Russia and India — as among the 'countries at strategic crossroads' whose policies and options the United States is seeking to influence.[20] One key component of America's strategy is to bind the three to U.S.-set international institutions and norms.

China's growing geopolitical weight is evident from its extensive and expanding economic ties with America. In fact, China — which already holds more than 10 per cent of the U.S. public debt — is becoming America's banker, as Washington remains heavily dependent on foreign cash, although its current-account deficit has in just a few years shrunk from nearly 7 per cent of its annual income to 3 per cent now. A creditor-debtor relationship between Washington and Beijing, along with China's growing sway over states around its periphery, holds major relevance for America's traditional allies, principally Japan and Taiwan, and new strategic partners, like India. After all, a banker has greater leverage over a customer than vice versa. But Chinese leverage is likely to stay limited. For instance, it is as much in China's interest as in America's to prop up the value of the dollar because if the dollar sinks, the worth of the Chinese dollar-denominated assets would plummet.

The U.S. and China have emerged as partners tied by such close interdependence that economic historians Niall Ferguson and Moritz Schularick have coined the term, 'Chimerica'[21]—a fusion like the less-convincing 'Chindia'. In fact, the recrudescence of the Sino-Japanese historical rivalry and Sino-Indian border tensions not only makes any externally driven balancing of China gratuitous at this time but also helps reinforce America's role as the main arbiter in Asia. Japan and China, as well as India and China, wish to prevent their political relations from going into a downward spiral, but the issues that bedevil their ties offer no easy solutions. In the years ahead, it is possible that the emerging generation of political leaders in Japan and India could favour the adoption of a more-assertive foreign and defence posture and be less willing to countenance a pushy China.

Too much is made about America's desire to use India to hold China in check. A durable U.S.–Indian partnership, however, can be built not on strategic opportunism but on shared national interests. Shared interests mean far more than shared democratic values. According to Henry Kissinger, 'Too often America's India policy is justified — occasionally with a wink — as way to contain China. But the reality has been that so far both India and America have found it in their interest to maintain a constructive relationship with China.... India will not serve as America's foil with China and will resent any attempts to use it in that role'.[22]

Any U.S. need to rope in India as an Asian balancer, in any case, has been mitigated by the emerging Sino–Japanese cold war. Through their rivalry, China and the economically powerful Japan will keep each other in check, without one gaining the upper hand over the other. Japan, by staying ensconced under a U.S. security and nuclear umbrella, offsets China's advantage as East Asia's sole possessor of both nuclear weapons and long-range ballistic missiles. But this comes at a considerable price — Japanese security dependency on Washington.

Strategic conflict in Asia will not be in U.S. interest, and America will try to do what it can to avert such a conflict. The United States would not want Japan or India to kowtow to an increasingly confident China that wishes to supplant America as the leading force on the continent. But the United States also would not want to see the rise of either a combative India or a Japan that is itching for a showdown with China in the East China Sea over the competing maritime and gas-exploration claims. Any Japan–China conflict would compel America, against its interests, to be on Tokyo's side because of its security commitments. Staying aloof and non-committal in such a situation would both wreck America's security relationship with Japan — centred on U.S. forward-deployment on Japanese soil — and damage its credibility with other military allies.

America's interests in Asia actually lie in hedging its future options and balancing the various powers. As the White House's national-security strategy report states, the United States, in the absence of big-power rivalries that divided the world in earlier eras, needs to take advantage of the contemporary 'absence of fundamental conflict between the great powers' to advance its interests.[23] The deepening strategic ties with India and a nascent defence relationship with Vietnam are examples of how America is seeking to imaginatively advance its interests in Asia.

The United States wishes to preserve its place at the centre of the universe, with other powers subject to its gravitational pull and being balanced by it against each other, at times through corrective U.S. interventions. That may explain why then U.S. Deputy Secretary of State Robert B. Zoellick in the autumn of 2005 called China a 'stakeholder' in the international system and urged it to show its commitment to maintaining an order forged primarily by the United States in the post-World War II period. What the United States is offering China is a minority stake in the U.S.-centred international system, on the condition that Beijing will work to uphold it. Seen in that light, being 'wary of authoritarian China while engaging with emerging China is a logical dualism' in U.S. policy.[24] That policy seeks to enmesh Beijing in multilateral institutions and norms even as Washington adopts strategic hedging against the risk of a hostile China.

Like it attempted in the past century, America would like to keep China and Japan in balance, without allowing either state's power capabilities to become unsurpassable by the other. Similarly, U.S. strategy is unlikely to stop employing Pakistan to countervail India, even as America seeks to frame an option to leverage its increasingly cosy ties with India against China. Through major bargaining chips — from arms sales to nuclear cooperation — the United States wishes to gain over India the kind of strategic influence it has secured over Pakistan, even if such a prospect looks daunting or remote. It is inevitable that, relative to Pakistan, America will continue to lavish more attention and praise on India, a country where U.S. businesses can make more money and U.S. strategic interests are greater.

China's rising economic importance for America does not mean that the U.S. economy has ceased to be closely tied to Japan. For long, Japan has run a large current-account surplus, thanks to brisk exports of electronics, cars and other goods. Any move by Japan to diversify its holdings of U.S. debt, which totalled about $725 billion in July 2009, would drive up U.S. yields. The ongoing recovery in Japan could actually encourage the Bank of Japan to rein in the ridiculously cheap Japanese cash sloshing around the global financial markets. The United States would be similarly concerned over possible constriction of foreign-money inflows from China, which overtook Japan in September 2008 to become the U.S. government's largest foreign creditor. China has ploughed as much as 70 per cent of its $2.3 tillion foreign-currency reserves into U.S. dollar-denominated assets, such as U.S. Treasury bills and corporate debt holdings. A Japanese or Chinese decision to suspend buying more Treasury notes or unload a portion of the hundreds of billions of dollars worth of such bills already held by Tokyo and Beijing would hit the U.S. economy hard.

Such low-yielding investments by Japan and China are a great boon to the U.S. economy, providing it cheap capital, helping to prop up the value of the dollar and effectively lending American consumers money to buy Asian exports. At the same time, such foreign-financed U.S. spending has also helped put limits on American leverage in certain areas. For example, it has constricted Washington's leverage to goad Beijing to increase the value of its currency, the yuan, which China has kept artificially low to underpin export-fuelled growth, attract foreign manufacturers and gain competitive trade advantage. Even so, China has begun to examine ways to cautiously reduce its exposure to the U.S. dollar while reassuring financial markets of its continued faith in the dollar.

So large is the American appetite for cheap money from abroad that before the 2008-09 global financial crisis put the brakes on unbridled borrowing, the U.S. external deficit was soaking up nearly 70 per cent of the excess funds saved by all the countries with current-account surpluses in the world combined. The Chinese and Japanese hoards of U.S. Treasury bills carry the risk of a repeat of Europe's experience from the 1970s. After having accumulated a huge mass of Treasury bills over two decades to help maintain fixed exchange-rate pegs in a style similar to China's today, West European states saw the value of their dollar savings contract in the 1970s, as spiralling oil prices and the Vietnam War costs fuelled U.S. inflation. China, which has the most to lose from a dollar crash, has called for the International Monetary Fund to find an alternative to the dollar as a global currency.

The converse dynamics drawing some Asian states closer to the United States also help shape Asian geopolitics. Japan's major financial and political support to the U.S. missile-defence programme, for instance, has come to symbolize its strengthened security relationship with Washington. Had China not resurrected historical grievances and purposely promoted anti-Japanese populist nationalism at home, it could have served its strategic interests better by seeking to wean Japan away from the security apron strings of the United States. Driving Japan further into the U.S. strategic camp has been a counterproductive outcome of China's heavy-handedness in policy — a result Beijing can still help roll back through a wiser course of action.

Indeed, in a mirror image of the short-lived four-nation tsunami relief coalition, the Asian line-up on America's missile-defence plans foreshadows the probable new global power alignments in the coming years, with Japan, India, Australia and the United States likely to be on the same strategic side. China cannot miss the strategic significance of such a potential quartet. At the same time, in an increasingly interdependent Asia, the interests of India or Japan can hardly be advanced if they are seen as engaged in efforts to reduce the promotion of security to a zero-sum game. Nor can excessive security reliance on the United States be in the interest of either Tokyo or New Delhi. Increasing, not constricting, their strategic leeway is the aim of India and Japan.

Major Challenges Ahead

In an Asia with several failing or problem states, China remains the biggest wild card despite its galloping economy. The most difficult question on the future make-up of Asian security is whether China will continue to grow stronger in a linear fashion. There is a basic contradiction in the two paths China is presently pursuing: political autocracy and market capitalism. In that sense, China is truly what it said it was when it absorbed Hong Kong: 'one country, two systems'. The longest-running autocratic regime in modern history survived 74 years in the Soviet Union. The Chinese communists have successfully retained a monopoly on power since 1949, even as the world has changed fundamentally.

How long can China's two systems co-exist in one country? Even China's free economy functions within a command economy, with the communist leadership anxious to maintain political and social stability through continued rapid progress. If market capitalism has helped the People's Republic to become the world's back factory or basic factory floor, political autocracy, as embodied by the Communist Party, is the bull in its own China shop, threatening to unleash a political cataclysm.

If Beijing manages to resolve the stark contradictions between the two systems, just the way Asian 'tigers' like South Korea and Taiwan made the transition to democracy without crippling turbulence, China could emerge as a peer competitor to the United States in the years ahead. But if the twin tracks of political autocracy and market capitalism prove inherently incompatible and collide at some future point, the consequences inescapably will be negative for China, as they were for Indonesia.

Even if the trajectories collide, it would not, however, mean the automatic collapse or paralysis of China. In that situation, China could still manage the adverse fallout in a way that preserves its unity and rising strength. China's challenge is that while it 'may achieve first-world status before India', it will have to steer clear of 'a political hard landing'.[25] China owes its rise as a major power to the free-market system, but maintains values that are not in harmony with that system. Its lack of any checks and balances in the political or corporate realm can hardly be a sound basis for long-term prosperity and stability. The more Beijing embraces values that go with a free-market system, the less likely it will confront a political hard landing.

China can be a positive influence in Asia. But it can just as easily become the biggest geopolitical problem. China's rise thus presents both an opportunity and a threat. The risk that China itself faces is that the more it globalizes, the more vulnerable it could become internally. That has made its autocrats wary of change and averse to any unregulated opening up of the country. The Internet by itself presents a formidable challenge to China's Marxist–Leninist–Maoist system because without the ubiquitous state censors and sophisticated filters, cyberspace could rapidly become a force for change. In contrast, India — a bastion of freedom in an Asian continent torn by Islamic fundamentalism and the shadow of potential Chinese hegemony — has little to lose and everything to gain by opening up to the rest of world.

As a pluralistic society that is a net exporter of culture, India can reap benefits aplenty from the process of globalization. India has a system whose openness, transparency and free avenues for expression are in harmony with its historical character as an assimilative civilization and with its traditions of tolerance. It is a land that supports varied social identities to flourish within a national framework founded on diversity, unlike China's.

Encouraging China to democratize and refrain from erecting another type of Great Wall to shut out the liberalizing elements of globalization will be a challenging task, given the ingenious ways Beijing has found to control and censor Internet content and regulate civil-society groups. One can find anything one wants on China's Internet: 'sex, fashion, business, travel, entertainment, romance. Anything, that is, except democracy, Tiananmen, Taiwan, human rights, Tibet and hundreds of other subjects'.[26] The Chinese leadership is wary of well-organized groups with popular appeal and foreign links and, therefore, seeks to subject them to stringent governmental oversight. Where it sees a threat, it is quick to crack down on any group, as its onslaught on the Falun Gong sect underscored.

Despite democracy being its greatest asset, India faces a different set of internal challenges. These challenges relate principally to internal cohesion and stability. India's strength — a multitude of diversities defining its rich social fabric — can be a drag and even weakness in the absence of good national leadership and able governance. Nowhere is India's frailty more apparent today than on internal security, which historically has been its Achilles heel. With one of the world's highest rates of terrorism, India today is battling underground extremists on multiple fronts: Pakistan-aided Islamists in Kashmir and elsewhere; Maoists rebels in a north–south corridor stretching from Nepal to its southeastern coastline; and ethno-linguistic separatists in the restive northeast region wedged between Burma, Bangladesh and China-annexed Tibet. It is thus critical for India to focus on internal security and consolidation.

A major cause of strategic friction in Asia is that China brooks no peer competition from any other Asian power.

It openly seeks to emerge as the main player on the continent. China's long-standing strategy has been to neutralize or deter the rise of peer competition, including from Japan (which it sees as having the advantage of enjoying U.S. military support) and India (whose 1998 nuclear-weapons tests jolted Beijing out of its smug complacency and belief that it could keep India confined south of the Himalayas through Pakistan-aided, low-level deterrence). While wanting to fashion a multipolar world, Beijing strives to be the sole pole in Asia, so that it is free to limit U.S. influence, keep India in check, bully Taiwan, shame Japan, divide ASEAN and make use of semi-failed states that serve as its clients. It is a friend of every despotic regime in Asia. It is also working to acquire forward-operating naval facilities and secure greater access to energy resources around India's periphery.

Another source of strategic discord in Asia is nuclear and missile proliferation. To be sure, few want weapons of mass destruction (WMD) falling into the hands of dangerous states or non-state actors. The possibility of terrorists getting hold of nuclear, biological or chemical weapons used to be the stuff of Hollywood melodramas. But after the September 11, 2001 terrorist attacks in the United States, that threat has become more plausible. In fact, U.S. President George W. Bush received a specific intelligence warning that the Al Qaeda planned to carry out a crude nuclear attack on Washington in October–November 2001 with radioactive material procured from Pakistan. 'We began to get serious indications that nuclear plans, material and know-how were being moved out of Pakistan,' Bush is quoted as saying in a book by Bob Woodward. 'It was the vibrations coming out of everybody reviewing the evidence'.[27]

Yet, as the cases of North Korea, Iran and Pakistan separately illustrate, the interests of the major players in Asia do not necessarily converge on non-proliferation matters, even if they put up the pretence of seeking common ground through dialogue. China's continued modernization of its nuclear and missile arsenals, and its WMD collaboration with Pakistan and missile aid to several states including North Korea and Iran, underscore the proliferation challenges in Asia. With its record of using Pakistan against India and North Korea against Japan, China even helped facilitate Pakistani–North Korean WMD and missile collaboration. It has for long played proliferation as a strategic card, with U.S. intelligence identifying it as the 'most significant supplier' of WMD goods and technology.

In fact, China has valued the proliferation tool as integral to its balance-of-power politics vis-à-vis India, Japan and the United States. It is an instrument that has helped Beijing win allies and boost leverage, as exemplified by the way it linked suspending its nuclear and missile transfers to Pakistan to U.S. concessions on theatre missile defences and arms sales to Taiwan. Even as China secured access to Australian uranium, notwithstanding concerns that it could divert the imports meant for its nuclear power stations to its atomic-weapons programme,[28] it sought to apply a different standard to New Delhi, opposing Australian uranium sales to India and the Indo–U.S. deal on civilian nuclear cooperation.

In the years ahead, the prime drivers of the security dynamics in Asia are likely to be the U.S.–China competition, the Sino–Japanese strategic antagonisms (which have already spilled out into the open) and the sharpening Sino–Indian rivalry. The foreign-policy challenge for Washington is to stave off a potential strategic threat from China while staying friendly with that country. Yet, there are already signs that such a challenge will not be easy to meet. China indeed has not made America's task easier by continually manoeuvring to expand its strategic advantages and by placing Taiwan under a permanent threat of force. In the event of aggression, the United States is sworn by the 1979 Taiwan

Relations Act to defend Taiwan, China's single largest investor.

The number of Chinese missiles targeted at Taiwan has increased by at least one hundred a year, as Beijing inducts new warships, strike aircraft and weapons to make it possible for its forces to capture vital ports and airfields on the island in the event of an invasion. In boosting its offensive and deterrent capabilities, it has established a credible military threat to Taiwan while continually raising the potential cost of any U.S. intervention in the Taiwan Strait. In contrast, efforts to upgrade Taiwan's own defences through planned purchase of U.S. submarines and anti-missile systems have stalled in the face of murky politics on the island, with the governing Kuomintang (KMT) party not averse to placing Taiwan in China's anaconda-like embrace.

Just as the U.S. –Soviet rivalry shaped global geopolitics for more than four decades up to the fall of the Berlin Wall, the U.S.–China strategic competition could greatly influence Asian and global geopolitics in the next four decades. The upside and downside — the yin and the yang — of the complex U.S.–China relationship will impinge on Asian security and prosperity like no other interstate relationship.

Even so, the Asian balance of power will inexorably change as other Asian powers rise. While the role of the United States will remain important in Asia for the foreseeable future, the relative weight of America in Asian affairs may decline regardless of the U.S.–China competition, if the China–Japan and India–China relationships are effectively managed and a unified Korea and an increasingly more assertive Russia emerge. The confident, petro-wealthy Russia of today is drastically different from the weak, Boris Yeltsin-led country that depended on the International Monetary Fund's largesse and yielded to the West on NATO expansion, intervention in the Balkans and other issues. America's ability to shape

Asian developments, despite retaining vast political influence and commercial leverage in Asia, appears headed towards decline.

Given China's size, population (a fifth of the human race) and economic dynamism, few can question or grudge its right to be a world power. In fact, such is China's sense of where it wishes to go that it cannot be deflected from its belief that it is destined to emerge as a great power. Yet, at the core of the challenge that an opaque China poses to equilibrium and stability in Asia is a need for Asian states to engineer discreet limits on the exercise of Chinese power. As the geographical hub of Asia sharing frontiers with 14 countries, China can engage many neighbours, unlike Japan and India, which are restricted to one zone. China has for years been taking calculated steps to boost its security and economic interests round its periphery. The same geographical advantage it has, however, can be an asset to other states in establishing a constellation of democracies round China that are tied together by mutually beneficial strategic partnerships.

Such a constellation can serve as a major stabilizing and coalescing force in Asia. Whenever a major power emerges, smaller states round its frontiers tend to slowly gravitate towards it, unless other important actors have helped establish power equilibrium on the continent. A constellation of cooperative democracies can institute such power stability in Asia and help ensure that the computation of various parts of China's role puts it always on the credit side of the ledger.

Minimize Mistrust, Maximize Cooperation

It is in the paramount interest of all the principal players in Asia — China, India, Japan, South Korea, Russia and the United States — to make sure that strategic competition between any two powers does not deteriorate into a major geopolitical flare-up or confrontation. The deepening mistrust and nationalistic chauvinism in Asia could create conditions that seriously harm the interests of all the major players. The common challenge thus is to find ways to minimize mutual mistrust and maximize avenues for reciprocally beneficial cooperation. But this can be done not by shying away from the contentious issues in Asia but by seeking to tackle them in a practical way.

Take the divisive issue of history. The emphasis on past grievances only engenders nationalistic hostility and, as seen from the trends in China, South Korea and Japan, creates congenial conditions for the virus of xenophobia to spread in such homogenized societies. Focusing on unsavoury history amplifies mistrust and runs counter to the liberalizing elements of globalization. An archetypal case was the Chinese state-run 'political education' campaign, launched in the 1990s, demonizing Japan for its 1931–45 occupation of Manchuria and China. That campaign laid the groundwork for the upsurge of deleterious nationalism and the deterioration of China's relations with Tokyo.

In order not to jeopardize stability and peace across Asia, sustained efforts need to be made to overcome the harmful historical legacies and the negative stereotyping of a rival state. China's communist leaders will have to refrain from using the history card against Japan, just as Japanese right-wing politicians, intent on reviving a spirit of militarism, need to stop peddling myths about the benevolence of Japan's imperial past.

When Britain and its apologists in its former colonies extol the benefits that British imperial rule allegedly bestowed upon the conquered peoples, it does not trigger the strong reaction that similar claims about the munificence of Japan's colonial past provoke in China and Korea. That is partly because a country like India has not kept alive the colonial-era history of British atrocities and abuses. Another reason is that India has no experience of being led by post-independence, ultra-nationalistic, politicians messianically determined to correct historical wrongs or reinterpret colonial history.

The international community cannot be a silent spectator to the motivated resurrection of unpleasant history today. Such revivalistic actions may be designed to bolster political legitimacy at home and whip up nationalism, but they harm regional growth and stability and challenge international norms on good-neighbourly conduct. A sustained Asian renaissance demands a more hospitable political atmosphere to help Asia sharpen its competitive edge and innovative skills through greater intraAsian cooperation and larger investments in the sciences.

The setting aside of historical issues and inculcation of positive political values in education are essential to the building of genuine, enduring interstate partnerships in Asia. Disputes over history textbooks, war museums, exhibits in museums and xenophobic cultural programming need to be addressed through bilateral or, where necessary, trilateral commissions. Nationalistic antagonisms ought to be calmed through governmental intervention and public education, along with the conscious promotion of competing ideas and open discourse. Ugly nationalism can be structurally constrained through internal mechanisms. The best bet against detrimental currents is a diversified civil society and the rule of law in the true sense of the term.

Priority should be given to a resolution of territorial or maritime disputes in Asia. The Asian strategic triangle cannot become stable without progress on that front. A first step to a settlement of any dispute is clarity on a line of control or appreciation of the 'no go' areas in order to eschew provocative or unfriendly actions. China's gunboat diplomacy in September 2005 across the median line in the East China Sea, for instance, only aided the re-election campaign of Japanese leader Junichiro Koizumi. In his five years in office, the jujitsu prime minister not only built popular support for revision of the pacifist Japanese

Constitution but also laid the foundation for the emergence of a more muscular Japan.

The best way for China and Japan to explore for hydrocarbons in the East China Sea is through joint development of fields there, given the intricate, difficult-to-resolve claims and legal ambiguities. Emulating the example of bilateral cooperative agreements set by disputants in the North Sea, Japan and China could jointly develop hydrocarbon deposits around the disputed Senkaku/Diaoyu Islands, which have become symbols of potent nationalism. As a first step, Beijing and Tokyo need to reach agreement not to change the status quo. Joint development of fields where the Sino–Japanese maritime-boundary claims overlap can help bridge the dispute between China's rights to the continental-shelf area, according to the UN Convention on the Law of the Sea, and Japan's lawful rights to an Exclusive Economic Zone (EEZ) that extends 370 kilometres to the west of the Ryukyu Islands chain in the Okinawa Prefecture.

Through a joint-development agreement under which they agree to share costs and benefits, China and Japan can positively transform the security environment in East Asia, and help establish regional cooperation and multilateral security mechanisms. With the East China Sea potentially holding up to 100 billion barrels of oil, Japan and China have a strong incentive to reach a compromise. A 2008 Sino-Japanese agreement-in-principle on joint development needs to be fleshed out and implemented.

The two most populous nations on earth, China and India, have been scowling at each other across a 4057-kilometre disputed frontier for more than half a century. Since 1981, India has been negotiating with China to settle the Indo–Tibetan frontier. These border talks are the longest between any two nations in modern world history. Yet, not only have the negotiations yielded no concrete progress on a settlement, but they also have failed so far to remove even the ambiguities plaguing the long line of control. Beijing has been so loath to clearly define the frontline that it suspended the exchange of maps with India several years ago. Consequently, India and China remain the only countries in the world not separated by a mutually defined frontline.

China's reluctance to fully define its long frontier with India may be linked to its strategy to keep its neighbour under strategic pressure, by pinning down a large number of Indian troops along the inhospitable slopes and valleys of the Himalayas. But through such reluctance China only advertises itself as a problem state for India. It has, for example, accepted the colonial-era McMahon Line with Burma but not with India. It treats the still-undefined line of control with India as a powerful lever in its hands. It has also not defined its 470-kilometre frontier with Bhutan, with crossborder Chinese incursions occurring periodically into both India and Bhutan.

The China–India frontline, without prejudice to rival territorial claims, can be clarified through a mutual exchange of maps showing each other's military positions. A Chinese disinclination to trade such maps translates into a greater aversion to clinch an overall border settlement. Rather than present itself as a practitioner of classical balance-of-power politics, China can profit more by fostering genuine political cooperation with New Delhi so that India is not driven into the U.S. strategic camp.

A China–India rapprochement fundamentally demands a resolution of the Tibet issue through a process of reconciliation and healing initiated by Beijing with its Tibetan minority. Such a process will aid China's own internal security. Despite decades of ruthless repression, China has failed to win over the Tibetan people, whose struggle for self-rule remains a model movement. As Desmond Tutu has reminded the world, 'there are no Tibetan suicide bombers, no Tibetan terrorists. This is because of the steadfast leadership of the Dalai Lama, one of the greatest men of peace the world has ever known, and his emphasis on the importance of nonviolence'.[29] Such is the suppression in Tibet that even having a photograph of the Dalai Lama constitutes a criminal offence. Yet the Tibetans have not lost their sense of mission or the will to regain their rights. As long as their spirit remains indomitable, there is always hope. Who thought in 1990 that the Central Asian republics would become free and that many of the Russians living there for long would have to leave?

It is an illusion that China and India can build enduring peace and cooperation without Beijing reaching out to Tibetans and solving the problem of Tibet. A problem that defines the origins of the China–India divide will stay at the centre-stage of that troubled relationship even if it were set aside indefinitely. China's own journey towards great-power status will be aided if it helped preserve Tibet's unique culture and religion, involved Tibetans in the development of their land and reached a deal to bring the Dalai Lama back from his exile in Dharamsala, India. Having ceased to be a political buffer between India and China, Tibet can become the political bridge between the two giants. With the Dalai Lama publicly expressing his readiness to accept a status for Tibet short of independence — as a genuinely autonomous region within the People's Republic — a placated Tibet can help bridge the China–India chasm.

Another Asian dispute — Taiwan — is an issue far larger than the size of that island's population and area. Whether Taiwan — a vibrant democracy today — continues to prosper under self-governance, or is beaten into submission or absorbed by the world's largest autocratic state, will determine the future make-up of China and of Asian security. Taiwan, sitting astride vital sea lanes, truly holds the key to whether China emerges as a stabilizing force or an arrogant power seeking unchallenged ascendancy in Asia.

By staking its claim to a role in the security of Taiwan,

Japan is signalling that it will not allow China to change East Asia's strategic balance in Beijing's favour. This signalling was best symbolized by the February 2005 U.S.–Japan security declaration that identified the peaceful resolution of the Taiwan issue as a shared strategic objective. Japan's interest to play a role in Taiwan's future is reflected in a growing view among Japanese politicians that Tokyo must come to the island's aid in the event of a Chinese invasion. A takeover of Taiwan will not only allow China to absorb the island's technology, weaponry and large foreign-exchange reserves, but it will also arm Beijing with the power to control shipping lanes to Japan and position missiles just 100 kilometres from the nearest Japanese territory.

Taiwan may be far from Indian shores but its political future also matters to India. Just as China lays claim to India's Arunachal Pradesh state, unmindful of the wishes of its people, it seeks to absorb Taiwan, irrespective of what the majority of Taiwanese want. In strategic terms, Taiwan can be to India what Pakistan is to China. Translated into policy that could entail close strategic collaboration between India and Taiwan, with the goal to aid each other's security through stared objectives and means and help build equilibrium in Asia. Economically, the new Taiwan–India Cooperation Council symbolizes the island's effort to reduce its economic dependence on mainland China, which accounts for some 70 per cent of Taiwan's accumulated offshore investment and has emerged as its largest import and export partner.

A new Indian strategic thrust towards Taiwan, however, may have to await a generational political change in India, most of whose present leaders are well past the retirement age. In the near- to medium-term, strategic cooperation between Japan and Taiwan appears more conceivable, despite occasionally insensitive Japanese rhetoric, such as Foreign Minister Taro Aso's reported remark in February 2006 that Taiwan owes its high educational standards to enlightened Japanese policies during the 50-year occupation that began when Tokyo grabbed the island as war booty in 1895. Japan and India cannot be oblivious to the prospect that a Beijing-obedient Taiwan may presage movement towards a Beijing-oriented Asia.

Time clearly is on Taiwan's side. For more than a century, Taiwan has been outside the control of mainland China. A continuation of the status quo for another quarter century will only bolster Taiwan's de facto independence, making it more difficult for Beijing to undo that. While playing for time, Taipei could continue to signal (by pushing the envelope without actually breaching the threshold) that it cannot be browbeaten by China. Assertiveness, in any case, cannot be the prerogative of one side. If Taiwan is to be told that it should not take any unilateral action to change the status quo, China too should get the same message, loud and clear, from the international community. If anything, China can profit by learning from Taiwan the value of establishing political linkage between free market and open society.

Energy is another critical area where strategic friction can be forestalled through shared Asian interests to safeguard energy supplies and maximize resource conservation and efficiency in order to underpin economic growth and commercial competitiveness. Such common interests can be the basis of a cooperative approach in Asia that emphasizes the development of secure new energy assets and the adoption of energy-saving technologies and methods. Japan, a leader in energy efficiency, can offer valuable assistance to the rapidly growing Asian economies. According to Japan's Natural Resources and Energy Agency, the Japanese industry's energy use is so efficient that it uses one-ninth the amount of oil that China does to generate the same profit.

A cooperative energy approach, of course, cannot be built without taming the two main Asian monsters —

resurgent nationalism and the recrudescence of fiery historical grievances. Such an approach also will not be possible if any power seeks to control an ever-larger percentage of the world's energy resources. The present zero-sum game on energy impedes the development of new oil and gas fields in a high-potential resource area — the East China Sea. Furthermore, it obstructs cooperation on bringing Russian oil and gas to consumers in Northeast Asia in a major way so that the region's reliance on the volatile Persian Gulf region could be reduced.

Undoubtedly, the path to energy security demands reliability and security of supply. As highlighted by Russia's two-day cut-off of gas supply to Ukraine at the beginning of 2006 and the consequent impact on supplies to Europe, even a brief supply disruption can badly rattle governments and financial markets. Moscow's use of the 'energy weapon' actually dates back to 1990, before the Soviet Union's disintegration, when it tried in vain to stifle independence movements in the Baltic states by suspending energy supplies. Two years later, it again played the same energy game in response to demands in the Baltic countries for the pullout of the remainder Russian forces. And in 1993–94, to back up varied political demands on Kiev, Moscow cut back gas supplies to Ukraine. Now Asia and Europe want Russia to open its gas production facilities and pipelines to foreign investors to help guarantee energy supplies to their markets.

If Russia, with its growing petro-wealth, has shown itself to be not a reliable supplier, how should energy importers classify the Irans, Nigerias, Bolivias and Venezuelas of the world? For any oil- or gas-importing nation, it is critical to ensure that, besides not becoming dependent on a sole supplier, any delivery arrangement it works out with an exporting state should be transparent, predictable and insulated from political shocks. That is as true of the proposed Iranian overland gas pipeline to India via Pakistan as it is of potential oil and gas supplies from the Russian Far East to Northeast Asia and the United States.

Interstate cooperation on energy can help stem escalating tensions in Asia while allowing the harvesting of new resources to aid prosperity. But energy cooperation cannot be institutionalized or sustained on a long-term basis without expanded political and security cooperation as well as increased transparency on military expenditures. The unremitting pace of China's ambitious military modernization even as its diplomacy becomes increasingly sophisticated indicates its intent to follow Theodore Roosevelt's dictum, 'Speak softly, but carry a big stick'. With opacity in planning and continuous, double-digit spending increases since before 1990, China's military build-up has advanced well beyond what most analysts envisaged just a decade ago.[30] Beijing's barely disguised ambition is to establish a blue-water navy ostensibly to secure its energy-supply lines. In that light, building interstate transparency in Asia on defence-spending levels there has become necessary to help set up multilateral maritime-security and energy-cooperation arrangements.

In fact, with Japan, China and India importing more than 95 per cent, 40 per cent and 77 per cent of their energy needs respectively, multinational cooperation on the security of sea lanes has become essential to avert strategic friction in Asia. Serious efforts are also needed to satisfactorily manage, if not settle, disputes over what are legitimate zones of energy exploration in open seas. An agreed code of conduct on naval and energy-exploration activities has to be a key component of such endeavours. Given the intense nationalistic passions aroused by the boundary disputes, the only realistic option is joint investment in and development of oil and gas fields in areas of overlapping maritime claim, like the East China Sea. The answer to the long running battle between Japan and China over the disputed oil and gas fields in the East China Sea cannot be unilateral drilling or production by either side. Yet a Chinese state-controlled upstream energy company, the China National Offshore Oil Corporation (CNOOC) Limited, announced in August 2006 that it had begun production in a gas field straddling the sea's median line.

Institutionalized energy and security cooperation in Asia will facilitate the commercial development of energy assets in the Russian Far East and make Russia a more attractive and secure supplier of oil and gas to Japan, South Korea and China than the Persian Gulf region. Northeast Asian states can provide the technical expertise and financial assistance Russia needs to develop oil and gas fields in its Far East. As the world's wealthiest country in natural resources, Russia is determined to use its energy assets to underpin its foreign-policy interests and re-emerge as a pivotal player on the world's geopolitical chessboard. At present, however, Russia is still struggling to lift its energy industry to Western standards. As demand for energy in Asia and Europe soars further, Russia's wealth and power are bound to grow. Russia has already come back as a force to reckon with, but with a new currency of power — its oil and gas. It has truly turned into an energy-producing superpower.

Asia as the Global Pivot

With Japan and India in no mood to play second fiddle to China, a much-needed reform of the United Nations Security Council could contribute to stability in the Asian strategic triangle. Even as China seeks to expand its global influence, Japan and India are aspiring to take on new international responsibilities, including a broader strategic role and a permanent seat on the Security Council. Beijing, however, is deeply suspicious and even resentful of their power pretensions, regarding India's 'Look East' policy, for instance, as part of an attempt to encroach on Chinese strategic space and to strategically link up with Japan.

The April 2005 anti-Japanese mob protests in China, although ostensibly linked to the controversy over Japanese schoolbooks, were intended to signal that Beijing would not allow Japan to become a Security Council permanent member.

The point is that as long as China insists on remaining Asia's sole permanent member in the Security Council, a more cooperative Asian political environment will be harder to create. China short-sightedly views the prospect of its Asian peers, Japan and India, joining the council's permanent membership as a strategic nightmare.[31] By seeking to keep them out, it only draws attention to its desire for unchallenged ascendancy in Asia.[32] Consequently, the issue of Security Council enlargement, already tied to the sharpening competition for global influence and resources, has now acquired the potential to determine the future strategic picture of the continent — a unipolar or multipolar Asia.

No strategic scenario probably worries China more than the possibility of a Washington–Tokyo–New Delhi axis. Such a bloc could help forestall the pre-eminence that China covets in Asia. New Delhi, on the other hand, sees no let-up in China's efforts to encircle India strategically through military tie-ups, access to naval facilities and transportation and energy links round its periphery.[33] China's accumulating power is also challenging Japanese security. Beijing will continue to plough more and more of its resources into activities and capabilities that New Delhi and Tokyo are likely to see as antithetical to their interests and security. Both India and Japan thus would like to lay down markers by which Chinese behaviour could be evaluated.

As ancient cultures with highly sophisticated arts and knowledge skills, China, India and Japan have impressive soft-power resources. Their political rise is helping to enhance their soft power globally. In fact, their cultural appeal has grown in Asia as America's soft power has decreased. But it is hard power that is influencing the strategic thinking and policy of China, India and Japan. In fact, Japan and India are learning from China that national security is not just about the level of defence spending and the quality of political and economic engagement with other states; rather it is also about the national ability and will to project power and assertively enlarge strategic space.

The intensifying competition between these and other players increases the risks of serious strategic miscalculations in Asia. The constant unleashing of nationalistic fury, for example, could damage the robust China–Japan commercial relationship, despite Beijing's conscious efforts to ensure that no lasting damage is caused to its booming trade with Tokyo or to the inflow of Japanese investments. Japan's own economic and political interests demand stable relations with Beijing. Indeed, Japan, India, Russia, America and the other players in Asia have an important stake in creating conditions that would ensure that China's rise remains a positive, not a negative, element in international relations.

The present resurgent nationalism, strategic antagonisms and hardening of popular sentiments in Asia are at odds with the global processes of greater economic integration in which Asian states are fully involved. Just as economies in the world have become more integrated through the trade of goods and services, the world's capital markets are now linked together. Sovereign debt markets in the largest economies trade as if they are in a single global market. Yet the new nationalism is incongruently visible not just in Asia but also elsewhere. It implicitly challenges the post-1945 world order that was built on international institutions designed to contain the demons of nationalism.

The rise of major strategic rivalries in Asia is more worrying because of the continent's conflicting political and strategic cultures and weak regional institutions.

China, India and Japan, in fact, epitomize three distinct strategic cultures. The evolving equations between and among them confirm that globalization, far from sweeping away national identities, is helping to reinforce them. As a consequence, replicating European-style integration in Asia appears more problematic than ever. Yet there is a great need in Asia for political pragmatism and judicious diplomacy to ensure that China, India and Japan emerge as positive forces in international politics. While it would be idealistic to expect China and Japan, and China and India, to become close friends, they need to at least strive for peaceful coexistence and deeper engagement. If these powers and the other Asian states eschew nationalism-mongering and develop long-term cooperation, Asia will truly prosper and become stronger as the global pivot.

The central challenge now is not so much to create an Asian Union as to find ways to stabilize major-power relationships in Asia and promote cooperative approaches that can tackle security, energy, territorial, environmental, developmental and history issues. Rather than become the scene of a new cold war, Asia can chart a more stable future for itself through shared security and prosperity among its states. An inability to resolve *all* the disputes and problems should not hold up cooperation on issues that can be addressed. Nor should competition discourage collaboration.

Given the fundamental diversity that persists in Asia and the discernible areas of strategic discord, ways need to be found to develop wider cooperative arrangements and institutions that build upon existing regional identities and mechanisms. Evolving common norms, rules and values is a prerequisite to an Asian order. If the changing balance of power is to promote stability and peaceful change, the establishment of institutions is necessary to build confidence, manage security, link bilateral and multilateral arrangements in a wider Asian web and blend regionalism with globalization. A stronger, more vibrant

Asia will emerge also from national policies that improve political participation of citizens, narrow down income gaps and increase social mobility.

A sustainable Asian order built on a balance among the market, culture and nature will necessarily pursue institutionalized multilateral approaches to various challenges, including on development, energy and security. Multilateral mechanisms to undertake a collective response to Asian problems and natural disasters must be devised, as Asia attempts to evolve into a more coherent entity within the context of globalization. A process of multilateral security cooperation will undeniably help underpin Asian interests. Asian multilateral cooperation is also needed to conserve freshwater ecosystems within a framework for sustainable development aimed at promoting efficient water use to address the growing shortages in several parts of Asia and to help protect endangered wildlife species. Cooperative interstate-river mechanisms are necessary, or else a new Great Game over water could unfold, given China's control over the source of most of Asia's major rivers — the Plateau of Tibet — and its projects to dam rivers upstream. In addition, the establishment of marine-protected areas has become necessary due to growing deep-ocean activities, such as bottom-trawling, that damage ecosystems and deplete or make extinct numerous species of fish.

In keeping with its emergent centrality in the world, Asia will help shape the future course of globalization. That makes it more important for Asian states to pursue policies that break free from history and are pragmatic, growth-oriented and forward-looking. IntraAsian trade and investment are so large that there is pressing need for partnerships between central banks and greater interstate cooperation on exchange rates, disputes over intellectual property rights and other issues. Asia should employ its vast savings and trade surpluses to finance development and consumption in Asian societies, rather than channelling capital flows largely outward, principally to U.S. assets. The common slogan in Asia ought to be, 'Make money, not war'. Nothing can shore up Asian security more than a genuine thaw in Sino–Japanese and Sino–Indian relations.

As the three main players, China, India and Japan can set a model for other states in Asia by establishing stable political relationships that put the accent on mutually beneficial cooperation. Without these powers taking the lead, it may not be possible to deal with the increasingly complex security, energy and development challenges facing Asia. All states in Asia stand to benefit from coordinated political and economic strategies in what is likely to be the Asian century. Deterrence, stability and peace have been at the heart of Asia's growing dynamism and prosperity. These elements need to be preserved and strengthened to help fully ripen the Asian renaissance.

Notes and References

1. China's trade surplus with the rest of the world tripled in 2005 alone.
2. GDP per capita figures are from World Bank, *2009 World Development Indicators* (Washington, D.C.: World Bank).
3. The theory of China's 'peaceful rise' originated in a book published in April 1998 by Chinese strategic scholar Yan Xuetong and three of his colleagues. The book discusses China's strategy to emerge as a great power without facing Cold War-style containment. The theory was quickly embraced by the communist leadership.
4. When the People's Liberation Army marched hundreds of miles south to annex independent Tibet and nibble at Indian areas, this action supposedly was neither expansionist nor forward policy. But when the ill-equipped and short-staffed Indian army belatedly sought to set up posts along its unmanned Himalayan frontier to try and stop further Chinese land grabs, Beijing and its Marxist friends in the world like Neville Maxwell dubbed it 'forward policy' and 'provocative'!

Maxwell's mind-blowing thesis was that India provoked the Chinese aggression. Neville Maxwell, *India's China War* (New York: Pantheon Books, 1970). Likewise, the Beijing military museum holds India responsible for the war, even as present-day Chinese textbooks paint India negatively.

5. Condoleezza Rice, 'Promoting the National Interest', *Foreign Affairs*, Vol. 79, No. 1 (January/February 2000), p. 54.
6. Arthur Herman, 'The Eagle and the Elephant', *Wall Street Journal*, March 7, 2006.
7. Rice, 'Promoting the National Interest'.
8. Pew Global Attitudes Project, *Confidence in Obama Lifts U.S. Image Around the World* (Washington, D.C.: Pew Research Centre, July 23, 2009).
9. http://news.bbc.co.uk/1/hi/world/americas/2994924.stm
10. Full official text of the Bush speech of March 3, 2006, in New Delhi, at:
http://www.whitehouse.gov/news/releases/2006/03/print/20060303-5.html
11. White House, *The National Security Strategy of the United States of America* (Washington, D.C.: White House, March 2006).
12. Amitav Acharya, 'Asia–Pacific: China's Charm Offensive in Southeast Asia', *International Herald Tribune*, November 8, 2003.
13. Lloyd Rudolph and Susanne Hoeber Rudolph, 'Why Bush Blinked', *The Times of India*, March 14, 2006.
14. R.N. Security and Hans de Vreij, 'Lubbers: CIA Asked Netherlands Not to Arrest Pakistani Nuclear Spy', Radio Netherlands, August 9, 2005, at:
http://www.radionetherlands.nl/currentaffairs/region/netherlands/ned050809?version=1
15. AFP dispatch dated September 10, 2005, quoting what the Amsterdam court's vice-president, Judge Anita Leeser, told Dutch news show, NOVA. 'Something is not right, we just don't lose things like that', Judge Leeser said on the show. 'I find it bewildering that people lose files with a political goal, especially if it is on request of the CIA. It is unheard of.'
16. The implicit recognition of India's nuclear-weapons programme is contained in the following language of the July 18, 2005 Joint Statement signed by President George W. Bush and Prime Minister Manmohan Singh in

Washington: 'The Prime Minister conveyed that, for its part, India would reciprocally agree that it would be ready to assume the same responsibilities and practices and acquire the same benefits and advantages as other leading countries with advanced nuclear technology, such as the United States. These responsibilities and practices consist of identifying and separating civilian and military nuclear facilities and programmes in a phased manner...'

17. America's trade deficit has ballooned to record levels (now about 6 per cent of its GDP) in the face of growing trade imbalances with China, Japan and Southeast Asian nations. In addition, America has a significant budget deficit that it finances through Treasury bonds. Over the past 25 years, there has been an important change, with foreign governments, rather than U.S. citizens, buying this U.S. debt. Now, approximately half of such government debt is held outside the United States, primarily by Japan, China and Southeast Asian nations.

18. Joseph S. Nye Jr., 'The Future of U.S.–China Relations', PacNet Newsletter No. 10, March 16, 2006.

19. Murray Herbert, 'China's Rising Clout Splits Republicans', *Wall Street Journal*, October 27, 2005, p. A4.

20. U.S. Department of Defence, *2006 Quadrennial Defence Review* (Washington, D.C.: Department of Defence, released February 3, 2006).

21. Niall Ferguson and Moritz Schularick, 'Chimerica and the Global Asset Market Boom', *International Finance* (December 2007).

22. Henry A. Kissinger, 'Anatomy of a Partnership', *Tribune* Media Services, March 10, 2006.

23. See Section VIII titled, 'Develop Agendas for Cooperative Action with the Other Main Centres of Global Power', in White House, *The National Security Strategy of the United States of America*.

24. Ross Terrill, 'Fearful Asymmetry', *Wall Street Journal*, April 24, 2006, p. A14.

25. Joydeep Mukherji, 'China, India, and the Fate of Globalization', *Standard and Poor's CreditWeek*, January 5, 2005, pp. 11–22.

26. Jonathan Mirsky, 'China's Tyranny Has the Best Hi-Tech Help', *International Herald Tribune*, January 16, 2006. Also,

Nicholas Bequelin, 'How China Controls the Internet', *BusinessWeek*, January 13, 2006.

27. Bob Woodward, *Bush at War* (New York: Simon & Schuster, 2002).

28. Australia's exports of uranium to China are to be covered by two accords signed on April 3, 2006 — the *Agreement Between the Government of Australia and the Government of the People's Republic of China for Cooperation in the Peaceful Uses of Nuclear Energy* and the *Agreement Between the Government of Australia and the Government of the People's Republic of China on the Transfer of Nuclear Material*. The accords incorporate Chinese assurances of peaceful use but do not carry any specific verification mechanisms. The non-profit Australian Conservation Foundation, for example, declared in a resolution on April 2, 2006: 'Australian uranium exports would facilitate diversion of China's limited uranium supplies into their ongoing nuclear-weapons programme, further regional insecurity and increase nuclear risks including unresolved nuclear waste management. China is an authoritarian state with a history of lack of accountability and non-compliance to a range of relevant nuclear and human rights treaties and conventions'.

29. Desmond Tutu, 'Following the Light of Truth', *International Herald Tribune*, June 1, 2006.

30. A reminder of that came in December 2005 when Japan's foreign minister, Taro Aso, told a news conference that China is 'a neighbouring country with one billion people, nuclear arms, and military spending that has shown double-digit growth for the last 17 years, with extremely little transparency'. He went on to say: 'It's becoming a considerable threat.'

31. In stridently opposing Tokyo's bid, China has felt no similar need to go against New Delhi's candidacy, because if Japan cannot join the Security Council as a permanent member, neither can India, because at issue is the inclusion of Japan, India, Germany and Brazil, plus two countries from Africa.

32. See J. Mohan Malik, 'Security Council Reform: China Signals Its Veto', *World Policy Journal* (Spring 2005).

33. According to one China expert, 'Sooner rather than later, China's military alliances and forward deployment of its

naval assets in the Pakistani, Bangladeshi and Burmese ports would leave India with no option but to respond in kind by seeking access to Cambodian (Sinhanoukville/Kompong Som), Vietnamese (Cam Ranh Bay), Taiwanese (Kao-hsiung) and Japanese (Okinawa) ports for the forward deployment of Indian naval assets to protect India's shipping and trade routes and access to energy resources from the Russian Sakhalin province'. Mohan Malik, 'China's Peaceful Ruse: Beijing Tightens Its Noose Round India's Neck', *Force*, December 10, 2005, available at: http://www.forceindia.net/chineseconundrumnext.asp

Agreement between the Republic of India and the People's Republic of China on Trade and Intercourse between Tibet Region of China and India (Peking, April 29, 1954)*

The Government of the Republic of India and the Central People's Government of the People's Republic of China,

Being desirous of promoting trade and cultural intercourse between Tibet Region of China and India and of facilitating pilgrimage and travel by the peoples of China and India,

Have resolved to enter into the present Agreement based on the following principles:

(1) mutual respect for each other's territorial integrity and sovereignty,

(2) mutual non-aggression,

---

*Also known as the Panchsheel [Five Principles] Agreement, this accord was to be the basis of friendly relations between India and China. Under the agreement, India gave up all extra-territorial rights and privileges it enjoyed in Tibet, formally recognizing Tibet to be a region of China. In return, however, it did not get China to recognize the then-existing Indo–Tibetan frontier. No sooner had the pact been signed than China began furtively encroaching on Indian territories. Eight years later, with the two sides not renewing the agreement at the end of its term despite a provision for its extension, the Panchsheel Principles went up in smoke when China invaded India.

(3)   mutual non-interference in each other's internal affairs,
(4)   equality and mutual benefit, and
(5)   peaceful co-existence.

And for this purpose have appointed as their respective Plenipotentiaries.

The Government of the Republic of India,

H.E. Nedyam Raghavan, Ambassador Extraordinary and Plenipotentiary of India accredited to the People's Republic of China; the Central People's Government of the People's Republic of China, H.E. Chang Han-fu, Vice-Minister of Foreign Affairs of the Central People's Government,

who, having examined each other's credentials and finding them in good and due form, have agreed upon the following:

Article I

The High Contracting Parties mutually agree to establish Trade Agencies:

(1)   The Government of India agrees that the Government of China may establish Trade Agencies at New Delhi, Calcutta and Kalimpong.

(2)   The Government of China agrees that the Government of India may establish Trade Agencies at Yatung, Gyantse and Gartok. The Trade Agencies of both Parties shall be accorded the same status and same treatment. The Trade Agents of both Parties shall enjoy freedom from arrest while exercising their functions, and shall enjoy in respect of themselves, their wives and children who are dependent on them for livelihood, freedom from search. The Trade Agencies of both Parties shall enjoy the privileges and immunities for couriers, mail-bags and communications in code.

Article II

The High Contracting Parties agree that traders of both countries known to be customarily and specifically engaged in trade between Tibet Region of China and India may trade at the following places:

(1) The Government of China agrees to specify (1) Yatung, (2) Gyantse and (3) Phari as markets for trade. The Government of India agrees that trade may be carried on in India, including places like (1) Kalimpong, (2) Siliguri and (3) Calcutta, according to customary practice.

(2) The Government of China agrees to specify (1) Gartok, (2) Pulanchung (Taklakot), (3) Gyanima-Khargo, (4) Gyanima-Chakra, (5) Ramura, (6) Dongbra, (7) Pulang-Sumdo, (8) Nabra, (9) Shangtse and (10) Tashigong as markets for trade; the Government of India agrees that in future, when in accordance with the development and need of trade between the Ari District of Tibet Region of China and India, it has become necessary to specify markets for trade in the corresponding district in India adjacent to the Ari District of Tibet Region of China, it will be prepared to consider on the basis of equality and reciprocity to do so.

Article III

The High Contracting Parties agree that pilgrimage by religious believers of the two countries shall be carried on in accordance with the following provisions:

(1) Pilgrims from India of Lamaist, Hindu and Buddhist faiths may visit Kang Rimpoche (Kailas) and Mavern Tso (Manasarovar) in Tibet Region of China in accordance with custom.

(2) Pilgrims from Tibet Region of China of Lamaist and Buddhist faiths may visit Banaras, Sarnath, Gaya and Sanchi in India in accordance with custom.

(3) Pilgrims customarily visiting Lhasa may continue to do so in accordance with custom.

Article IV

Traders and Pilgrims of both countries may travel by the following passes and route: (1) Shipki La pass, (2) Mana pass, (3) Niti pass, (4) Kungri Bingri pass, (5) Darma pass and (6) Lipu Lekh pass. Also, the customary route leading to Tashigong along the valley of the Shangatsangpu (Indus) River may continue to be traversed in accordance with custom.

Article V

For travelling across the border, the High Contracting Parties agree that diplomatic personnel, officials and nationals of the two countries shall hold passports issued by their own respective countries and visas by the other Party except as provided in Paragraphs 1, 2, 3 and 4 of this Article.

(1) Traders of both countries known to be customarily and specifically engaged in trade between Tibet Region of China and India, their wives and children who are dependent on them for livelihood and their attendants will be allowed entry for purposes of trade into India or Tibet Region of China, as the case may be, in accordance with custom on the production of certificates duly issued by the local government of their own country or by its duly authorized agents and examined by the border check-posts of the other Party.

(2) Inhabitants of the border districts of the two countries who cross the border to carry on petty trade or to visit friends and relatives may proceed to the border districts of the other Party as they have customarily done heretofore and need not be restricted to the passes and route specified in Article IV above and shall not be required to hold passport, visas or permits.

(3) Porters and mule team drivers of the two countries who cross the border to perform necessary transportation services need not hold passports issued by their own country, but shall only hold certificates good for a definite period of time (three months, half a year or one year) duly issued by the local government of their own country or by its duly authorized agents and produce them for registration at the border check-posts of the other Party.

(4) Pilgrims of both countries need not carry documents of certification but shall register at the border check-posts of the other Party and receive a permit for pilgrimage.

(5) Notwithstanding the provisions of the foregoing paragraphs of this Article, either Government may refuse entry to any particular person.

(6) Persons who enter the territory of the other Party in accordance with the foregoing paragraphs of this Article may stay within its territory only after complying with the procedures specified by the other Party.

Article VI

The present Agreement shall come into effect upon ratification by both Governments and shall remain in force for eight (8) years. Extension of the present Agreement may be negotiated by the two Parties if either Party requests for it six (6) months prior to the expiry of the Agreement and the request is agreed to by the other Party.

DONE in duplicate in Peking on the twenty-ninth day of April, 1954 in Hindi, Chinese and English languages, all texts being equally valid.

NEDYAM RAGHAVAN,
Plenipotentiary of the Government of India

CHANG HAN-FU,
Plenipotentiary of the Central People's Republic of China.

NOTES EXCHANGED

Peking, April 29, 1954

Note from India

Your Excellency Mr Vice-FOREIGN MINISTER. In the course of our discussions regarding the Agreement on Trade and Intercourse between Tibet Region of China and India, which has been happily concluded today, the Delegation of the Government of the Republic of India and the Delegation of the Government of the People's Republic of China agreed that certain matters be regulated by an exchange of notes. In pursuance of this understanding, it is hereby agreed between the two Governments as follows:

(1) The Government of India will be pleased to withdraw completely within six (6) months from date of exchange of the present notes the military escorts now stationed at Yatung and Gyantse in Tibet Region of China. The Government of China will render facilities and assistance in such withdrawal.

(2) The Government of India will be pleased to hand over to the Government of China at a reasonable price the postal, telegraph and public telephone services together with their equipment operated by the Government of India in Tibet Region of China. The concrete measures in this regard will be decided upon through further negotiations between the Indian Embassy in China and the Foreign Ministry of China, which shall start immediately after the exchange of the present notes.

(3) The Government of India will be pleased to hand over to the Government of China at a reasonable price the twelve (12) rest houses of the Government of India in Tibet Region of China. The concrete measures in this regard will be decided upon through further negotiations between the Indian Embassy in China and the Foreign Ministry of China, which shall start immediately after the exchange of the present notes. The Government of China agrees that they shall continue as rest houses.

(4) The Government of China agrees that all buildings within the compound walls of the Trade Agencies of the Government of India at Yatung and Gyantse in Tibet Region of China may be retained by the Government of India. The Government of India may continue to lease the land within its Agency compound walls from the Chinese side. And the Government of India agrees that the Trade Agencies of the Government of China at Kalimpong and Calcutta may lease lands from the Indian side for the use of the Agencies and construct buildings thereon. The Government of China will render every possible assistance for housing the Indian Trade Agency at Gartok. The Government of India will also render

every possible assistance for housing the Chinese Trade Agency at New Delhi.

(5) The Government of India will be pleased to return to the Government of China all lands used or occupied by the Government of India other than the lands within its Trade Agency compound walls at Yatung. If there are godowns and buildings of the Government of India on the abovementioned lands used or occupied and to be returned by the Government of India and if Indian traders have stores, godowns or buildings on the above mentioned lands so that there is a need to continue leasing lands, the Government of China agrees to sign contracts with the Government of India or Indian traders, as the case may be, for leasing to them those parts of the land occupied by the said godowns, buildings or stores and pertaining thereto.

(6) The Trade Agents of both Parties may, in accordance with the laws and regulations of the local governments, have access to their nationals involved in civil or criminal cases.

(7) The Trade Agents and traders of both countries may hire employees in the locality.

(8) The hospitals of the Indian Trade Agencies at Gyantse and Yatung will continue to serve personnel of the Indian Trade Agencies.

(9) Each Government shall protect the person and property of the traders and pilgrims of the other country.

(10) The Government of China agrees, so far as possible, to construct rest houses for the use of pilgrims along the route from Pulanchung (Taklakot) to Kang Rimpoche (Kailas) and Mavern Tso (Manasarovar); and the Government of India agrees to place all possible facilities in India at the disposal of pilgrims.

(11) Traders and pilgrims of both countries shall have the facility of hiring means of transportation at normal and reasonable rates.

(12) The three Trade Agencies of each Party may function throughout the year.

(13) Traders of each country may rent buildings and godowns in accordance with local regulations in places under the jurisdiction of the other Party.

(14) Traders of both countries may carry on normal trade in accordance with local regulations at places as provided in Article II of the Agreement.

(15) Disputes between traders of both countries over debts and claims shall be handled in accordance with local laws and regulations.

On behalf of the Government of the Republic of India I hereby agree that the present Note along with Your Excellency's reply shall become an agreement between our two Governments which shall come into force upon the exchange of the present Notes. I avail myself of this opportunity to express to Your Excellency Mr Vice-Foreign Minister, the assurances of my highest consideration.

N.RAGHAVAN, Ambassador Extraordinary and Plenipotentiary of the Republic of India.

Note from China

Your Excellency Mr AMBASSADOR:

I have the honour to receive your note dated April 29, 1954 which reads: [*Not repeated here.*]

On behalf of the Central People's Government of the People's Republic of China, I hereby agree to Your Excellency's note, and your note along with the present note in reply shall become an agreement between our two Governments, which shall come into force upon the exchange of the present notes. I avail myself of this opportunity to express to Your Excellency, Mr Ambassador, the assurances of my highest consideration.

CHANG HAN-Fu. Vice Minister, Ministry of Foreign Affairs, People's Republic of China.

NOTIFICATION OF RATIFICATION BY BOTH SIDES ON AUGUST 17, 1954

To: His Excellency Mr CHOU EN-LAI, Minister for Foreign Affairs, Central People's Government of the People's Reublic of China, Peking. (Original in Chinese.)

EXCELLENCY, I have the honour to state that WHEREAS an agreement between the Government of the Republic of India and the Central People's Government of the People's Republic of China on trade and intercourse between Tibet region of China and India was signed at Peking on the 29th Day of April, 1954, by the respective plenipotentiaries of the two Governments, namely,

For the Government of the Republic of India. His Excellency Nedyam Raghavan, Ambassador Extraordinary and Plenipotentiary of India.

For the Central People's Government of the People's Republic of China, His Excellency Chang Han-fu, which Agreement is reproduced, word for word, in the Annexure here.

AND WHEREAS the Government of the Republic of India has ratified this Agreement on the 3rd June 1954. I request you to convey information of the said ratification to the Central People's Government of the People's Republic of China. I avail myself of this opportunity to renew to you, Excellency, the assurances of my highest consideration.

NEDYAM RAGHAVAN. Ambassador of the Republic of India.

To: His Excellency PANDIT JAWAHARLAL NEHRU, Minister for External Affairs, Government of Republic of India, New Delhi

EXCELLENCY,

I have the honour to inform you that the Agreement between the People's Republic of China and the Republic of India on Trade and Intercourse between Tibet Region of China and India, which was signed at Peking on the 29th of April, 1954, by Chang Han-fu, Vice-Minister, Ministry of Foreign Affairs, Central People's Government of the People's Republic of China, for the Central People's Government of the People's Republic of China and Nedyam Raghavan, Ambassador Extraordinary and Plenipotentiary of the Republic of India to the People's Republic of China, for the Government of the Republic of India, was subsequently ratified on the 3rd June, 1954, by the Central People's Government of the People's Republic of China. I hereby request you to convey information of the said ratification to the Government of India.

The Agreement is reproduced, word for word, in the Annexure hereto. I avail myself of this opportunity to renew to you, Excellency, the assurances of my highest consideration.

(Sd.) YUAN CHUNG-HSIEN
Ambassador Extraordinary and Plenipotentiary of the People's Republic of China.

The Indian Parliament's Resolution on China
(November 14, 1962)*

This House notes with deep regret that, in spite of the uniform gestures of goodwill and friendship by India towards the People's Government of China on the basis of recognition of each other's independence, non-aggression and non-interference and peaceful co-existence, China has betrayed this goodwill and friendship and the Principles of Panchsheel which had been agreed to between the two countries, and has committed aggression and initiated a massive invasion of India by her armed forces.

This House places on record its high appreciation of the valiant struggle of men and officers of our armed forces while defending our frontiers, and pays its respectful homage to the martyrs who have laid down their lives in defending the honour and integrity of our motherland.

This House also records its profound appreciation of the wonderful and spontaneous response of the people of India to the emergency and the crisis that has resulted from China's invasion of India.

---

*This resolution, moved while the Chinese aggression was on, was unanimously passed by the Indian Parliament, with the pledge to 'drive out the aggressor from the sacred soil of India, however long and hard the struggle may be'.

It notes with deep gratitude this mighty upsurge amongst all sections of our people for harnessing all our resources towards the organization of an all-out effort to meet this grave national emergency. The flame of liberty and sacrifice has been kindled anew and a fresh dedication has taken place to the cause of India's freedom and integrity.

This House gratefully acknowledges the sympathy and the moral and material support received from a large number of friendly countries in this grim hour of our struggle against aggression and invasion.

With hope and faith, this House affirms the firm resolve of the Indian people to drive out the aggressor from the sacred soil of India, however long and hard the struggle may be.

Joint Communiqué of the Government of Japan and the Government of the People's Republic of China (September 29, 1972)*

Prime Minister Kakuei Tanaka of Japan visited the People's Republic of China at the invitation of Premier of the State Council Chou En-lai of the People's Republic of China from September 25 to September 30, 1972. Accompanying Prime Minister Tanaka were Minister for Foreign Affairs Masayoshi Ohira, Chief Cabinet Secretary Susumu Nikaido and other government officials.

Chairman Mao Tse-tung met Prime Minister Kakuei Tanaka on September 27. They had an earnest and friendly conversation.

Prime Minister Tanaka and Minister for Foreign Affairs Ohira had an earnest and frank exchange of views with Premier Chou En-lai and Minister for Foreign Affairs Chi Peng-fei in a friendly atmosphere throughout on the question of the normalization of relations between Japan and China and other problems between the two countries as well as on other matters of interest to both sides, and agreed to issue the following Joint Communiqué of the two Governments:

Japan and China are neighbouring countries, separated only by a strip of water with a long history of traditional

---

*Restoring diplomatic relations between Japan and China and acknowledging the People's Republic of China to be the sole Government of China, this joint communiqué also ended intergovernmental claims for World War II reparations.

friendship. The peoples of the two countries earnestly desire to put an end to the abnormal state of affairs that has hitherto existed between the two countries. The realization of the aspiration of the two peoples for the termination of the state of war and the normalization of relations between Japan and China will add a new page to the annals of relations between the two countries.

The Japanese side is keenly conscious of the responsibility for the serious damage that Japan caused in the past to the Chinese people through war, and deeply reproaches itself. Further, the Japanese side reaffirms its position that it intends to realize the normalization of relations between the two countries from the stand of fully understanding 'the three principles for the restoration of relations' put forward by the Government of the People's Republic of China. The Chinese side expresses its welcome for this.

In spite of the differences in their social systems existing between the two countries, the two countries should, and can, establish relations of peace and friendship. The normalization of relations and development of good-neighbourly and friendly relations between the two countries are in the interests of the two peoples and will contribute to the relaxation of tension in Asia and peace in the world.

(1) The abnormal state of affairs that has hitherto existed between Japan and the People's Republic of China is terminated on the date on which this Joint Communiqué is issued.

(2) The Government of Japan recognizes that Government of the People's Republic of China as the sole legal Government of China.

(3) The Government of the People's Republic of China reiterates that Taiwan is an inalienable part of the territory of the People's Republic of China. The Government of Japan fully understands and respects this stand of the Government of the People's Republic of China, and it firmly maintains its stand under Article 8 of the Potsdam Proclamation.

(4) The Government of Japan and the Government of the People's Republic of China have decided to establish

diplomatic relations as from September 29, 1972. The two Governments have decided to take all necessary measures for the establishment and the performance of the functions of each other's embassy in their respective capitals in accordance with international law and practice, and to exchange ambassadors as speedily as possible.

(5) The Government of the People's Republic of China declares that in the interest of the friendship between the Chinese and the Japanese peoples, it renounces its demand for war reparation from Japan.

(6) The Government of Japan and the Government of the People's Republic of China agree to establish relations of perpetual peace and friendship between the two countries on the basis of the principles of mutual respect for sovereignty and territorial integrity, mutual non-aggression, non-interference in each other's internal affairs, equality and mutual benefit and peaceful co-existence.

The two Governments confirm that, in conformity with the foregoing principles and the principles of the Charter of the United Nations, Japan and China shall in their mutual relations settle all disputes by peaceful means and shall refrain from the use or threat of force.

(7) The normalization of relations between Japan and China is not directed against any third country. Neither of the two countries should seek hegemony in the Asia–Pacific region and each is opposed to efforts by any other country or group of countries to establish such hegemony.

(8) The Government of Japan and the Government of the People's Republic of China have agreed that, with a view to solidifying and developing the relations of peace and friendship between the two countries, the two Governments will enter into negotiations for the purpose of concluding a treaty of peace and friendship.

(9) The Government of Japan and the Government of the People's Republic of China have agreed that, with a view to further promoting relations between the two countries and to expanding interchanges of people, the two

Governments will, as necessary and taking account of the existing non-governmental arrangements, enter into negotiations for the purpose of concluding agreements concerning such matters as trade, shipping, aviation and fisheries.

Done at Peking, September 29, 1972

Prime Minister of Japan
Minister for Foreign Affairs of Japan
Premier of the State Council of the People's Republic of China
Minister for Foreign Affairs of the People's Republic of China

Treaty of Peace and Friendship between Japan and the People's Republic of China (August 12, 1978)*

Japan and the People's Republic of China,

Having recalled with satisfaction that, since the issuance of the joint statement by the Government of Japan and the Government of the People's Republic of China on September 29, 1972 at Beijing, friendly relations between the Governments and the peoples of the two countries have developed extensively on a new basis,

Affirming that the aforementioned joint statement constitutes the basis for relations of peace and friendship between the two countries and that the principles set out in that statement should be strictly observed,

Affirming that the Charter of the United Nations should be fully respected,

Desiring to contribute to the peace and security of Asia and the world,

Seeking to strengthen and develop peaceful and friendly relations between the two countries,

Have decided to conclude a treaty of peace and friendship and have, for this purpose, appointed as their Plenipotentiaries:

---

*This pact took four years to negotiate. It was signed on August 12, 1978 and came into effect on October 23, 1978.

For Japan, the Minister of Foreign Affairs, Sunao Sonoda
For China, the Minister for Foreign Affairs, Huang Hua

The Plenipotentiaries of both Parties, having exchanged their full powers, and found them in good and due form, have agreed as follows:

Article 1

(1) The Contracting Parties shall develop lasting relations of peace and friendship between the two countries on the basis of mutual respect for the principles of sovereignty and territorial integrity, mutual non-aggression, non-intervention in each other's internal affairs, mutual benefit and peaceful co-existence.

(2) In accordance with the aforementioned principles and the principles of the Charter of the United Nations, the Contracting Parties affirm that, in their mutual relations, they will use peaceful means to settle all disputes and will refrain from the use of force or the threats of the use thereof.

Article 2

The Contracting Parties declare that neither Party will seek hegemony within the Asian and Pacific region or in any other region and that both shall oppose any attempt by any other country or group of countries to establish such hegemony.

Article 3

The Contracting Parties, motivated by the spirit of good neighbourliness and friendship and in accordance with the principles of mutual benefit and non-interference in each other's internal affairs, shall foster contacts and endeavours involving the peoples of the two countries with a view to furthering economic and cultural relations between the two countries.

Article 4

This Treaty shall not affect the relations either Contracting Party maintains with third countries.

Article 5

(1) This Treaty is subject to ratification and shall enter into force on the day of the exchange of the instruments of ratification at Tokyo. This Treaty shall remain in force for 10 years and thereafter until the statement of termination provided for in paragraph 2 of this article is made.

(2) Upon the expiration of the initial ten-year period or at any time thereafter, either Contracting Party may terminate this Treaty by informing the other Contracting Party in writing one year beforehand of its intention to do so.

IN WITNESS WHEREOF, the Plenipotentiaries have signed this Treaty and affixed thereto their seals.

Done at Beijing, August 12, 1978, in duplicate, in the Japanese and Chinese languages, both texts being equally authentic.

For Japan: SUNAO SONODA
For the People's Republic of China: HUANG HUA

Agreement on the Maintenance of Peace and Tranquillity along the Line of Actual Control in the India–China Border Areas (Beijing, September 7, 1993)*

The Government of the Republic of India and the Government of the People's Republic of China (hereinafter referred to as the two sides) have entered into the present Agreement in accordance with the Five Principles of mutual respect for sovereignty and territorial integrity, mutual non-aggression, non-interference in each other's internal affairs, equality and mutual benefit and peaceful co-existence and with a view to maintaining peace and tranquillity in areas along the line of actual control in the India–China border areas.

(1) The two sides are of the view that the India–China boundary question shall be resolved through peaceful and friendly consultations. Neither side shall use or threaten to use force against the other by any means. Pending an ultimate solution to the boundary question

---

*This accord was signed when Indian Prime Minister P.V. Narasimha Rao visited Beijing. Both sides agreed to maintain 'peace and tranquillity' along the Line of Actual Control, a line China has refused to fully define, let alone delineate, as a way to maintain military pressure on India.

between the two countries, the two sides shall strictly respect and observe the line of actual control between the two sides. No activities of either side shall overstep the line of actual control. In case personnel of one side cross the line of actual control, upon being cautioned by the other side, they shall immediately pull back to their own side of the line of actual control. When necessary, the two sides shall jointly check and determine the segments of the line of actual control where they have different views as to its alignment.

(2) Each side will keep its military forces in the areas along the line of actual control to a minimum level compatible with the friendly and good neighbourly relations between the two countries. The two sides agree to reduce their military forces along the line of actual control in conformity with the requirements of the principle of mutual and equal security to ceilings to be mutually agreed. The extent, depth, timing, and nature of reduction of military forces along the line of actual control shall be determined through mutual consultations between the two countries. The reduction of military forces shall be carried out by stages in mutually agreed geographical locations sector-wise within the areas along the line of actual control.

(3) Both sides shall work out through consultations effective confidence–building measures in the areas along the line of actual control. Neither side will undertake specified levels of military exercises in mutually identified zones. Each side shall give the other prior notification of military exercises of specified levels near the line of actual control permitted under this Agreement.

(4) In case of contingencies or other problems arising in the areas along the line of actual control, the two sides shall deal with them through meetings and friendly consultations between border personnel of the two countries. The form of such meetings and channels of communications between the border personnel shall be mutually agreed upon by the two sides.

(5) The two sides agree to take adequate measures to ensure that air intrusions across the line of actual control do

not take place and shall undertake mutual consultations should intrusions occur. Both sides shall also consult on possible restrictions on air exercises in areas to be mutually agreed near the line of actual control.

(6) The two sides agree that references to the line of actual control in this Agreement do not prejudice their respective positions on the boundary question.

(7) The two sides shall agree through consultations on the form, method, scale and content of effective verification measures and supervision required for the reduction of military forces and the maintenance of peace and tranquillity in the areas along the line of actual control under this Agreement.

(8) Each side of the India–China Joint Working Group on the boundary question shall appoint diplomatic and military experts to formulate, through mutual consultations, implementation measures for the present Agreement. The experts shall advise the Joint Working Group on the resolution of differences between the two sides on the alignment of the line of actual control and address issues relating to redeployment with a view to reduction of military forces in the areas along the line of actual control. The experts shall also assist the Joint Working Group in supervision of the implementation of the Agreement, and settlement of differences that may arise in that process, based on the principle of good faith and mutual confidence.

(9) The present Agreement shall come into effect as of the date of signature and is subject to amendment and addition by agreement of the two sides.

Signed in duplicate at Beijing on the Seventh day of September 1993 in the Hindi, Chinese and English languages, all three texts having equal validity.

R.L. Bhatia, Minister of State for External Affairs, Republic of India
Tang Jiaxuan, Vice-Foreign Minister, People's Republic of China

Agreement between the Government of the Republic of India and the Government of the People's Republic of China on Confidence-Building Measures in the Military Field along the Line of Actual Control in the India–China Border Areas (New Delhi, November 29, 1996)*

The Government of the Republic of India and the Government of the People's Republic of China (hereinafter referred to as the two sides),

Believing that it serves the fundamental interests of the peoples of India and China to foster a long-term good-neighbourly relationship in accordance with the five principles of mutual respect for sovereignty and territorial integrity, mutual non-aggression, non-interference in each other's internal affairs, equality and mutual benefit and peaceful co-existence,

Convinced that the maintenance of peace and tranquillity along the line of actual control in the India–China border areas accords with the fundamental interests of the two peoples and will also contribute to the ultimate resolution of the boundary question,

---

*This accord, signed when Chinese President Jiang Zemin visited New Delhi, prohibited certain military activities at specific distances from a line of control that has remained largely undefined.

Reaffirming that neither side shall use or threaten to use force against the other by any means or seek unilateral military superiority,

Pursuant to the Agreement between the Government of the Republic of India and the Government of the People's Republic of China on the Maintenance of Peace and Tranquillity along the Line of Actual Control in the India–China Border Areas, signed on 7 September, 1993,

Recognizing the need for effective confidence-building measures in the military field along the line of actual control in the border areas between the two sides,

Noting the utility of confidence-building measures already in place along the line of actual control in the India–China border areas,

Committed to enhancing mutual confidence and transparency in the military field, Have agreed as follows:

Article I

Neither side shall use its military capability against the other side. No armed forces deployed by either side in the border areas along the line of actual control as part of their respective military strength shall be used to attack the other side, or engage in military activities that threaten the other side or undermine peace, tranquillity and stability in the India–China border areas.

Article II

The two sides reiterate their determination to seek a fair, reasonable and mutually acceptable settlement of the boundary question. Pending an ultimate solution to the boundary question, the two sides reaffirm their commitment to strictly respect and observe the line of actual control in the India–China border areas. No activities of either side shall overstep the line of actual control.

Article III

The two sides agree to take the following measures to reduce or limit their respective military forces within mutually agreed geographical zones along the line of actual control in the India–China border areas:

(1) The two sides reaffirm that they shall reduce or limit their respective military forces within mutually agreed geographical zones along the line of actual control in the India–China border areas to minimum levels compatible with the friendly and good neighbourly relations between the two countries and consistent with the principle of mutual and equal security.

(2) The two sides shall reduce or limit the number of field army, border defence forces, paramilitary forces and any other mutually agreed category of armed force deployed in mutually agreed geographical zones along the line of actual control to ceilings to be mutually agreed upon. The major categories of armaments to be reduced or limited are as follows: combat tanks, infantry combat vehicles, guns (including howitzers) with 75 mm or bigger calibre, mortars with 120 mm or bigger calibre, surface-to-surface missiles, surface-to-air missiles and any other weapon system mutually agreed upon.

(3) The two sides shall exchange data on the military forces and armaments to be reduced or limited and decide on ceilings on military forces and armaments to be kept by each side within mutually agreed geographical zones along the line of actual control in the India–China border areas. The ceilings shall be determined in conformity with the requirement of the principle of mutual and equal security, with due consideration being given to parameters such as the nature of terrain, road communication and other infrastructure and time taken to induct/deinduct troops and armaments.

Article IV

In order to maintain peace and tranquillity along the line of actual control in the India–China border areas and to prevent any tension in the border areas due to misreading by either side of the other side's intentions:

(1) Both sides shall avoid holding large-scale military exercises involving more than one Division (approximately 15,000 troops) in close proximity of the line of actual control in the India–China border areas. However, if such exercises are to be conducted, the strategic direction of the main force involved shall not be towards the other side.

(2) If either side conducts a major military exercise involving more than one Brigade Group (approximately 5000 troops) in close proximity of the line of actual control in the India–China border areas, it shall give the other side prior notification with regard to type, level, planned duration and area of exercise as well as the number and type of units or formations participating in the exercise.

(3) The date of completion of the exercise and deinduction of troops from the area of exercise shall be intimated to the other side within five days of completion or deinduction.

(4) Each side shall be entitled to obtain timely clarification from the side undertaking the exercise in respect of data specified in Paragraph 2 of the present Article.

Article V

With a view to preventing air intrusions across the line of actual control in the India–China border areas and facilitating overflights and landings by military aircraft:

(1) Both sides shall take adequate measures to ensure that air intrusions across the line of actual control do not take place. However, if an intrusion does take place, it should cease as soon as detected and the incident shall be promptly investigated by the side operating the aircraft. The results of the investigation shall be immediately communicated, through diplomatic channels or at border personnel meetings, to the other side.

(2) Subject to Paragraphs 3 and 5 of this Article, combat aircraft (to include fighter, bomber, reconnaissance,

military trainer, armed helicopter and other armed aircraft) shall not fly within ten kilometres of the line of actual control.

(3) If either side is required to undertake flights of combat aircraft within ten kilometres from the line of actual control, it shall give the following information in advance to the other side, through diplomatic channels:

(a) Type and number of combat aircraft;

(b) Height of the proposed flight (in metres);

(c) Proposed duration of flights (normally not to exceed ten days);

(d) Proposed timing of flights; and

(e) Area of operations, defined in latitude and longitude.

(4) Unarmed transport aircraft, survey aircraft and helicopters shall be permitted to fly up to the line of actual control.

(5) No military aircraft of either side shall fly across the line of actual control, except by prior permission. Military aircraft of either side may fly across the line of actual control or overfly the other side's airspace or land on the other side only after obtaining the latter's prior permission after providing the latter with detailed information on the flight in accordance with the international practice in this regard.

Notwithstanding the above stipulation, each side has the sovereign right to specify additional conditions, including at short notice, for flights or landings of military aircraft of the other side on its side of the line of actual control or through its airspace.

(6) In order to ensure flight safety in emergency situations, the authorities designated by the two sides may contact each other by the quickest means of communications available.

Article VI

With a view to preventing dangerous military activities along the line of actual control in the India–China border areas, the two sides agree as follows:

(1) Neither side shall open fire, cause bio-degradation, use hazardous chemicals, conduct blast operations or hunt with guns or explosives within two kilometres from the line of actual control. This prohibition shall not apply to routine firing activities in small arms firing ranges.

(2) If there is a need to conduct blast operations within two kilometres of the line of actual control as part of developmental activities, the other side shall be informed through diplomatic channels or by convening a border personnel meeting, preferably five days in advance.

(3) While conducting exercises with live ammunition in areas close to the line of actual control, precaution shall be taken to ensure that a bullet or a missile does not accidentally fall on the other side across the line of actual control and cause harm to the personnel or property of the other side.

(4) If the border personnel of the two sides come in a face-to-face situation due to differences on the alignment of the line of actual control o any other reason, they shall exercise self-restraint and take all necessary steps to avoid an escalation of the situation. Both sides shall also enter into immediate consultations through diplomatic and/or other available channels to review the situation and prevent any escalation of tension.

Article VII

In order to strengthen exchanges and cooperation between the military personnel and establishments in the border areas along the line of actual control, the two sides agree:

(a) To maintain and expand the regime of scheduled and flag meetings between their border representatives at designated places along the line of actual control;

(b) To maintain and expand telecommunication links between the border meeting points at designated places along the line of actual control;

(c) To establish step-by-step medium and high-level contacts between the border authorities of the two sides.

Article VIII

(1) Should the personnel of one side cross the line of actual control and enter the other side because of unavoidable circumstances like natural disasters, the other side shall extend all possible assistance to them and inform their side, as soon as possible regarding the forced or inadvertent entry across the line of actual control. The modalities of return of the concerned personnel to their own side shall be settled through mutual consultations.

(2) The two sides shall provide each other, at the earliest possible, with information pertaining to natural disasters and epidemic diseases in contiguous border areas which might affect the other side. The exchange of information shall take place either through diplomatic channels or at border personnel meetings.

Article IX

In case a doubtful situation develops in the border region, or in case one of the sides has some questions or doubts regarding the manner in which the other side is observing this Agreement, either side has the right to seek a clarification from the other side. The clarifications sought and replies to them shall be conveyed through diplomatic channels.

Article X

(1) Recognizing that the full implementation of some of the provisions of the present Agreement will depend on the two sides arriving at a common understanding of the alignment of the line of actual control in the India–China border areas, the two sides agree to speed up the process clarification and confirmation of the line of actual control. As an initial step in this process, they are clarifying the alignment of the line of actual control in those segments where they have different perceptions. They also agree to exchange maps indicating their respective perceptions of the entire alignment of the line of actual control as soon as possible.

(2) Pending the completion of the process of clarification and confirmation of the line of actual control, the two sides shall work out modalities for implementing confidence-building measures envisaged under this Agreement on an interim basis, without prejudice to their respective positions on the alignment of the line of actual control as well as on the boundary question.

Article XI

Detailed implementation measures required under Article I to Article X of this Agreement shall be decided through mutual consultations in the India–China Joint Working Group on the Boundary Question. The India–China Diplomatic and Military Expert Group shall assist the India–China Joint Working Group in devising implementation measures under the Agreement.

Article XII

This Agreement is subject to ratification and shall enter into force on the date of exchange of instruments of ratification. It shall remain in effect until either side decides to terminate it after giving six months' notice in writing. It shall become invalid six months after the notification.

This Agreement is subject to amendment and addition by mutual agreement in writing between the two sides.

Signed in duplicate in New Delhi on November 29, 1996 in the Hindi, Chinese and English languages, all three texts being equally authentic. In case of divergence, the English text shall prevail.

Japan–China Joint Declaration on Building a Partnership of Friendship and Cooperation for Peace and Development (November 26, 1998)*

In response to an invitation extended by the Government of Japan, President Jiang Zemin of the People's Republic of China made an official visit to Japan as a State Guest from 25 to 30 November 1998. On the occasion of this historically significant first visit to Japan by a President of the People's Republic of China, President Jiang met with His Majesty the Emperor of Japan, and held an intensive exchange of views with Prime Minister Keizo Obuchi on the international situation, regional issues and the overall Japan–China relationship. They attained a broad common view and, based on the success of this visit, declared as follows:

Both sides shared the view that as the world in the post-Cold War era continues to undergo great changes towards the creation of a new international order, further economic globalization is deepening interdependence and security dialogue and cooperation are making constant progress. Peace and development remain major issues facing the human society. It is therefore the common wish of the international community to build a new international political and economic order which is fair and rational, and to

---

*The third of three bilateral agreements that were to guide Sino–Japanese relations, this joint declaration was made during the visit to Japan by President Jiang Zemin – the first by a Chinese head of state.

strive for a peaceful international environment in the twenty-first century that is even more firmly rooted.

Both sides reaffirmed that the principles of mutual respect for sovereignty and territorial integrity, mutual non-aggression, non-interference in each other's internal affairs, equality and mutual benefit and peaceful co-existence, as well as the principles of the Charter of the United Nations, are the basic norms for relations between states.

Both sides positively evaluate the efforts made by the United Nations to preserve world peace and to promote the economic and social development of the world, and believe that the United Nations should play an important role in building and maintaining a new international order. Both sides express support for the reforms of the United Nations including the reform of the Security Council, in order for the United Nations to further embody the common wish and collective will of all Members in its activities and policy decision-making process.

Both sides stress the importance of the ultimate elimination of nuclear weapons, and oppose the proliferation of nuclear weapons in any form whatsoever, and furthermore, strongly call upon the nations concerned to cease all nuclear testing and nuclear arms race, in order to contribute to the peace and stability of the Asian region and the world.

Both sides believe that both Japan and China, as nations influential in the Asian region and the world, bear an important responsibility for preserving peace and promoting development. Both sides will strengthen coordination and cooperation in the areas such as international politics, international economy, and global issues, thus positively contributing to the endeavour for the peace and development of the world aimed at the progress of humanity.

Both sides believe that, after the Cold War, the Asian region has continued to move towards stability and the regional cooperation has deepened further. In addition, both sides are convinced that this region will exert greater influence on international politics, economics and security and will continue to play an important role in the coming century.

Both sides reiterate that it is the unshakable fundamental policy of the two countries to maintain the peace of this region and to promote its development, and that they will not seek hegemony in the Asian region and settle all disputes by peaceful means, without recourse to the use or threat of force.

Both sides expressed their great interest in the current financial crisis in East Asia and the ensuing difficulties for the Asian economy. At the same time, both sides recognize that the economic foundation of this region is sound, and firmly believe that by advancing rational adjustment and reform based on experiences, as well as by enhancing regional and international coordination and cooperation, the economy of Asia will definitely overcome its difficulties and continue to develop. Both sides affirmed that they would positively meet the various challenges that they faced, and would respectively make their utmost efforts towards promoting the economic development of the region.

Both sides believe that stable relations among the major nations of the Asia–Pacific region are extremely important for the peace and stability of this region. Both sides shared the view that they would actively participate in all multilateral activities in this region, such as the ASEAN Regional Forum, promote coordination and cooperation, and support all measures for enhancing understanding and strengthening confidence.

Both sides reviewed the bilateral relationship since the normalization of relations between Japan and China, and expressed satisfaction with the remarkable development in all areas, including politics, economics, culture and personnel exchanges. Further, both sides shared the view that under the current situation cooperation between the two countries is growing in importance, and that further strengthening and developing the friendly and cooperative relations between the two countries not only serve the fundamental interests of their peoples, but also positively contribute to the peace and development of the Asia–Pacific region and the world as a whole. Both sides reaffirmed that the Japan–China relationship is one of the most important bilateral relationships for the respective country, deeply recognized the role and responsibility of both countries in achieving peace and development, and expressed their resolve to establish a partnership of friendship and cooperation for peace and development towards the twenty-first century.

Both sides restated that they will observe the principles of the Joint Communiqué of the Government of Japan and the

Government of the People's Republic of China, issued on September 29, 1972 and the Treaty of Peace and Friendship between Japan and the People's Republic of China, signed on 12 August 1978, and reaffirmed that the above-mentioned documents will continue to be the most important foundation for the bilateral relations.

Both sides are of the view that Japan and China share a history of friendly exchanges spanning more than 2000 years, as well as a common cultural background, and that it is the common desire of the peoples of the two countries to continue this tradition of friendship and to further develop mutually beneficial cooperation.

Both sides believe that squarely facing the past and correctly understanding history are the important foundation for further developing relations between Japan and China. The Japanese side observes the 1972 Joint Communiqué of the Government of Japan and the Government of the People's Republic of China and the 15 August 1995 Statement by former Prime Minister Tomiichi Murayama. The Japanese side is keenly conscious of the responsibility for the serious distress and damage that Japan caused to the Chinese people through its aggression against China during a certain period in the past and expressed deep remorse for this. The Chinese side hopes that the Japanese side will learn lessons from the history and adhere to the path of peace and development. Based on this, both sides will develop long-standing relations of friendship.

Both sides shared the view that expanding personnel exchanges between the two countries is extremely important for advancing mutual understanding and enhancing mutual trust.

Both sides confirmed an annual visit by a leader of either country to the other, the establishment of a Tokyo–Beijing hotline between the two Governments, and the further enhancement of personnel exchanges at all levels, in particular among the younger generation who will shoulder the heavy burden of the future development of the two countries.

Both sides shared the view that, based on the principles of equality and mutual benefit, they will formulate long-term, stable, cooperative economic and trade relations, and will further expand cooperation in such areas as high technology, information, environmental protection, agriculture and infrastructure. The Japanese side reiterated that a stable, open and developing China is significant for the peace and development of the Asia–Pacific region and the entire world, and restated its policy of continuing cooperation and assistance for the economic development of China. The Chinese side expressed its gratitude for the economic cooperation extended by Japan to China. The Japanese side reiterated that it will continue to support China's efforts for the early accession to the WTO.

Both sides positively evaluated the beneficial role played by their bilateral security dialogue in increasing mutual understanding, and shared the view that they would further strengthen this dialogue mechanism.

The Japanese side continues to maintain its stand on the Taiwan issue which was set forth in the Joint Communiqué of the Government of Japan and the Government of the People's Republic of China and reiterates its understanding that there is one China. Japan will continue to maintain its exchanges of private and regional nature with Taiwan.

Both sides affirmed that, based on the principles of the Joint Communiqué of the Government of Japan and the Government of the People's Republic of China and the Treaty of Peace and Friendship between Japan and the People's Republic of China, and following the spirit of seeking common major benefits while setting aside minor differences, they would work to maximize their common interests and minimize their differences, and, through friendly consultations, appropriately handle the issues, differences of opinion and disputes which currently exist and may arise in the future, thereby avoiding any restraint or obstacle to development of friendly relations between the two countries.

Both sides believe that through establishment of a partnership of friendship and cooperation for peace and development, the bilateral relations will enter a new level of development. To this end, a wide range of participation and sustained effort not only of both Governments, but also of the peoples of both countries, is essential. Both sides firmly believe that, if the peoples of both countries, hand-in-hand, thoroughly demonstrate the spirit shown in this Declaration, it will not only contribute to the friendship of the peoples of both countries for generations to come, but also make an important contribution to the peace and development of the Asia–Pacific region and of the world.

Declaration on Principles for Relations and Comprehensive Cooperation between the Republic of India and the People's Republic of China (Beijing, June 23, 2003)*

At the invitation of Premier of the State Council of the People's Republic of China H.E. Wen Jiabao, Prime Minister of the Republic of India H.E. Atal Bihari Vajpayee paid an official visit to the People's Republic of China from 22 to 27 June 2003.

During this visit, Premier Wen Jiabao held talks with Prime Minister Vajpayee. Their Excellencies President Hu Jintao of the People's Republic of China, Chairman Jiang Zemin of the Central Military Commission, Chairman Wu Bangguo of the Standing Committee of the National People's Congress and Vice President Zeng Qinghong of the People's Republic of China held separate meetings with Prime Minister Vajpayee. The talks and meetings were held in a sincere and friendly atmosphere.

Leaders from both countries noted with satisfaction the progress made over recent years in bilateral relations. This is conducive not only to their respective development, but also to regional

---

*This declaration, made during Indian Prime Minister Atal Bihari Vajpayee's visit to China, shifted India's position on Tibet by describing the Chinese-labelled 'Tibetan Autonomous Region' as 'part of the territory' of the People's Republic of China. A memorandum was also signed during the visit to open trade between Tibet and Sikkim through Nathula Pass.

stability and prosperity. The two sides recalled the historical depth of their friendly contacts. India and China are the two largest developing countries of the world with centuries-old civilization[s], unique history and similar objectives. Both noted that the sustained economic and social development in the two countries, representing one-third of humanity is vital for ensuring peace, stability and prosperity not only in Asia but also in the whole world.

The two sides agreed that India and China have a mutual desire for good neighbourly relations and have broad common interests. They agreed to fully utilize the substantial potential and opportunities for deepening mutually beneficial cooperation.

Friendship and cooperation between the two countries meet the need to:

- promote the socio-economic development and prosperity of both India and China;
- maintain peace and stability regionally and globally;
- strengthen multipolarity at the international level; and
- enhance the positive factors of globalization.

Both sides affirmed that they would abide by the following principles, promote a long-term constructive and cooperative partnership and, on this basis, build a qualitatively new relationship:

- Both sides are committed to developing their long-term constructive and cooperative partnership on the basis of the principles of Panchsheel, mutual respect and sensitivity for each other's concerns and equality;
- As two major developing countries, India and China have a broad mutual interest in the maintenance of peace, stability and prosperity in Asia and the world, and a mutual desire in developing wider and closer cooperation and understanding in regional and international affairs;
- The common interests of the two sides outweigh their differences. The two countries are not a threat to each other. Neither side shall use or threaten to use force against the other; and
- Both sides agree to qualitatively enhancing the bilateral relationship at all levels and in all areas while addressing

differences through peaceful means in a fair, reasonable and mutually acceptable manner. The differences should not be allowed to affect the overall development of bilateral relations.

Both sides agreed to hold regular high-level exchanges between the two countries. This will greatly enhance mutual understanding and expand bilateral relations. With a view to deepening their coordination and dialogues on bilateral, regional and international issues, both sides agreed on the need for annual meetings between Foreign Ministers of the two countries. They also agreed that personnel exchanges and friendly contacts between ministries, parliaments and political parties of the two countries should be further enhanced.

The two sides welcomed the positive momentum of bilateral trade and economic cooperation in recent years and shared the belief that continued expansion and intensification of India–China economic cooperation is essential for strengthening bilateral relations.

Both sides shared the view that existing complementarities between their two economies provide an important foundation and offer broad prospects for further enhancing their economic relations. In order to promote trade and economic cooperation, both sides will take necessary measures consistent with their national laws and rules and international obligations to remove impediments to bilateral trade and investment. They reaffirmed the importance of the ministerial meeting of the Joint Economic Group (JEG) and agreed to hold the next (seventh) JEG meeting within the year.

The two sides will set up a compact Joint Study Group (JSG) composed of officials and economists to examine the potential complementarities between the two countries in expanded trade and economic cooperation. The JSG would also draw up a programme for the development of India–China trade and economic cooperation for the next five years, aimed at encouraging greater cooperation between the business communities of both sides. The Group should present a study report and recommendations to the two Governments on measures for comprehensive trade and economic cooperation by the end of June 2004.

The two countries will launch a financial dialogue and cooperation mechanism to strengthen their dialogue and coordination in this sector.

The two sides agreed to enhance cooperation at the World Trade Organization, which is not only to mutual benefit but also in the broader interest of developing countries. The two sides will hold dialogues on a regular basis in this regard.

Historical and cultural links between India and China will be strengthened, inter alia, through the promotion of exchanges in culture, education, science and technology, media, youth and people-to-people relations. They agreed to set up Cultural Centres in each other's capitals and facilitate their establishment.

Both sides will work towards the enhancement of direct air and shipping links, tourism, exchange hydrological data in flood season on common rivers as agreed, cooperation in agriculture, dairy, food processing, health and other sectors.

They agreed on the need to broaden and deepen defence exchanges between the two countries, which will help enhance and deepen the mutual understanding and trust between the two armed forces. They confirmed that the exchange of visits by their Defence Ministers and of military officials at various levels should be strengthened.

The two sides exchanged views on the India–China boundary question and expounded their respective positions. They reiterated their readiness to seek a fair, reasonable and mutually acceptable solution through consultations on an equal footing. The two sides agreed that pending an ultimate solution, they should work together to maintain peace and tranquillity in the border areas, and reiterated their commitment to continue implementation of the agreements signed for this purpose, including the clarification of the Line of Actual Control.

The two sides agreed to each appoint a Special Representative to explore from the political perspective of the overall bilateral relationship the framework of a boundary settlement.

The Indian side recognizes that the Tibet Autonomous Region is part of the territory of the People's Republic of China and reiterates that it does not allow Tibetans to engage in anti-China political activities in India. The Chinese side expresses its appreciation for the Indian position and reiterates that it is firmly opposed to any attempt and action aimed at splitting China and bringing about 'independence of Tibet'.

The Indian side recalled that India was among the first countries to recognize that there is one China and its one China policy remains unaltered. The Chinese side expressed its appreciation of the Indian position.

India and China recognized the primacy of maintaining international peace. This is a prerequisite for the socio-economic development of all developing countries, including India and China. The world is marked by diversity. Every country has the right to choose its own political system and path to development. As two major developing countries, India and China acknowledged the importance of their respective roles in the shaping of a new international political and economic order. The international community must help the developing countries to eliminate poverty and narrow the gap between the North and the South through dialogue and cooperation so as to achieve common prosperity.

The two sides acknowledged the vital importance of the role of the United Nations in world peace, stability and development. They are determined to continue their efforts in strengthening the UN system. They reaffirmed their readiness to work together to promote reform of the UN. In reform of the UN Security Council, priority should be given to enhancing representation of the developing countries.

Both sides stood for continued multilateral arms control and disarmament process, undiminished and equal security for all at progressively lower levels of armament and for multilateral negotiations aimed at nuclear disarmament and elimination of nuclear weapons. They are firmly opposed to introduction of weapons in outer space, use or threat of force against space-based objects and support cooperation in development of space technology for peaceful purposes.

The two sides recognized the threat posed by terrorism to them and to global peace and security. They resolutely condemned terrorism in any form. The struggle between the international community and global terrorism is a comprehensive and sustained one, with the ultimate objective of eradication of terrorism in all regions. This requires strengthening the global legal framework against terrorism. Both sides shall also promote cooperation on counterterrorism through their bilateral dialogue mechanism.

India and China face special and similar challenges in their efforts to protect the environment while simultaneously forging ahead with rapid social and economic development of their countries. In this context, the two sides agreed to work together in a practical manner to cooperate on preserving the environment and ensuring sustainable development and to coordinate positions on climate change, biodiversity and other issues in relevant multilateral fora.

The two sides supported multilateral cooperation in Asia, believing that such cooperation promotes mutually beneficial exchanges, economic growth as well as greater cohesion among Asian countries. The two sides viewed positively each other's participation in regional and subregional multilateral cooperation processes in Asia.

The two sides stated that the improvement and development of India–China relations is not targeted at any third country and does not affect either country's existing friendly relations and cooperation with other countries.

The two sides agreed that the official visit of the Prime Minister of India to the People's Republic of China has been a success, has contributed to enhancing mutual understanding and trust between the Governments, leaders and peoples of the two countries, and marks a new step forward in strengthening the all-round cooperation between India and China in the new century.

Prime Minister Vajpayee invited Premier Wen Jiabao to visit India at a mutually convenient time and conveyed to President Hu Jintao an invitation from President Abdul Kalam to visit India. The Chinese side accepted the invitations with appreciation. The dates of the visits will be settled through diplomatic channels.

On behalf of the Government and the people of India, H.E. Prime Minister Atal Bihari Vajpayee thanked the Government and the people of China for the warm welcome received by him and his delegation.

Signed in Beijing on 23 June 2003 in the Hindi, Chinese and English languages.

Atal Bihari Vajpayee   Wen Jiabao
Prime Minister   Premier of the State Council
The Republic of India   The People's Republic of China

Memorandum between the Government of the Republic of India and the Government of the People's Republic of China on Expanding Border Trade (Beijing, June 23, 2003)*

The Government of the Republic of India and the Government of the People's Republic of China (hereinafter referred to as the two sides),

With a view to promoting the development of friendly relations between the two countries and two peoples,

Pursuant to the Memorandum between the Government of the Republic of India and the Government of the People's Republic of China on the Resumption of Border Trade signed on 13 December 1991, and Protocol on Entry and Exit Procedures for Border Trade signed on 1 July 1992,

Desirous of opening another pass on the India–China border and setting up an additional point on each side for border trade,

Have agreed as follows:

---

*Signed during Prime Minister Atal Bihari Vajpayee's visit to China, this memorandum opened the way to the resumption of trade with India through the strategic Nathula Pass in Chumbi Valley, located at the tri-junction of Sikkim, Bhutan and Tibet.

Article I

The Indian side agrees to designate Changgu of Sikkim state as the venue for border trade market; the Chinese side agrees to designate Renqinggang of the Tibet Autonomous Region as the venue for border trade market.

Article II

The two sides agree to use Nathula as the pass for entry and exit of persons, means of transport and commodities engaged in border trade. Each side shall establish checkpoints at appropriate locations to monitor and manage their entry and exit through the Nathula Pass.

Article III

All the provisions of the Memorandum on the Resumption of Border Trade signed between the two Governments on 13 December 1991 and the Protocol on Entry and Exit Procedures for Border Trade signed between the two Governments on 1 July 1992 under the Memorandum shall also be applicable to the border trade through the Nathula Pass.

Article IV

This Memorandum may be amended or supplemented by agreement in writing between the two sides.

Article V

This Memorandum shall come into force as from the date of its signature and shall be valid during the validity of the Memorandum on Resumption of Border Trade signed between the two Governments in New Delhi on 13 December 1991.

Done in Beijing on 23 June 2003 in two originals each in the Hindi, Chinese and English languages, the three texts being equally authentic.

Protocol between the Government of the Republic of
India and the Government of the People's Republic of
China on Modalities for the Implementation of
Confidence-Building Measures in the Military Field
along the Line of Actual Control in the India–China
Border Areas (New Delhi, April 11, 2005)*

The Government of the Republic of India and the Government
of the People's Republic of China (hereinafter referred to as the
two sides),

Recalling that both sides are committed to developing their
long-term constructive and cooperative partnership on the basis
of the Five Principles of Peaceful Co-existence, mutual respect
and sensitivity for each other's concerns and aspirations, and
equality,

Reaffirming that the two sides seek a fair, reasonable and
mutually acceptable settlement of the boundary question,

Reaffirming their commitment that, pending an ultimate solution
to the boundary question, both sides shall strictly respect and
observe the Line of Actual Control in the India–China border areas,

Noting the utility of confidence-building measures already
in place along the Line of Actual Control in the India–China
border areas,

---

*This protocol seeks to define and amplify certain provisions of the
1996 confidence-building agreement while it repeats verbatim some
of the bilateral commitments in the 1996 accord.

Recognizing that the maintenance of peace and tranquillity along the Line of Actual Control in the India–China border areas accords with the fundamental interests of the two sides, and will facilitate the process of early clarification and confirmation of the alignment of the Line of Actual Control,

Convinced of the need for agreed modalities for the implementation of confidence-building measures between the two sides in the military field along the Line of Actual Control in the India–China border areas, and

Recalling further the relevant provisions of the Agreement on the Maintenance of Peace and Tranquillity along the Line of Actual Control in the India–China Border Areas signed in September 1993 and Agreement on Confidence-Building Measures in the Military Field along the Line of Actual Control in the India–China Border Areas signed between the two sides in November 1996,

Have agreed on the modalities as follows:

Article I

In accordance with Article II of the Agreement on Confidence-Building Measures in the Military Field along the Line of Actual Control in the India–China Border Areas signed between the two sides in November 1996, the two sides should strictly respect and observe the Line of Actual Control and work together to maintain peace and tranquillity in the border areas.

Article II

In accordance with Article IV of the Agreement on Confidence-Building Measures in the Military Field along the Line of Actual Control in the India–China Border Areas signed between the two sides in November 1996,

(a) Both sides shall avoid holding large-scale military exercises involving more than one Division (approximately 15,000 troops) in close proximity to the Line of Actual Control. However, if such exercises are to be conducted, the strategic direction of the main force involved shall not be towards the other side.

(b) If either side conducts a military exercise involving more than one Brigade Group (approximately 5000 troops) in close proximity to the Line of Actual Control, it shall not be targeted against the other side. The side undertaking the exercise shall give, through Flag Meetings, the other side prior intimation 15 days in advance of the exercise with regard to type, level, planned duration and area of exercise as well as the number and type of units or formations participating in the exercise.

(c) Each side shall be entitled to obtain timely clarification within 15 days from the side undertaking the exercise in respect of data specified in paragraph (b) above of the present article, through Flag Meetings.

Article III

In accordance with Article V of the Agreement on Confidence-Building Measures in the Military Field along the Line of Actual Control in the India–China Border Areas signed between the two sides in November 1996,

(a) In the event of an alleged air intrusion of its controlled airspace by the military aircraft of the other side, either side may seek a Flag Meeting within 48 hours of the alleged air intrusion in order to seek a clarification. The investigation shall be completed by the other side and its results communicated through a Flag Meeting within a period of four weeks.

(b) If a military aircraft of either side is required to fly across the Line of Actual Control or to overfly the airspace of the other side, prior permission shall be sought from the other side according to procedures and formats to be mutually agreed upon.

(c) If a military or civilian aircraft of either side is required to fly across the Line of Actual Control or to land on the other side of the Line of Actual Control in an emergency situation, the two sides will ensure flight safety in such situations by adhering to procedures to be mutually agreed upon.

Article IV

In accordance with Article VI of the Agreement on Confidence-Building Measures in the Military Field along the Line of Actual Control in the India–China Border Areas signed between the two sides in November 1996, if the border personnel of the two sides come to a face-to-face situation due to differences on the alignment of the Line of Actual Control or any other reason, they shall exercise self-restraint and take all necessary steps to avoid an escalation of the situation. To this end, they shall follow the procedures as given below:

(a) Both sides shall cease their activities in the area, not advance any further, and simultaneously return to their bases.

(b) Both sides shall then inform their respective Headquarters and, if necessary, enter into immediate consultations through border meetings or diplomatic channels so as to prevent an escalation of the situation.

(c) Throughout the face-to-face situation, neither side shall use force or threaten to use force against the other.

(d) Both sides shall treat each other with courtesy and refrain from any provocative actions. Neither side shall put up marks or signs on the spots.

Article V

In accordance with Article VII of the Agreement on Confidence-Building Measures in the Military Field along the Line of Actual Control in India–China Border Areas signed between the two sides in November 1996,

(a) Both sides shall hold two additional border meetings each year at Spanggur Gap in the Western Sector, Nathula Pass in the Sikkim Sector and Bum La in the Eastern Sector respectively in celebration of the National Day or Army Day of either side. Specific arrangements shall be decided through consultation between the border forces of the two sides.

(b) Both sides agree in principle to expand the mechanism of border meeting points to include Kibithu-Damai in the Eastern Sector and Lipulekh Pass/Qiang La in the Middle Sector. The precise locations of these border meeting points will be decided through mutual consultations.

(c) Both sides shall conduct exchanges between the relevant Military Regions of China and Army Commands of India. Specific arrangements shall be decided upon through mutual consultations between the relevant agencies under the Ministries of Defence of the two sides.

(d) Both sides shall strengthen exchanges between institutions of training of the two armed forces, and conduct exchanges between institutions of sports and culture of the two armed forces. Specific arrangements shall be decided upon through mutual consultations between the relevant agencies under the Ministries of Defence of the two sides.

Article VI

In accordance with Article VIII of the Agreement on Confidence-Building Measures in the Military Field along the Line of Actual Control in the India–China Border Areas signed between the two sides in November 1996,

(a) In case the personnel of one side in the border areas cross over to the other side due to *force majeure* such as natural disasters:

(i) The side having discovered it should promptly contact and notify the other side;

(ii) The personnel crossing over to the other side should, in the light of the prevailing circumstances, take measures to return to their own side or proceed to places designated by the other side en route to return to their own side;

(iii) The receiving side will provide all possible assistance to the personnel from the other side and ensure their earliest possible return; and

(iv) At the request of the side affected by the natural

disaster, the other side may consider all possible measures to help alleviate the situation.

(b) In order to prevent infectious diseases in specific areas on either side in the border areas from spreading to the other side:

  (i) Both sides should share relevant information promptly through border meetings or diplomatic channels;

  (ii) Each side should take measures to prevent the spread of diseases from spilling onto the other side; and

  (iii) At the request of the side suffering from spread of infectious diseases, the other side may consider all possible measures to help alleviate the situation.

Article VII

The Protocol shall enter into force on the date of signature of this Protocol and will automatically be rendered invalid if the Agreement on Confidence-Building Measures in the Military Field along the Line of Actual Control in the India–China Border Areas signed between the two sides in November 1996 ceases to be in force. Subject to agreement after mutual consultations between the two sides, the Protocol may be amended and supplemented at any time.

Done in duplicate in New Delhi on April 11, 2005 in the Hindi, Chinese and English languages, all three texts being equally authentic. In case of any divergence, the English text shall prevail.

For the Government of the Republic of India
For the Government of the People's Republic of China
New Delhi, April 11, 2005

Agreement between the Government of the Republic of India and the Government of the People's Republic of China on the Political Parameters and Guiding Principles for the Settlement of the India–China Boundary Question (New Delhi, April 11, 2005)*

The Government of the Republic of India and the Government of the People's Republic of China (hereinafter referred to as the two sides),

Believing that it serves the fundamental interests of the peoples of India and China to foster a long-term constructive and cooperative partnership on the basis of the Five Principles of Peaceful Co-existence, mutual respect and sensitivity for each other's concerns and aspirations, and equality,

Desirous of qualitatively upgrading the bilateral relationship at all levels and in all areas while addressing differences through peaceful means in a fair, reasonable and mutually acceptable manner,

Reiterating their commitment to abide by and implement the Agreement on the Maintenance of Peace and Tranquillity along the Line of Actual Control in the India–China Border Areas, signed

---

*Nearly a quarter century after China–India border talks began in 1981, six 'guiding principles' for a settlement of the still-festering frontier dispute were identified during the 2005 New Delhi visit of Chinese Premier Wen Jiabao.

on 7 September 1993, and the Agreement on Confidence-Building Measures in the Military Field along the Line of Actual Control in the India–China Border Areas, signed on 29 November 1996,

Reaffirming the Declaration on Principles for Relations and Comprehensive Cooperation between India and China, signed on 23 June 2003,

Recalling that the two sides have appointed Special Representatives to explore the framework of settlement of the India–China boundary question and the two Special Representatives have been engaged in consultations in a friendly, cooperative and constructive atmosphere,

Noting that the two sides are seeking a political settlement of the boundary question in the context of their overall and long-term interests,

Convinced that an early settlement of the boundary question will advance the basic interests of the two countries and should therefore be pursued as a strategic objective,

Have agreed on the following political parameters and guiding principles for a boundary settlement:

Article I

The differences on the boundary question should not be allowed to affect the overall development of bilateral relations. The two sides will resolve the boundary question through peaceful and friendly consultations. Neither side shall use or threaten to use force against the other by any means. The final solution of the boundary question will significantly promote good neighbourly and friendly relations between India and China.

Article II

The two sides should, in accordance with the Five Principles of Peaceful Co-existence, seek a fair, reasonable and mutually acceptable solution to the boundary question through consultations on an equal footing, proceeding from the political perspective of overall bilateral relations.

Article III

Both sides should, in the spirit of mutual respect and mutual understanding, make meaningful and mutually acceptable adjustments to their respective positions on the boundary question, so as to arrive at a package settlement to the boundary question. The boundary settlement must be final, covering all sectors of the India–China boundary.

Article IV

The two sides will give due consideration to each other's strategic and reasonable interests, and the principle of mutual and equal security.

Article V

The two sides will take into account, inter alia, historical evidence, national sentiments, practical difficulties and reasonable concerns and sensitivities of both sides, and the actual state of border areas.

Article VI

The boundary should be along well-defined and easily identifiable natural geographical features to be mutually agreed upon between the two sides.

Article VII

In reaching a boundary settlement, the two sides shall safeguard due interests of their settled populations in the border areas.

Article VIII

Within the agreed framework of the final boundary settlement, the delineation of the boundary will be carried out utilizing means such as modern cartographic and surveying practices and joint surveys.

Article IX

Pending an ultimate settlement of the boundary question, the two sides should strictly respect and observe the line of actual control and work together to maintain peace and tranquillity in the border areas. The India–China Joint Working Group and the India–China Diplomatic and Military Expert Group shall continue their work under the Agreements of 7 September 1993 and 29 November 1996, including the clarification of the line of actual control and the implementation of confidence-building measures.

Article X

The Special Representatives on the boundary question shall continue their consultations in an earnest manner with the objective of arriving at an agreed framework for a boundary settlement, which will provide the basis for the delineation and demarcation of the India–China boundary to be subsequently undertaken by civil and military officials and surveyors of the two sides.

Article XI

This Agreement shall come into force as of the date of signature and is subject to amendment and addition by mutual agreement in writing between the two sides.

Signed in duplicate in New Delhi on 11 April 2005, in the Hindi, Chinese and English languages, all three texts being equally authentic. In case of divergence, the English text shall prevail.

For the Government of the Republic of India
For the Government of the People's Republic of China
New Delhi, 11 April 2005

Index